ALSO BY ED WARD

The History of Rock & Roll, Volume One: 1920–1963
Rock of Ages
(coauthored with Geoffrey Stokes and Ken Tucker)
el Bloomfield: The Rise and Fall of an American Guitar Hero
The Bar at the End of the Regime (ebook)
Two Blues Stories: Fiction by Ed Ward (ebook)

THE HISTORY

ROCK & F

volume two

Mich

THE HISTORY OF
ROCK & ROLL

volume two

1964–1977

The Beatles, the Stones, and the Rise of Classic Rock

ED WARD

FLATIRON
BOOKS
NEW YORK

THE HISTORY OF ROCK & ROLL, VOLUME 2. Copyright © 2019 by Ed Ward. All rights reserved. Printed in the United States of America. For information, address Flatiron Books,
120 Broadway, New York, NY 10271.

www.flatironbooks.com

Designed by Steven Seighman

The Library of Congress Cataloging-in-Publication Data is available upon request.

ISBN 978-1-250-16519-0 (hardcover)
ISBN 978-1-250-16997-6 (ebook)

Our books may be purchased in bulk for promotional, educational, or business use. Please
contact your local bookseller or the Macmillan Corporate and Premium Sales Department at
1-800-221-7945, extension 5442, or by email at MacmillanSpecialMarkets@macmillan.com.

First Edition: November 2019

10 9 8 7 6 5 4 3 2 1

To Margaret Moser, 1954–2017
She Lived It

CONTENTS

THE HISTORY OF

ROCK & ROLL

volume two

chapter zero
THE STORY SO FAR

Selection at Village Music, Mill Valley, California, circa 1980
(Photo by Mush Evans; courtesy of John Goddard)

The coming of rock and roll to postwar America was just one of the many shocks that era gave the world at the time, but it wasn't so much the screaming teenage girls (they'd appeared with Frank Sinatra in the '40s) or the sexually suggestive records (they'd been coming out all along) that seemed to threaten society. It was the fact that, as the form rose in popularity and began to become the default style of popular music in America, it wasn't the wise elders of the music business who were calling the shots. You could groom a nice teenage boy, give him good material, put him on television, and promote the hell out of his records and still be met with indifference by the very kids you were trying to sell him to. This had never happened before: those kids were supposed to be passive consumers. Also, in the beginning, the real pioneers—Elvis Presley, Jerry Lee Lewis, Little Richard, Fats Domino, Chuck Berry (who was almost thirty when his career began), et al.—were a few years older than their young fans, but as the 1950s faded into the 1960s, this gap began to narrow. At first, the emerging teen stars such as Ricky Nelson and Brenda Lee were carefully managed so as not to offend parents, but with Nelson in particular, there were a lot of kids who saw him on his parents' TV show each week and thought, "I could do that." Maybe, maybe not. Those backup musicians were also kids, but they had experience in the studios, particularly guitarist James Burton, who'd found his way to Hollywood via the country circuit and was on other people's records at the same time, most notably laying the snaky guitar line on Dale Hawkins's "Suzy Q." But some kids just flat out *could* "do that": Buddy Holly went to see Elvis when Presley played Lubbock on his first tour of Texas, talked to him between sets, and found a kindred spirit. It would take Holly and his group, the Crickets, a bit longer before they were joining Elvis on the charts, but it would happen.

And on the rhythm and blues charts, lots of the vocal groups' singers were young—Frankie Lymon and the Teenagers really *were* teenagers, and the Chantels' Arlene Smith was thirteen when she sang "Maybe." But for many white teens, that was an unknown world.

This would last for only a short time: television awaited, ready to start beaming images of these new young performers nationwide on Dick Clark's ABC network dance party show, *American Bandstand,* which aired in the dead zone of late afternoon (right after school), and although the performers never played live but instead mimed to their records, they were at least visible. So were the ultra-hip—or so they appeared—Philadelphia kids who gathered at the studio to dance the latest dances on the show while wearing the latest clothes. This spawned imitators, shows that localized the phenomenon and also had touring acts on to play live when they could. The downside of *Bandstand* was that when a few Philadelphia-based people (such as Dick Clark, the show's host, and some of his music biz cronies) decided they could safely take the reins of this teen phenomenon, they perpetrated those nice teenage boys and foisted them on an audience that had lost Elvis to the army, Jerry Lee Lewis and Chuck Berry to sex scandals, and Little Richard to the ministry.

But in the West, they weren't buying this. For one thing, starting in Seattle in the mid-'50s, combos that were all electric guitars and drums, like the Ventures, the Wailers, and Paul Revere and the Raiders, were the rage, albeit for the most part only locally. This band template made its way south, where a virtuoso guitarist, Richard Monsour (who, like his father, worked in the aircraft industry just south of Los Angeles), relaxed by enjoying a sport that had sprung up after the war: surfing. He also had the itch to perform professionally, and with his father's help, he formed a band, cut some records, and instituted weekly dances in Balboa Beach. Rechristened Dick Dale, Monsour and his band, the Deltones, referenced surfing in the title of their first hit, "Let's Go Trippin'" (*tripping* being simply a slang term the kids he knew used for surfing), and wound up with a hit. Soon, surfing instrumentals were being recorded in LA and selling well even in places with no surf—and no ocean, come to that.

In nearby Hawthorne, California, a bunch of kids, three brothers and a couple of others, had been rehearsing vocal group music and, of course, hanging out at the beach, although only one of them, Dennis Wilson, actually surfed. He snapped to an intriguing fact: none of these records had words. Nobody was actually *singing* about surfing. Soon, his brother Brian was writing lyrics, and through their father's connections, the group signed with Capitol Records, which, having lost its big stars Frank Sinatra and Dean Martin to Warner Bros., was desperate for hits. With the Wilsons' group, the Beach Boys, it got them.

This wasn't the only "I can do that" movement going, though. Starting in the mid-'50s, New York, Boston, Chicago, Philadelphia, and Denver, and college campuses all over the country, started seeing a new wave of folk revivalism. There had been one in the 1930s, fueled largely by left-wing politics and the labor movement, that had led to the ascendance of the Weavers, who had heavily orchestrated hits in the early '50s and were brought down by the Red Scare. Performers in this new movement often shared those politics, wedding them to the current struggle for civil rights and nuclear disarmament, but their music also had a whiff of scholarship to it, largely influenced as it was by a six-LP set on Folkways Records, the *Anthology of American Folk Music*, which had been compiled by an eccentric named Harry Smith. The three double-album packages, labeled "Ballads," "Social Music," and "Songs," exposed a world of rural recordings only thirty-five years old that had vanished almost entirely. The *Anthology*, and various bootlegs of country blues 78s, prompted college-age amateur researchers to head South to see if some of these people were still alive—they were—and to record them and bring them back to play concerts. The researchers also learned instrumental techniques, and many of them began playing themselves. For older teens who were becoming disillusioned with the insipidity of current pop music, this was a great way to plug into a nationwide network of like-minded individuals: show up with a guitar or a banjo and you'd meet interesting people. Some, such as teenage Robert Zimmerman, who'd left the town of Hibbing, Minnesota, for college, not only warmed to the local folk scene but also decided to start writing their own songs, mostly about injustice and contemporary society, but that hung on traditional melodies the way '30s protest singer Woody Guthrie had done. Soon enough, Zimmerman, who'd rechristened himself Bob Dylan, was off to New York City to try to make it in the folk clubs there.

This folk thing also started appearing on the radio and the charts, at first with a group called the Kingston Trio, whose main repertoire wasn't folk music at all but show tunes and other sophisticated composed songs that had a wide appeal to college kids. The trio's freak hit, however, was their arrangement of a genuine folk song, "Tom Dooley," by a banjo player named Frank Proffitt. The Kingston Trio's basic configuration spawned a number of other commercial folk groups, as well as Peter, Paul and Mary, who bridged the gap between pure commercialism and the underground with their first hit, Bob Dylan's "Blowin' in the Wind." These groups managed to set off yet another folk revival, in England: the skiffle craze. The idea of easily portable instruments and good-time sing-alongs caught on with the bohemian crowd in London's Soho, as well as on British college campuses and among the country's nuclear disarmament crowd. The skifflers' repertoire was largely American folk music from the first American folk revival, heavy on hokum tunes and songs that the black singer Lead Belly had recorded in the '30s.

The skiffle fad spread like crazy in Britain, which had largely missed the first wave of rock and roll (and whose attempts to replicate it ranged from lame to horribly embarrassing). Soon, singers such as Nancy Whiskey and Lonnie Donegan were climbing the British charts.

Donegan even had an American hit with "Rock Island Line," a Lead Belly tune, and an even bigger one with a music hall tune, the unfortunately unforgettable "Does Your Chewing Gum Lose Its Flavour (On the Bedpost Overnight)?" But the key to skiffle's popularity was its simple demands: a couple of guitars and a bass made from a length of wash line and a lead-lined tea chest, which you could pick up behind your local grocer's—anyone, it seemed, could do it. It soon spread out of London and all over Britain, even to Liverpool, in the north of England, where a skiffle band called Johnny and the Moondogs tried, with little success, to adapt rock-and-roll tunes to the form. The group's leader, John Lennon, was obsessed with rock and roll, and haunted local record shops seeking out records to hear in the shop's listening booth and shoplift or, if he had to, buy. Before a Moondogs performance at a church fête in Liverpool, a friend of Lennon's introduced him to a kid named Paul McCartney, who had a similar obsession. McCartney had a friend who was a much better guitarist than he or Lennon but who was younger than them: George Harrison. Soon, an actual rock-and-roll band began to form. They needed work, they needed a drummer, and, well, they needed a lot of things.

Back in London, the jazz scene, which had inadvertently given birth to the skiffle scene, also developed another subgenre, blues, which several players attempted to play as break music at jazz gigs, most notably Alexis Korner and Graham Bond, who'd been listening to Muddy Waters and Sonny Boy Williamson, Chicago bluesmen with current American hits. This produced an interesting phenomenon: young fans were coming to hear them, not the main band, and had a cultish interest in the music these older men were playing. Soon, Korner had broken away from his regular employer to form Blues Incorporated, with a regular club gig that began attracting young fans of what they called rhythm and blues. One of the loudest of these fans was a young man from the suburbs named Brian Jones, who wrote impassioned letters to the music press advocating for rhythm and blues and sat in with Korner on harmonica. Eventually, Korner introduced the young fanatic to two other kids, Michael Jagger and Keith Richards, who'd bonded over their love for blues on the Chess label (including Chuck Berry), and the three holed up together in a miserable flat in Chelsea working things out. Their personnel still fluid, they eventually debuted in a South London club as the Rollin' Stones.

This book starts a little while after that. The Beach Boys have established themselves as genuine hit makers, not just faddish promoters of fun in the sun; the Beatles have conquered England; and Capitol, which owned the rights to both of them, still needed hits. It passed on the Beatles' first records, but in late 1963, it decided to give them a whirl. The Rolling Stones would take longer but would inspire another rush of I-can-do-that from teens eager to make their own music. The music business, the music scene, and youth culture itself were about to be transformed.

There's a lot more complexity to the backstory here, and you should seek out and read volume one of this history to find it, which doesn't mean you won't get a great story if you start with this one. More important, readers who were there when all this happened will note some curious omissions or underplaying of events toward the end of this volume: disco, electronic pop, and a small revolution in country music, to state the most glaring examples. There's a reason for this. It became evident during the writing of this volume that a third, and final, volume would be necessary to treat these and other developments with the detail and care they needed. This final volume is in the process of being written.

Another thing: the period treated in this book saw a massive outpouring of popular music. It is more than likely that some of your favorite artists from this period aren't mentioned or are treated with a lack of the detail you may feel they deserve. There's a reason for this: since this period saw the rise of the rock press, it also saw the rise of writers who felt they were capable of treating these subjects in great detail. You could fill several bookshelves with nothing but Beatles books, Stones books, Grateful Dead books, books on labels, books on individual albums, books on posters and album covers, as well as books of criticism and theory. I urge you to read further on topics that interest you: books consulted in the writing of this one are listed in the bibliography, but it's far from an exhaustive one. This book is an overview, nothing more. Its purpose is to show how movements arise, how they interact with their intended audiences, and how they die. And so, on to December 1963.

chapter one

YOUR SONS AND YOUR DAUGHTERS ARE BEYOND YOUR COMMAND

A Fab Four, definitely not authorized Beatles product
(Photo courtesy of Debbie Hudson Baddin, from her collection)

The world of American popular music changed forever on December 26, 1963, although nobody realized it at the time. Oh, there had been ads in the trade magazines showing four disembodied haircuts floating above the words "The Beatles Are Coming!" but so what? Hype was the lifeblood of the record business, and all it meant was that Capitol Records had (perhaps reluctantly) given in to its British parent company's Parlophone subsidiary and decided to put out a record by an act who'd already had records out on two other U.S. labels—records Capitol had passed on. But it was undeniable that the lads were shifting units at home, so it couldn't hurt to try the act out in the States: the band had a new record out, "I Want to Hold Your Hand," and in the new year, Capitol would give it a shot.

It got beaten by Carroll James, a disc jockey at Washington, DC's WWDC-AM, who got a British Overseas Airways Corporation flight attendant friend to slip him a British copy. Listeners seemed to like it, but it wasn't for sale. TV host Jack Paar said he'd be showing film of the Beatles on his January 3 show, and that other notable TV host Ed Sullivan announced that he'd have them on his Sunday night shows on February 9 and 16.

The start of a new year is always an occasion for optimism, though, and the record biz trade magazine *Billboard* ran a big black headline on its January 4 issue (*Billboard* appears in print several days earlier than dated): FORECAST 1964 AS HOTTEST YEAR YET. Well, one would expect nothing less, but in this case it was right: two weeks later, the headline was BRITISH BEATLES HOTTEST CAPITOL SINGLES EVER. This had data behind it: "I Want to Hold Your Hand" had broken into the charts at an unprecedented 45, orders for the record had passed the million mark (200,000 of which had to be farmed out to an RCA pressing plant), and Capitol was hoping to present the Beatles with a gold record when their plane landed in February.

By the next week, war had been declared. Vee-Jay, the Chicago-based rhythm-and-blues label, had licensed a couple of Beatles tracks that Capitol had passed on in 1963, and was now claiming that it had the band under contract, filing injunctions against Capitol and Swan, a sketchy Philadelphia label that had issued "She Loves You," which Vee-Jay had passed on. Capitol, for its part, filed an injunction against Vee-Jay, and Swan looked on as "She Loves You" broke into the charts at 69. The Beatles themselves were preparing for the American tour the way they knew best: by playing a residency at the Olympia the-ater in Paris from January 16 to February 4, sharing the bill with American singer Trini Lopez and French yé-yé singer Sylvie Vartan. The French reviews were lousy, but manager Brian Epstein kept get-ting reports from New York that made them irrelevant.

On February 7, the first-class Pan Am lounge at Heathrow filled up with the Beatles party: the four group members; Epstein; Tony Barrow, a newspaperman from Liverpool who'd covered them from the beginning; Neil Aspinall, another close friend from Liverpool; Mal Evans, who'd become their roadie; and surprisingly, John Len-non's no-longer-secret wife, Cynthia. Rounding out the first-class cabin once they got on were Phil Spector and the Ronettes (one of whom was dating George Harrison)—Spector was hoping to be able to spend the flight convincing them to let him produce a Beatles record; Maureen Cleave, a British journalist who'd written about the band extensively; a reporter for the Liverpool *Echo* confusingly named George Harrison; and some Capitol Records guys who'd handle the landing logistics, or so they hoped. Back in tourist class was a gaggle of British businessmen who were hoping that the long flight would give them a chance to talk to Brian about making deals on Beatles merchandise. Fat chance—the flight attendants refused to take their notes into first class. Finally, Dezo Hoffmann, the official Beatles photographer, took pity on them and gave them the name of David Jacobs, the London solicitor who looked after the Beatles' and Epstein's affairs. As the plane came in for a landing, they noticed a huge crowd on the tarmac, and it wasn't until Spector took out some binoculars and said, "Look! Look! They're holding up Beatles banners!" that the passengers snapped to what was happening. The noise was insane, as was the size of the crowd, but with the help of the NYPD, they all made it into a huge hall, where a crowd of two hundred journalists awaited the Beatles' first American press conference.

Brian Sommerville, their press secretary, had flown in two days earlier to coordinate things with Capitol, and was waiting at the table with the microphones after the band cleared customs. According to eyewitnesses, the hostility in the room was palpable. The screaming hordes outside notwithstanding, there was an undercurrent of resentment for these weird-looking foreign punks who'd taken an American invention and used it to become millionaires. There was a thrum of conversation, eye-watering amounts of cigar smoke, and a constant flashing of cameras. Finally, Sommerville, a former navy commander, said, "Shut up! Just shut up!" and the Beatles all said, "Yeah, shurrup!" And the Americans did, and applauded. Then the questions began. "Are you going to get a haircut in America?" was the first, fielded by Lennon: "We had one yesterday." "Will you sing something for us?" John again: "We need money first." After a few more witticisms of the sort the boys would soon perfect, it was into the limos—Paul had his hair grabbed by a reporter who was trying to take off his nonexistent wig—and off to the Plaza Hotel, which had begged New York's other hotels to take the group upon learning that Brian's description of "businessman" for each of them wasn't quite accurate. Over the next few days, the Beatles were essentially captive there, although by some superhuman feat of jet lag avoidance, on that first night, Paul managed to go to the Playboy Club, and the Lennons and Ringo went down to the Peppermint Lounge to see what it was all about. Ringo wasn't recognized, while John and Cynthia beat a hasty retreat. Anyway, nobody was twisting: the house band was doing Beatles songs.

The next day, the band did a rehearsal at CBS Studios for the Sullivan show, except for George, who'd come down with a sore throat and was being ministered to by his sister—she'd married an American and lived in the Midwest—and on the night of February 9, they did the show, viewed by seventy million people. It didn't sound all that hot, since this was the era before stage monitors, and there were also all those shrieking girls, but it did the trick: Beatlemania was now nationwide, and that night, a baton was passed as Ed Sullivan opened their segment of the show by reading a telegram wishing them luck, signed by Elvis Presley and "Colonel Tom" Parker, Elvis's manager.

The next day, another press conference, this time at the Plaza Hotel. It went on long enough that the band ordered (and was served) lunch midway through it. The next day, they were scheduled to go to Washington, DC, which hadn't initially been on the schedule, but given that they'd been paid only three thousand dollars for the Sullivan show, Epstein had decided they needed to make a bit of cash. There was a snag: one reason so many people had seen them Sunday night was that a huge snowstorm had hit the Northeast, and nobody went out. It snowed all through the next day, and was still snowing the morning they were supposed to head to Washington. A quick round of phone calls resulted in a private car being added to a Washington-bound train that would arrive in plenty of time for them to get set up and rehearse, and that night they took the stage before a large audience in the Coliseum, introduced by Carroll James, after which they went to a party thrown for them at the British embassy, where they were treated like a novelty—enough so that a woman felt entitled to walk up to Ringo and snip off a piece of his hair with her nail scissors. They soldiered on, though, heading back to New York City for two shows at Carnegie Hall, and then to Miami Beach for the next Sullivan show. On February 22, they got back on a plane to England, leaving chaos in their wake. But they had a film to make.

A new landscape had been opened up. For one thing, the demographics were different: retailers reported that really young kids were coming in to buy a Beatles record or two but nothing else. And then there were the toys: Brian Epstein was trying hard to control the amount of Beatlesploitation merchandise on the market, but although (for instance) there were authorized Beatles wigs for sale, you couldn't stop people from selling a shaggy mop without explicitly connecting it with the band—and selling it cheaper. And there were loads of records coming out: the Swans' "The Boy with the Beatle Hair," Donna Lynn's "My Boyfriend Got a Beatle Haircut" and the Buddies' instrumental "The Beatle" were just the first in a torrent that culminated at year's end with ventriloquist puppets Tich and Quackers's "Santa, Bring Me Ringo." Record companies that had missed on the Beatles settled for British bands in general: Epic was the first, releasing "Glad All Over," by the Dave Clark Five, in January and advertising it as "Mersey Beat!" thereby ingeniously rerouting Liverpool's iconic River Mersey to London, the Five's home. Laurie Records signed Gerry and the Pacemakers, another Brian Epstein client; while Kapp had the Searchers, Atco the Fourmost, and Liberty both Billy J. Kramer and the Dakotas and the Swinging Blue Jeans—all of whom were Liverpool bands (oddly, the Merseybeats went unsigned in America). Nearby, Manchester's Hollies were also on Liberty, MGM snagged Newcastle's Animals, and London was represented by the Shadows on Atlantic, the Zombies on Parrot, and, oh yes, the Rolling Stones on London. The relentless torrent of English bands reached a kind of pathetic end in May 1965, when a trio called Ian and the Zodiacs released an album with the three guys pictured with a speech bubble that read, "We're new! We're from England! We have a new sound!" By then, nobody cared; there was enough choice for the moment.

During the Beatles' transatlantic flight in February, George Harrison the guitarist remarked to George Harrison the Liverpool journalist, "They've got everything over there," meaning the United States. "What do they want *us* for?" The answer to that question has been discussed ad nauseam, but he had a point. There were other cultural currents flowing, and they'd be important to the changing face of popular music in America and England and very much to the Beatles themselves.

Folk music, for one thing. What had started with the Kingston Trio and Peter, Paul and Mary on the one hand and the New Lost

City Ramblers on the other was now an established part of the music business. What might be called hootenanny bands were everywhere, with groups such as the Knob Lick Upper 10,000, the Serendipity Singers, the Back Porch Majority, the Folkwomen, and the Chad Mitchell Trio releasing albums that mixed sing-along tunes with solo numbers for a featured singer. These groups were popular as live acts on college campuses, although most didn't seem to sell many records. Another part of the folk movement was the "authentic" crowd, which included songwriters modeling themselves on Bob Dylan's stance in his latest album, *The Times They Are a-Changin'*, a collection of mostly protest songs, like the title tune, "With God on Our Side," and "When the Ship Comes In." (*Billboard* said of the album, "General theme is one of forlorn sadness and dismay at man's fight with life.") These included former journalist Phil Ochs, American Indian activist Buffy Sainte-Marie, left-wing housewife Malvina Reynolds, and of course Pete Seeger, who made a mini-hit out of Reynolds's rather obvious slam at suburbia, "Little Boxes." There were also loads of folk artists just writing songs and singing selected folk material. Ian and Sylvia were a Canadian duo who sang folk tinged with country, occasionally in Quebecois French; the Greenbriar Boys tried out urban bluegrass and scored with folkies; and Folkways was releasing material by newly found traditional performers like Roscoe Holcomb and Dock Boggs. Contributing to the ongoing folkie discussion of "Can/should white men sing/play the blues" were Dave Van Ronk; Minneapolis's Koerner, Ray and Glover; and John Hammond, the son of the man who'd signed Bob Dylan to Columbia. And if you were committed to authenticity but needed comic relief, there was the Jim Kweskin Jug Band out of Boston, featuring two wonderful singers, Geoff and Maria Muldaur; and New York's distinctly odd Holy Modal Rounders. None of these folks were selling many records, either, although the cumulative effect of their prodigious output and popularity on campuses and in folkie circles probably generated money. As for artists who were okay with the "authenticists," there was Joan Baez (never off the charts since her first album) and (grudgingly, occasionally) Peter, Paul and Mary, who astonished the biz by selling huge numbers of their double-LP live album, *In Concert*.

In fact, the rediscovery and discovery of older performers was a vital part of what would happen next. In June 1964, a sportswriter and folk fan named Dick Waterman and two other guys tracked down Eddie J. "Son" House, a legendary Delta bluesman, in Rochester, New York, of all places. Excited to get him to perform at that year's Newport Folk Festival, which was imminent, they made the approach only to find that another group of fans had tracked down Nehemiah "Skip" James, yet another legendary figure who'd been only a name on rare records up to then. The two legends would join Mississippi John Hurt, who'd been found the previous year and, like the other two, still had all his virtuosity intact, as well as a gentle charisma that magnetized audiences. (The story that a fan played one of Hurt's records to classical guitar icon Andrés Segovia, who declared that there were two guitarists playing, is, alas, not true.) Not only did Ralph Rinzler, the mandolinist of the Greenbriar Boys, track down the Folkways *Anthology* star Clarence Ashley and invite him to New York to play in a concert organized by Friends of Old Time Music, a nonprofit he'd organized, but when Ashley showed up, he had in tow a much younger man from his town, Arthel "Doc" Watson, who confounded folk guitarists with his speed and accuracy and went on to become a beloved folk performer. It was the realization that these old-timers had recorded these records in what seemed a far-off time but was actually a mere thirty-five years ago at most that gave new strength to the "authentic" wing of the folk movement.

Seemingly a million miles from folkdom was soul music. The civil rights movement is associated with the folk hymn "We Shall Overcome," discovered by folklorist Guy Carawan and rewritten and popularized by Pete Seeger, but Chicago's Impressions, led by Curtis Mayfield, were not only having hits but having hits with carefully encoded freedom messages that echoed 1964's passage of the Civil Rights Act. Their remarkable string of records started with "It's All Right" in late 1963, which was followed by "I'm So Proud" (supposedly about the singer's girlfriend), "Keep On Pushing," and "Amen" in 1964 (taken from the soundtrack of the film *Lilies of the Field*, which gave Sidney Poitier his first Oscar), and laid it all out in the open with "People Get Ready" in 1965, a mix of gospel fervor and determination that became an instant classic. Mayfield was brave: the black church was still not fully behind Martin Luther King Jr. (nor, needless to say, were older white people), and few other performers dared to be so forthright, although the Vibrations' "My Girl Sloopy" lived on the bad side of town, and some associated Martha and the Vandellas' "Dancing in the Street" with summer race riots—a bit of a stretch. But the other great song of the movement was on the flip side of Sam Cooke's dance tune "Shake." "A Change Is Gonna Come" has a leisurely pace and optimism that could have come from the pen of Dr. King himself: it had been a long time coming, but a change was going to come.

Cooke was rethinking things, though. He announced that he was quitting the road to concentrate on SAR, the label he'd set up with his manager, J. W. Alexander, and playing a waiting game: his staff producers, Hugo and Luigi, hadn't renewed their contract with RCA and had moved to Roulette. Soon, RCA would need new material, and maybe Cooke thought he could get someone who would help him inject a little more soul into the material. He had plans: he had an idea for a blues album, with material by the likes of Muddy Waters and John Lee Hooker. He'd released "Shake" and "A Change Is Gonna Come." A 1963 date at the Harlem Square Club in Miami was recorded and shelved, and when it was released many years later, it showed a much grittier side of Sam, one that Otis Redding, for one, revered. Who knows where 1965 would take him? But we'll never know. On the night of December 11, he went out alone, eventually meeting up with some business friends at Martoni's, a showbiz restaurant. During the course of the evening, he noticed a pretty young girl, Elisa Boyer, sitting with some musicians he knew, and she noticed him, too. They wound up going for a drive together, and she suggested they go to a nice hotel in Hollywood, but Sam knew a place where musicians went and you didn't get hassled. By the time they pulled up at the Hacienda Motel, 2:30 in the morning, Sam was pretty loaded. In the room, he started acting odd, tearing Boyer's clothes off. She retreated to the bathroom, only to find out the lock didn't work. She came back out to find Sam naked. He then went into the bathroom, and when he came out, Boyer and all Sam's clothes except his jacket had disappeared. He went to the motel office wearing the sports jacket and nothing else, apparently under the impression that the manager, Bertha Lee Franklin, was hiding Boyer. She denied it, and Sam started breaking down the office door. It didn't take long for the door to shatter, and he lurched in, looking all over for the girl and then attacking Franklin. They tussled for a while, and she grabbed the gun she kept in the office; it wasn't like this hadn't happened before. Sam went for the gun, and Franklin's first shot went into the ceiling. She shot again. Her third shot went into his chest, the bullet going through his heart and his lungs. "Lady, you shot me," Sam said and ran at her. She picked up a stick and hit him over the head. He fell to the floor, dead. The case was ruled a justifiable homicide and Franklin was never charged.

Had Cooke lived, SAR would have had stiff competition from Motown, which was just about to enter its first classic period and was aiming to be, as its label would soon claim, "the sound of young America." Its founder, Berry Gordy (although deeply committed to civil rights personally), wasn't looking to alienate anyone with political statements. Nineteen sixty-four, after all, was the year of the Temptations' "The Way You Do the Things You Do," "The Girl's Alright with Me," and "Girl (Why You Wanna Make Me Blue)"; Marvin Gaye's "You're a Wonderful One," "Baby Don't You Do It," and "How Sweet It Is to Be Loved By You" (just to mention the ones that were strong pop crossovers); the Marvelettes' "Too Many Fish in the Sea"; Mary Wells's "My Guy"; and most important for Gordy, the long-anticipated breakthrough of the "no-hit" Supremes, who finally found gold that summer with "Where Did Our Love Go," followed swiftly by "Baby Love," "Come See About Me," and, continuing the streak into '65, "Stop! In the Name of Love" and "Back in My Arms Again." Motown was putting out enough classics that wonderful records such as the Velvelettes' "He Was Really Saying Something" just got lost, and the label's first hit maker, Mary Wells, felt she was being ignored and refused to re-sign with Gordy, going on to 20th Century Fox and obscurity. It was also the year of the first Motortown Revue tour overseas. Rumor around Hitsville U.S.A. was that the Revue would soon be playing the Copa.

As for other soul music, it was carrying on as always. In Memphis, Bobby "Blue" Bland knocked out three R&B top 10 hits in a row, including the masterful "Share Your Love with Me," and his closest competitor, Little Milton, had the biggest hit of his career with "We're Gonna Make It," which mixed romance with a bit of black pride. In Chicago, deep soul vocalist Mitty Collier followed "Let Them Talk" with "I Had a Talk with My Man," written by gospel superstar James Cleveland. In New Orleans, Irma Thomas had her long-awaited breakthrough with "Wish Someone Would Care," only to have her brilliant follow-up, "Time Is On My Side," squashed by the Rolling Stones' version, while the classic girl group the Dixie Cups topped the pop charts with "Chapel of Love" in 1964, and had a very odd hit the next year with "Iko Iko," an irresistible bit of percussion overlaid with bizarre lyrics: a traditional Mardi Gras Indian chant. And in Memphis, Stax was struggling to survive, which meant developing Otis Redding as a hit maker and trying to have some hits with Booker T. and the M.G.'s, who'd swapped out their original bassist, Lewis Steinberg, for Donald "Duck" Dunn, a childhood friend of guitarist Steve Cropper, which made all the difference. But nothing really paid off until December 1964, when Redding released a two-sided smash, "That's How Strong My Love Is" backed with "Mr. Pitiful." Still, Stax had great hopes for the young man, and for a duet that Atlantic (which was now distributing Stax) had found in Miami: Sam and Dave.

Atlantic was doing its bit for the development of soul with Solomon Burke, whose "Everybody Needs Somebody to Love" once again reminded people that he was also an ordained minister, while the Drifters' "Under the Boardwalk" was one of the hottest singles of 1964's summer, Johnny Moore's lead vocal suggesting that he'd be there on a blanket with his baby, thereby proving that surfing wasn't the only recreation you could get at the beach. The Impressions' former lead singer, Jerry Butler, duetted with Betty Everett on the slow jam "Let It Be Me," while Maxine Brown protested "Oh No Not My Baby," and Little Anthony and the Imperials kept the old-school vocal group sound alive with "I'm On the Outside (Looking In)," "Goin' Out of My Head," and "Hurt So Bad," not bad for a group that had

had its first hit in 1958. The Larks told us how to do "The Jerk," and they were quickly joined by Motown's own Miracles, who further urged teens to "Come On Do the Jerk."

But it was the Brits who were grabbing all the attention. The Beatles had rushed back to England to get to work on their movie, which had been written by a Welsh screenwriter, Alun Owen, and would be directed by an American living in London, Richard Lester, who'd won John Lennon's heart by directing television shows and films with a comedy troupe, the Goons, whose records the Beatles' producer, George Martin, had made. As a hastily assembled book of John's writings, *A Spaniard in the Works,* showed, Lennon adored them almost to the point of imitation. The Beatles' film was not (thank heavens) called *The Beatles,* as early reports would have it, but *A Hard Day's Night,* after a malapropism Ringo had uttered, and it took all of six and a half weeks to shoot. Actually, it might as well have been called *The Beatles,* because that's a good summary of the plot: the Beatles come to London to shoot a television program and are met by Beatlemania. And that's it. The result, however, is a tribute to the band, Richard Lester, and Alun Owen, who managed to hang fantasy, stunning cinematic technique, and, of course, the band's singing and playing onto these bare bones.

There's a fifth major character, Paul's grandfather (played by Wilfrid Brambell), a tall, cadaverous gentleman who is anarchic and has to be carefully watched. The band is holed up in a hotel, where their managers want them to sign photos and answer fan mail while they go out to get the TV station ready. Each Beatle is moved by Grandfather's incitement to revolt, and each has various adventures. There is a press conference, of course, with food and drink, none of which the various Beatles can lay hands on. And there is the all-important rehearsal, which the boys barely make. Finally, of course, the show goes on. And that's that.

But it's more than that. For one thing, if you went to see the Beatles in real life then, you never really got close to the action, you couldn't hear anything because of the primitive sound setup onstage and the

screaming girls, and it was unlikely you saw any of their faces. Going
to this movie, though, you saw everything bigger than life, and heard
it all in studio-mixed sound. Lester's use of handheld cameras, where
the cameramen ran along with the band, particularly in the scenes
where the boys are pursued by screaming fans (male and female, recruited mostly from various performing arts schools—young Philip
Collins, a talented drummer, is visible in the audience of the climac-
tic TV show), add speed to the film, so that when it pauses for a set
piece, it's just a matter of time until another rush comes along. And
shooting it in black-and-white made it look like a newsreel, or television.

The "British Invasion," as it became known—the phrase, as far as can
be determined, was first used in this regard on page four of *Billboard*'s
March 21, 1964 issue—would, of course, become reality only if there
were other British artists having hits, which was by no means certain
at the time. Columbia, for instance, put out an album, *The Exciting
Liverpool Sound*, containing dud tracks by Sonny Webb and the Cas-
cades, Ian and the Zodiacs, Ringo's former band Rory Storm and the
Hurricanes, Faron's Flamingos, and others. Labels that had already
signed English acts wondered how they'd get them on the charts. In
that same 1964 issue of *Billboard*, the Beatles, on four different labels
(including MGM's issue of the Tony Sheridan recordings from Hamburg), occupied slots 1, 2, 3, 7, 14, 42, 58, and 79. But it could be
done: the Dave Clark Five didn't seem to have much problem with
"Glad All Over"; Chad and Jeremy, a quiet duo hyped as "the Oxford
Sound," did okay in the teeth of Beatlemania with "Yesterday's Gone"
and better that summer with "A Summer Song"; and the Animals'
"House of the Rising Sun" (based on the version on Bob Dylan's first
album) tussled with "A Hard Day's Night" to reach the top slot in
August.

For their part, the Rolling Stones, despite not having ridden the
Invasion's coattails with single hits, nonetheless decided to come to
the States in June to tour. There was the obligatory press conference—
Their hair? "This is a style set by Charles the First." Influences? "Bo
Diddley and Chuck Berry"—and an appearance on the Les Crane

show *Night Line,* a decided step or two down from Sullivan, after which they flew to Los Angeles, where another TV show, *The Hollywood Palace,* with Dean Martin making hostile remarks about their appearance, awaited them: after Larry Griswold, an acrobat, did his act, Martin said, "That's the father of the Rolling Stones; he's been trying to kill himself ever since." Then, after a trip to RCA Studios, where they met Phil Spector's arranger, Jack Nitzsche, with whom they would later record, they took a bus to their first gig, at San Bernardino's Swing Auditorium, which was a success. Less so the next one: two days at the Teen Fair of Texas, in San Antonio, where they shared the bill with country star George Jones, some trained monkeys, and Bobby Vee, who, unlike the audience, was impressed. The crowds at the next few shows, in Minneapolis, Omaha, and Detroit, numbered in the mid-hundreds. The Stones barely paid attention: on June 10 and 11, they were off, and scheduled to record at no less a shrine than 2120 South Michigan Avenue, Chicago: Chess Studios, where their idols had recorded the records that had brought the Stones together. During their time there they recorded fourteen tracks, met Chuck Berry, Buddy Guy, and Muddy Waters—"That guitar player ain't bad," Waters observed of Brian Jones—and got to talk to Bo Diddley on the phone. Then it was back to New York, overnight at a hotel, and home to London.

They returned to the States in October, though, for a can't-miss opportunity. A young TV director, Steve Binder, had hooked up with a guy named Joseph E. Bluth, who'd invented a high-definition television camera he called "Electronovision," for the purpose of recording shows—his first was Richard Burton's Broadway production of *Hamlet*—and showing them via closed circuit in movie theaters. This was all funded by a guy named Bill Sargent, who had some money to spend. Sargent had founded the Home Entertainment Company for pay-TV in the home, and had gone on to found another company, Subscription Television Inc., which provided closed-circuit sports events for theaters. After expanding his scope with Burton's *Hamlet,* he decided that his next project would be a concert launching an international nonprofit that would do annual concerts to raise money for music scholarships. Thus, the first Teen Age Music International (T.A.M.I.) Show was conceived. What with the invading Brits and the hot young black acts in America, it seemed like the perfect time to do this, so Sargent got Jack Nitzsche to put together a studio band while he booked the talent: Chuck Berry, backed by Liverpudlians Gerry and the Pacemakers; Smokey Robinson and the Miracles; Marvin Gaye; Lesley Gore; Jan and Dean; the Beach Boys; Brits Billy J. Kramer and the Dakotas; the Supremes; Boston's Barbarians, whose drummer had only one hand and held his other stick in a hook; and, well, the climax: Sargent ordered the Rolling Stones to close the show. This terrified them, and justly so: immediately preceding them would be James Brown, who put on his typical energetic show, boiled down to four songs, including the cape routine. He'd show *them*. Recorded at the Santa Monica Civic Auditorium over two days, October 28 and 29, the *T.A.M.I. Show* was presented at some LA theaters on November 14, and made available nationwide the next month; it was released in Britain as *Teen Age Command Performance* or *Gather No Moss*. Not long afterward, the whole shebang collapsed for lack of funds, squabbles over rights, and the fact that the show hadn't made much money. Teen Age Music International was never heard from again, and for those who hadn't seen it in the theater, the *T.A.M.I. Show* remained a delicious rumor. Released on DVD in 2009, it's a revelation: Billy J. Kramer turned out to be a wonderful performer. Chuck Berry, who was rumored to have caused some of the production's shortfall by demanding his fee in cash before he'd even plug in (a longstanding policy of his then and later that apparently caught the producers by surprise) still had it. Lesley Gore was superb with her proto-feminist anthem "You Don't Own Me." The Motown folks were backed not only by the Motortown Revue band but also by Nitzsche's crew, which included studio stalwarts Glen Campbell and Leon Russell on guitar and piano, along with Jimmy Bond on bass, Hal Blaine on drums, and Phil Spector's tenor saxophonist "Teenage" Steve Douglas. And James Brown's band was so hot that in the film, one can catch Glen Campbell craning his neck to see just what the hell is going on. The Stones overcame their nervousness enough to do a good closer, and to show there were no hard feelings, Brown invited them to see his whole show at the Apollo the next weekend, an offer they were smart enough to accept.

And what was mainstream pop music doing to defend itself against the Invasion? Carrying on with business as usual, for the most part. The smart money noticed that the Brits seemed to appeal mostly to younger females. While their little sisters fantasized over which Beatle they loved the most, boys lusted after cars, and one of the great hot-rod records, "Dead Man's Curve," by Jan and Dean, referred to a real stretch of Sunset Boulevard where, in 1966, cowriter Jan Berry would have an automobile accident that nearly cost him his life.

Another thing that was going full steam was so-called "girl group" records, which cut across all kinds of categories. Motown's Marvelettes and Velvelettes certainly qualified, as did the Shirelles and most of Phil Spector's output to date: the Crystals, the Ronettes, Darlene Love.

Teen Pan Alley, the young New York songwriters who mostly worked for Aldon Music, had provided both content and performers, as its demo-cutting Cookies began to have hits together and solo— Little Eva was a Cookie, as was Earl-Jean, whose "I'm into Something Good" was covered by Herman's Hermits—and there were even single female singers, including Lesley Gore, who started 1964 with "You Don't Own Me" (and, in June, graduated from high school as an honor student), who partook of the "girl group sound" while not being part of a group. The most baroque of all of them, though, was the Shangri-Las, two sets of sisters (two of them twins) from Long Island produced by the mysterious Spector wannabe George "Shadow" Morton. Their first two singles were notable for their spoken parts and their sound effects: "Remember (Walking in the Sand)" had seagulls, and "Leader of the Pack" was about a boy who horrifies the lead singer's parents because he leads a motorcycle gang. The climax is when she witnesses his death: a long skid, the girlfriend (in her thickest Long Island accent) saying, "Loogoud, loogoud, *loogoud!*" followed by a mighty crash. It was arguably the most action-packed two minutes and fifty-two seconds on the charts all year.

Nineteen sixty-four was also the year of the "Louie Louie" scandal.

Back in 1957, Richard Berry, a veteran LA R&B singer, had tried to jump on the cha-cha wagon with the simple three-chord lament in faux-Jamaican dialect about a separated pair of lovers. Berry played guitar in all sorts of bands, and he'd freely adapted his ditty from "El Loco Cha Cha," which he'd played with a band in East LA, who'd learned it from a record by one René Touzet. Berry's record company, in its wisdom, hid "Louie Louie" on the B-side of yet another version of "You Are My Sunshine," and Berry had to wait a bit longer for a hit. Meanwhile, the record attained cult status in the Pacific Northwest, where, spurred by the success of the Ventures, guitar bands started springing up, some with vocalists. The Kingsmen were one such band, from Portland, Oregon, and their recording of "Louie, Louie" on a tiny local label, Jerden, started selling so well that Scepter's subsidiary Wand licensed it, and it went all the way to number two in November 1963. Guitarist Jack Ely was not an outstanding vocalist, though; what carried the song was its instrumental power. Boys who bought the record strained to make out the lyrics—it was a natural for a beginning band to play—and thought they heard all kinds of things. The governor of Indiana, who apparently had nothing else to worry about, ordered radio stations in his state to ban the "pornographic" record, and the song's publisher offered a thousand dollars to anyone who could find anything suggestive in the lyrics. Eventually, the FBI got involved, and of course the record and the Kingsmen's albums sold and sold and sold in the teeth of Beatlemania. Kingsmen rivals Paul Revere and the Raiders (who had also recorded the song) released "Louie Go Home" in March.

Regular pop music, too, was still very much in evidence, with Broadway's *Hello, Dolly!* soundtrack selling great guns and Louis Armstrong's recording of the title tune dethroning the Beatles (if only for a week). Barbra Streisand's ubiquitous "People" was a notable mainstream hit, while singers such as Dusty Springfield and Dionne Warwick were working with great writers like Burt Bacharach. Nashville was also providing fine pop music, via Roy Orbison, who hit the top 10 twice with the operatic "It's Over" and the rock-inflected "Pretty Woman"; while the goofy Roger Miller, an old running buddy of Willie Nelson's and a veteran, like Nelson, of Ray Price's band, started hitting the charts with novelty songs such as "Dang Me," "Chug-a-Lug," and the song that made his fortune, "King of the Road." In November, Capitol Records announced the "Teen Underground" movement: "Don't tell your rock and roll friends that you listen to the good music things," their campaign said. Once you'd joined, you got a keychain with a "secret number" that entitled you to discounts at the Sight and Sound chain of record and audio stores. No word about any takers, though.

For the most part, things were calming down, and in *Billboard*'s November 7, 1964, issue, it was noted that for the first time that year the Beatles didn't have a song on the singles chart. Not that the British Invasion was over: in November, the Rolling Stones had their first top 10 single, a cover of Irma Thomas's "Time Is On My Side," followed in short order by *12×5*, the album containing some of the cuts they'd recorded at Chess Studios. Another crucial album that came out late in the year was *Another Side of Bob Dylan*, which contained not a single protest song but reflected some on Dylan's breakup with Suze Rotolo, the girl on the cover of his *Freewheelin'* album, as well as more abstract and mysterious stuff. There was no single, but Johnny Cash, who was a rabid Dylan fan, released one of the songs, "It Ain't Me Babe," with his wife, June Carter, duetting. It went top 10 country but didn't really disturb pop radio much.

Nineteen sixty-four was also the year Chuck Berry got out of prison. Chess had kept his career alive by releasing some of the tunes he'd recorded before, as well as a couple of albums, and he basked in the admiration of the Rolling Stones when they were in Chicago. Radio still considered him poison, though, and his first post-prison single, "Nadine," didn't bother the top 10. Although the follow-up, "No Particular Place to Go," scraped the bottom slot, his "teenage wedding" song, "You Never Can Tell," fared less well, and "Promised Land," a coded tale of driving cross-country while black, didn't do well at all. And that was almost it for Chuck Berry. Of the other pioneers, Jerry Lee Lewis was slowly, painfully reinventing himself as a country singer, while also playing incendiary live shows, including one that was recorded at the Beatles' old haunt, the Star-Club in Hamburg, where Lewis was backed by the Liverpudlian Nashville Teens; the album remained unreleased in the United States for years. Little Richard emerged from the seminary and rerecorded his hits for Vee-Jay to widespread indifference; Carl Perkins was on the road with Johnny Cash; Fats Domino was putting out records every couple of months that hit the bottom of the charts and then disappeared; and Elvis—well, Elvis was making movies and releasing soundtrack albums, and at Christmas his sultry version of the old Ernest Tubb classic "Blue Christmas" battled it out with Brenda Lee's "Rockin' Around the Christmas Tree" for holiday hit status. As for the classic record labels, King finally won its injunction against Smash for continuing to release James Brown's records—he'd had a smash for the latter with "Out of Sight"—only to put the label (and, most important, its music publishing wing, Lois Music, which owned such numbers as "Fever" and "The Twist") up for sale. Syd Nathan, King's founder, who was living in Florida, said he was looking forward to doing a lot more fishing. It seemed to be going around: the Beatles announced that their next film would be shot in the Bahamas.

The British didn't stop invading. The names were getting odder now. It started with the Kinks, a London band whose drummer had been in the Rolling Stones for a brief moment. They had launched a nasty piece of aggression entitled "You Really Got Me" into the top 10 in September 1964; followed it up swiftly after Christmas with the scarcely less primitive "All Day and All of the Night," another top 10 hit; and made it a trifecta with "Tired of Waiting for You" in the spring. The band sounded like it had one foot in the Beatles' rawer stuff and the other in the "Louie Louie" camp. They were all set to make it big, but Ray and Dave Davies, the brothers who started the band, fought constantly with each other and other musicians, and their violent behavior got them banned from the United States by the American Federation of Musicians in late spring, so they spent the next few years invading via vinyl only.

The next weird name was Them, a combo of roughnecks from Belfast whose first U.S. single, "Gloria," didn't do all that well but eventually wormed its way into the eardrums of the kind of kids who started bands. Their next single, "Here Comes the Night," was written by their producer, Bert Berns, and did considerably better. The band's front man, Ivan Morrison, whose friends called him Van, had a spooky intensity as a performer. And if Them wasn't a confusing enough name, how about another London band, the Who? "Anyway, Anyhow, Anywhere" didn't go anywhere, but "I Can't Explain" bothered the bottom of the charts in March 1965. Rumor was they had a great live show, but they weren't going to tour overseas until they had a hit, which might take a while. Then there were the Zombies, whose cheery songs such as "She's Not There" and "Tell Her No" partook of a Beatle-y flavor and zipped into the top 10. And, of course, the Beatles and the Stones helped keep the balance of payments lopsided, too, the latter starting an unfortunate trend that British bands would continue by releasing a Staple Singers song, "The Last Time," and taking credit for writing it themselves.

And then there was the British Invasion band that wasn't: Huey P. Meaux, the Houston-based producer who specialized in taking Texas and Louisiana acts onto the charts, and who had a lucrative leasing deal with Mercury for when those bands got too big for his own labels to handle, was in a funk. "I had Dale and Grace at number one, Paul and Paula in the top 10, Barbara Lynn coming up fast and then the Beatles hit and bang! I was out of business," he remembered years later, characteristically exaggerating his successes. As he told the story, he got a bunch of Beatles records, a case of cheap wine, and a portable record player, and rented three rooms in a motel, staying in the middle one so he wouldn't disturb any neighbors. "After a couple of days of drinking and listening to those records over and over, it hit me: the beat was *on the beat*! Just like the Cajun music my pappy used to play!" Again, this is kind of hard to parse, but Meaux did have a solution: a kid from San Antonio who'd been pestering him. This time when the kid came to Houston asking to record, Huey had an answer: "Grow you some fuckin' hair, get a band, and let's record some of this shit." Thus, Doug Sahm, a multi-instrumentalist who'd come up in the San Antonio clubs playing country, blues, and R&B with racially and culturally integrated bands, grabbed four other guys from more or less the same background and drove them to Houston. Meaux was very happy: the band looked good, sounded good, and Sahm had intuited that a kind of Tex-Mex beat was what he'd been asked for, so he had some songs ready to go. The best was one called "She's a Body Mover," but Meaux nixed that title, and it became "She's About a Mover." That didn't make sense, but the record was perfect for the times. To cash in on the British Invasion, Meaux called them the Sir Douglas Quintet, thinking that sounded English. The record took off, almost making the top 10 in the spring of 1965, and the band's disguise worked until they got to Los Angeles, where Trini Lopez, a kind of frenetic folk act, was hosting a television program they were booked for. Introducing them, he noted that he'd thought they were British, but backstage he'd gotten talking to them and discovered that they, like him, were from Texas! It really didn't make much difference: their subsequent records didn't sell as well, and a 1966 pot bust put a temporary end to their story. Nor were they the only Texans making noise: The Bobby Fuller Four had been the biggest thing in El Paso, recording regional hits on local labels. Feeling the town was too small to contain them, they'd moved to LA just in time for Beatlemania. Four clean-cut young guys who all played guitars and sang was just what everyone wanted, and soon they were the house band at the Sunset Strip's hottest nightclub, the Whisky a Go Go. After flopping on Liberty with the superb "Let Her Dance," backed with "Another Sad and Lonely Night," they formed Mustang Records and had a top 10 hit with "I Fought the Law," written by ex-Cricket Sonny Curtis. They followed it up with an update of "Love's Made a Fool of You," by Curtis's ex-employer Buddy Holly. The Fuller Four did television, broke into film with *The Ghost in the Invisible Bikini,* and might have seriously challenged the Brits had Bobby Fuller not been found dead, covered in gasoline, in his mother's car in July 1966. No serious investigation of the death was attempted until the twenty-first century, and even then, the results were muddled; suffice it to say nobody believes it was a suicide.

On March 13, 1965, the *Billboard* top 10 singles were "Eight Days a Week," by the Beatles; "My Girl," by the Temptations; "Stop! In the Name of Love," by the Supremes; "This Diamond Ring," by Gary Lewis and the Playboys (Gary was Jerry Lewis's son); "The Birds and the Bees," by Jewel Akens (a one-hit wonder from Houston); "King of the Road," by Roger Miller; "Ferry Cross the Mersey," by Gerry and the Pacemakers; "Can't You Hear My Heartbeat," by Herman's Hermits; "The Jolly Green Giant," by the Kingsmen; and "Hurt So Bad," by Little Anthony and the Imperials. The list that year was an amazing cross section of where American pop music taste was at that point. It was also about to get upset in a big way: among the single releases that week was something called "Subterranean Homesick Blues," by Bob Dylan—with an electric band behind him. It wasn't Dylan's first venture into rock and roll; he'd released something called "Mixed Up Confusion" in 1962, only to see it swiftly withdrawn by Columbia, which figured their folk star playing electric was a bad idea. Most of his fans had never gotten to hear it. But this—another very abstract lyric chanted above a single chord—was another matter entirely. "Subterranean Homesick Blues" started ascending the charts while Dylan himself packed for a quick solo acoustic tour of England, from April 30 to May 10. He took along a filmmaker, D. A. Pennebaker, to shoot the tour onstage and off. The film, *Dont Look Back,* wouldn't open until May 17, 1967.

By then, things would be very, very different.

chapter two

ANNUS MIRABILIS II: HELP FROM MY FRIENDS

Pre–Family Dog, Red Dog Saloon veterans throw a benefit,
Christmas 1965. *(Author's collection)*

A great number of things happened in June 1965, enough to make one wonder if it would be prudent to consult an astrologer for an explanation. Some of them were decades in the making, some mere years, and others spur-of-the-moment. But in retrospect there's little doubt that this was an earthshaking month.

One of the events had its genesis one night when three friends were in a small cabin nestled in a played-out silver mine in Silver City, Nevada, just south of Reno, that its owner, Don Works, had dubbed the Zen Mine, doubtless a pun on Shunryu Suzuki's popular book *Zen Mind, Beginner's Mind*. Works had moved there several years earlier to be near the Paiute and Washoe practitioners of his adopted religion, the Native American Church, which included peyote sessions. Milan Melvin, a man who wore many hats in this era, remembers a 1963 peyote session at Works's place in which Native Americans and young white people, including Chandler Laughlin, a wandering entrepreneur of folk-friendly coffeehouses, participated in an event that bound together a nascent community. But this evening in early 1965, nothing so spiritual was going on at the Zen Mine. It was just Works, Laughlin, and a rich kid named Mark Unobsky gathered at a table playing the board game Risk and smoking pot to the point where they didn't notice they were socked in by a blizzard.

Unobsky had left Memphis for San Francisco to play the folk clubs and had fallen in with a questionable crowd. His father, who thought it high time the young man learned to stand on his own two feet, had told him he was cutting off his allowance but would spot him up to five thousand dollars to help get a business going. While passing the time snowed in that night, Unobsky explained his situation, and Works told him about a big building four miles up the road, in the ghost town of Virginia City, another casualty of the Comstock Lode silver-mining frenzy. It had been a real Wild West joint, a hotel with a capacious bar on the ground floor, featuring a stage. Only a four-hour drive from San Francisco, it was an ideal weekend destination and a fine place for a vacation, and Works thought it could be had for almost nothing. Both Laughlin and Unobsky suddenly had a vision of a great place for touring folkies, not to mention the San Francisco crowd they both ran with. Unobsky later bought the place, hired carpenters and plumbers, painted it red, and christened it the Red Dog Saloon. He hired Jenna Worden, a French-trained chef, to prepare meals, and sent Laughlin to San Francisco to select furnishings. Fortunately for them, a luxe movie palace, the Fox Theatre, had just gone out of business, and its velvet curtains and other fixtures were for sale cheap.

While he was in town visiting friends on Pine Street, Laughlin met a young guy with very long blond hair wearing Edwardian clothing from one of the many thrift shops in the quiet neighborhood in which he lived, down at the tail end of Haight Street, where it ended at Golden Gate Park. The young man, George Hunter, said he had a band but not a folk band: it was a rock-and-roll band called the Charlatans. The band's piano player, Michael Ferguson, had recently run a store called Magic Theater for Madmen Only, selling antique clothes, odd objects with some age on them, and possibly other things. What Hunter neglected to tell Laughlin was that the band had never played—never even rehearsed, in fact—but Laughlin was already entranced by how cozily they fit into the look that was a-building at the Red Dog. He asked them what they were doing for the summer, and when they said they had no plans, he hired them unheard as the house band.

Meanwhile, in Virginia City, things were moving quickly: Ellen

Harmon, an old friend of Laughlin's, was installed as dishwasher, and her friend Luria Castell, a longtime political activist who'd gone to Cuba for the sugar harvest, handled the books. Alton Kelley, an artist, went up to supervise the construction; and an itinerant folk singer from Seattle, Lynne Hughes, dressed up as *Gunsmoke*'s Miss Kitty and helped out in a number of capacities while Don Works tended bar. On June 21, the doors were thrown open to the public, such as it was, and on the way in they passed Washoe Joe, 385 pounds of Indian wearing a top hat and a velvet sash that announced that it had belonged to the Rainbow Girls, whoever they were. Joe was the bouncer, but he was rarely called upon to bounce. On opening night, the sheriff paid a visit and, following local custom, walked up to the bar and told Works he'd like to check his pistol. Works picked it up, pointed it at the ceiling, squeezed the trigger, and the gun went off. "Seems to work," he told the nonplussed lawman.

Many a tale has been told about what went on at the Red Dog that summer, and many of them are retold in Don Works's daughter Mary's documentary film, *Rockin' at the Red Dog*. Among the undeniable things that happened, though, was that the Charlatans became an actual rock-and-roll band, and a lot of people formed bonds that would prove to be lifelong. Also, in late September, as the winds that would bring the blizzards started, Alton Kelley, Luria Castell, Ellen Harmon, and Lynne Hughes drove back to San Francisco wishing they could keep alive the spirit of the summer they'd just lived through. As it happened, the opportunity to do that awaited them. And how.

London was fairly humming with activity. In retrospect, this was predictable: food rationing didn't end in England until 1954, when the Beatles' generation was in its early teens, and the whole British Invasion cohort grew up with a world of choices Britain hadn't enjoyed in a long time, as well as a feeling of being entitled to make those choices. The country's prosperity promoted a mushrooming of leisure, and that meant an expanded involvement in the arts. This included poetry, and young poets, inspired by the American Beats of the 1950s, sprang up in London and Liverpool, with one of their London meeting points being Better Books, on Charing Cross Road, whose paperback section was managed by a poet from Montana named Bill Butler, who ceded the job to Barry Miles, known to all as simply Miles, in January 1965. Miles was well attuned to the British and American cultural undergrounds, and soon odd mimeographed poetry magazines started appearing in the shop, as well as, inevitably, those who wrote them. Miles initiated poetry readings there, so he wasn't as surprised as he might have been when Allen Ginsberg showed up in June. A reading was swiftly arranged, and the place was jammed, with most of the audience listening from the sidewalk, where Scottish Dylan wannabe Donovan busked until the reading started. Ginsberg's presence in London—he'd gotten there via Cuba, which expelled him for immorality to Czechoslovakia, where he was a huge hit and crowned King of the May, and thence to London—was a bona fide event, and he arrived for the end of Bob Dylan's acoustic tour (and appears, dressed as a rabbi, in the proto–rock video for "Subterranean Homesick Blues" in the film *Dont Look Back*), crashing with Miles and his wife, Sue. Ginsberg was about to turn thirty-nine on June 3, and Miles threw a party at which John Lennon and George Harrison showed up. A few days afterward, Ginsberg found out that his fellow Beat poet Lawrence Ferlinghetti was coming to town, and that another, Gregory Corso, was in Paris. Dissident Soviet poet Andrei Voznesensky was also due in, so why not have a group poetry reading?

Obviously, Better Books was out—it held only fifty people—and Ginsberg's friend Barbara Rubin asked, "What's the biggest joint in town?" Sue Miles said she thought it was the Royal Albert Hall, whereupon Rubin ran to the phone at the front of the shop and booked it. There was the matter of the four-hundred-pound rent, which was miraculously found, and on June 11, 1965, the doors opened and the wildest assemblage of humanity so far seen under one roof in England trooped in and took their seats. Someone had gone to Floral Street, in Covent Garden, and commandeered all the unsold flowers and brought them to the reading, so not only was there a huge bouquet onstage, but people were handed flowers on the way in. Wine bottles and joints went from hand to hand. R. D. Laing, the radical psychiatrist, brought a bunch of his patients. A young Indian politician, Indira Gandhi, attended, as did Nobel poetry laureate Pablo Neruda, whom Ginsberg unsuccessfully tried to coax into the event. To everyone's disappointment, Voznesensky, whose KGB minder had him under observation, declined to read. No matter: there were British and American poets aplenty, and the people in the audience, who were from all over England and farther—people are known to have hitchhiked in from Inverness, Scotland—looked around and wondered that there were so *many* like them. Who would have imagined it? And what would happen next?

Some of the answer to that, as well as the background to both these events, began on the afternoon of April 16, 1943, when Dr. Alfred Hofmann, a thirty-seven-year-old chemist working for Sandoz Pharmaceuticals in Basel, Switzerland, was researching plant compounds to aid difficult childbirth. Running through a number of derivatives of lysergic acid, present in ergot, a fungus that grows on rye, he accidentally ingested a tiny amount of the twenty-fifth derivative toward the end of his workday and, hanging up his lab coat, got on his bicycle to go home. Within minutes, he felt a growing intoxication, which blossomed into a complex experience of oceanic feeling of oneness with his surroundings. The effects lasted well into the evening, and he woke up the next day feeling changed for the better: Dr. Hofmann had just taken the first LSD trip. He realized the possibilities for psychopharmacology, and wrote up a paper for his employers, who began producing the compound in limited quantities for researchers in Prague; Weyburn, Saskatchewan; Cambridge, Massachusetts; and Palo Alto, California, among other places.

Research into the drug's effects was different in each place. Prague and Harvard were concentrating on its use as an aid in psychiatry, although a Harvard religion professor also became an informal researcher. At Stanford University in California, studies by the CIA's secretive MK-Ultra team was seeking to weaponize the drug, figuring that spraying it on enemy troops would immobilize them. In Saskatchewan, the research was also psychological in nature, concentrating on treating chronic alcoholics, with whom they managed an astounding 80 percent cure rate: "Bill W," cofounder of Alcoholics Anonymous, credited his LSD experiences with solidifying the ideas in AA's Big Book, the fellowship's central text. Inevitably, word of this powerful, seemingly benign agent spread. A lot of the press it received was due to an eccentric, wealthy inventor named Al Hubbard, who managed to talk Dr. Humphry Osmond in Saskatchewan out of a supply of the drug so that he could spread it to "captains of industry and princes of the church," in Osmond's words. Henry Luce, chairman of Time-Life publishers, was an early convert, and Cary Grant's psychiatrist administered some to him, causing the Hollywood star to become an advocate. Hubbard flew around in his private plane with a briefcase full of LSD, which was still legal. Needless to say, various Harvard and Stanford students volunteered for the research, and soon they, too, were proselytizing. If only there were a way to get some!

Well, there was: make it yourself. The main problem was the molecule's complexity. You couldn't just brew up a batch with the ease you could make home-brewed beer. It took precision measuring equipment and a few laboratory pieces, and the dose, measured in micrograms, had to be carefully watched. This was a challenge to a scientifically inclined young man from a prominent Kentucky family, Augustus Owsley Stanley III, who, as an undergraduate at Berkeley, started making it in his home. He was lucky to have a small fortune to draw on and a girlfriend who was a chemistry grad student. His lab equipment was state-of-the-art, his LSD pure and unadulterated. As adventurous Berkeleyites began using it, word got down to Palo Alto, where veterans of the MK-Ultra tests had enjoyed the drug but didn't have a source. Owsley (as he was invariably known) went down there and met novelist Ken Kesey, an enthusiast. Kesey soon gathered around him a group of friends dubbed the Merry Pranksters, causing some consternation in the conservative Stanford community, but with the drug still legal, there wasn't much they could do. LSD use also spread to college students in San Francisco itself, who mostly lived in the Charlatans' neighborhood, and in the summer of 1965, it made its way to Virginia City.

LSD was spreading among a crowd that was already conversant

with marijuana, a drug that had long been on the jazz scene (Louis Armstrong was a vocal advocate for the stuff), as well as among Mexicans and West Indians. Far milder in its effects, it was used to enhance music listening and sex, or just to brighten up the day. Marijuana, and its derivative hashish, was also popular among young rebels in England, thanks to its large West Indian and subcontinental populations, and the Beatles were no doubt exposed to it by Lord Woodbine, the West Indian sidekick of their first manager, Allan Williams. They were more interested in alcohol and amphetamines at first, but in April 1965, John Lennon, George Harrison, and their wives were having dinner with a cosmetic dentist, John Riley, who had posh offices on Harley Street and was treating them for the aftereffects of Britain's notoriously bad dental care. Riley had spent time studying in Chicago, where he had apparently run into one of Al Hubbard's people and was now an enthusiast—albeit not a well-informed one. At the meal's conclusion, Riley produced some LSD and introduced it into everyone's coffee. As anyone in LSD circles would have noted, this was not a smart or prudent thing to do, and as the two Beatle couples careened off into the London night, they had little idea what had happened. They soon found out, and in fact, the experience, and the four's correctly perceived instinct to ride out the trip together— they wound up at George's house—was most likely the genesis of the title song of the new film they'd begun work on: no longer *Eight Arms to Hold You,* it became *Help!* (Contrary to Beatle fan lore, the later song "Dr. Robert" was about another celebrity-chasing physician.)

Another momentous event in June 1965 was the release of a new Rolling Stones single, which was a decisive move away from their R&B-influenced past. Keith Richards apparently wrote it in his sleep: "I had no idea I'd written it, it's only thank God for the little Philips cassette player," he writes in his autobiography. "The miracle being that I looked at the cassette player in the morning and I knew I'd put in a brand-new tape in the previous night and I saw it was at the end. Then I pushed rewind and there was 'Satisfaction.' It was just a rough idea." Mick Jagger wrote the lyrics poolside while they were on tour in

Florida, and they nipped up to Chess Studios to record some numbers, but "Satisfaction" wasn't up to snuff. Two days later, they were in RCA Studios in LA, and for some reason, Richards put his electric guitar through a Gibson fuzztone, an effects box that surf musicians had used since the beginning. Back in England, their manager, Andrew Loog Oldham, went nuts when he heard it, and he put it out. Richards had thought it was a demo and had wanted horns to play the fuzztone line. Given that it went to number one ten days after its release in England, though, he was plenty happy with it.

And then there was Bob Dylan, who'd nipped off for his British tour in May, leaving behind the cautiously electric hit single "Subterranean Homesick Blues" and an album, *Bringing It All Back Home*, with the single as the lead track on the all-electric side one. Fans (the ones who didn't write him off for the electric material immediately) were mesmerized, not only by the abstract yet powerful lyrics—just who was he saying good-bye to in "It's All Over Now, Baby Blue"?— but also by the album cover, showing the star in a navy-blue continental suit and a dress shirt with French cuffs, holding a gray kitten, while behind him, an elegant woman in a red pantsuit (his manager's wife, Sally Grossman) lounges on a fainting couch staring into the camera. Scattered about are LPs by Lotte Lenya, Eric von Schmidt, Robert Johnson, and Lord Buckley (plus *Another Side of Bob Dylan* in the fireplace) and, among other things, a fallout shelter sign and a copy of *Time* magazine with Lyndon Johnson on the cover. Stream-of-consciousness liner notes on the back are placed by some photos, including one of Dylan and Joan Baez.

"Subterranean Homesick Blues" stalled at 39, but Dylan's music was still storming the charts with help from a new Los Angeles band, the Byrds, who'd coalesced at the Troubadour, a folk club whose bar was a major hangout for local folk talent during the daytime. Jim McGuinn, a Chicago folkie who'd lately worked as music director for Bobby Darin and Judy Collins and had appeared on Collins's album *3*, was an opening act at the Troubadour, singing Beatles songs with an acoustic guitar, an idea he'd had while playing folk clubs in New York City. He was approached by another of the regulars, Gene Clark, about starting a duo like Peter and Gordon. While trading songs and harmonizing under a stairwell at the club, they were heard by another regular. David Crosby was from a showbiz family and had just recently left a super-square hootenanny band run by Les Baxter, a big-band leader who usually had several types of combos working under his name. Crosby had already hooked up with Jim Dickson, a manager who thought he was a perfect solo artist and who'd been cutting demos on him at World Pacific Studios, where Dickson had a deal for free recording time. After their meeting at the Troubadour, Crosby appeared with McGuinn and Clark, and Dickson flipped: these guys were going places. They tossed around some names—the Beefeaters seemed British enough—but the band was still evolving. After seeing *A Hard Day's Night*, McGuinn had the answer: an electric twelve-string guitar like George Harrison played in the film! They were scarce, and only one company, Rickenbacker, made them, but he got one. A young bluegrass musician, Chris Hillman, and a guy who sometimes played congas at folk clubs, Michael Clarke, rounded out the band. Elektra took a chance with a Beefeaters single, but the label wasn't really in the singles business yet. Dickson went to work, and in 1964, the band, now called the Byrds, got a deal with Columbia. As Peter, Paul and Mary had done with his acoustic songs, the Byrds plunged into Dylan's new electric stuff, and by June 1965, their twelve-string-driven single of *Bringing It All Back Home*'s "Mr. Tambourine Man" was topping the charts.

But Dylan wasn't sitting still, either, and for his next move, he reached out to a guitarist he'd met years ago in Chicago. Michael Bloomfield was a rich kid, and could have been heir to a large restaurant-supply fortune, but all he was interested in was the guitar. He'd immersed himself in blues—naturally enough; he was living in Chicago—and soon fell into the orbit of a bunch of young white kids who felt the same way. Most of them had been introduced to what was going on around them by weekly parties at the University of Chicago, which were eventually taken over by two students, Paul Butterfield and Elvin Bishop. Nonstudents Nick Gravenites and Norman Dayron also participated, and occasionally local stars such as Little Walter sat in. There was no stigma to playing electric instruments on the Chicago folk scene, although some folkies (Bloomfield, for one) were more interested in finding blues stars from the '30s who'd been forgotten. Eventually, though, Butterfield and Bishop hooked up with two guys, Jerome Arnold and Sam Lay, who'd been Howlin' Wolf's rhythm section and started playing around town as the Paul Butterfield Blues Band. A white-led electric blues band of such authenticity was a real find, and Elektra Records grabbed them. The band asked Bloomfield to join, as a pianist, for sessions in April 1965, but they didn't work out. Then Bloomfield got a call from Dylan. "I don't know where he got my number," Bloomfield said, "but he said, 'I'm making a record. Do you want to play on it?'" So, on June 15, Bloomfield went into New York City's Columbia Studio A with a bunch of session men (including Al Kooper, who'd been called as a guitarist but who, upon hearing Bloomfield warming up, sat down behind a Hammond B3 organ and hoped he wouldn't be called upon to do anything but play chords) and producer Tom Wilson, and with the only instructions from Dylan being "Don't play any of that B.B. King shit," recorded "Like a Rolling Stone." Columbia released it immediately, buying two full pages in *Billboard* to announce it: "A 6-MINUTE SINGLE? WHY NOT? when you have 6 minutes of BOB DYLAN singing his great new song 'LIKE A ROLLING STONE' ON COLUMBIA RECORDS." Initially released in early July in two parts on a 45 (on red plastic, no less), it didn't really pick up steam until Columbia acceded to radio listeners' demands that it be played all the way through all at once, and became an inescapable hit.

"Folkswinging Wave On—Courtesy Rock Groups" was the headline in the June 12 issue of *Billboard,* and the article cited Dylan, the Byrds, the Rising Sons, Sonny and Cher, and the "Living Spoonful" as proof. The Rising Sons were heroes of the Troubadour set, featuring relocated Boston folkie Taj Mahal (real name Henry Fredericks) and a teenage guitar whiz named Ryland P. Cooder. Sonny and Cher were bandwagon hoppers extraordinaire, with former Specialty Records talent scout Sonny Bono and his much younger wife, Cherilyn Sarkisian, having recorded under other names (including Caesar and Cleo) in the past.

The Lovin' Spoonful, based in New York City, was fronted by John Sebastian, the son of a first-call harmonica studio musician. Sebastian, who wrote lovely songs influenced by jug band music, was supported by a band that had fallen together in the apartment/salon of New York's queen of folkie networking, Cass Elliot. She'd introduced Sebastian and Canadian folkie Zal Yanovsky, who'd been in her folk group, the Mugwumps, and soon the band was playing at the Night Owl Café in Greenwich Village. Had their label had more oomph, the *Billboard* article might have added Richard and Mimi Farina, whose new Vanguard album mixed acoustic and light electric backing on their songs: he was a poet and novelist; she was Joan Baez's younger sister.

Not everybody was folkswinging, of course. The British were still invading, with Them releasing the soon-to-be classic "Gloria"; the Kinks, "Set Me Free"; the Who, "Anyway, Anyhow, Anywhere" (these last two produced by Shel Talmy, an American who'd let a friend talk him into going to London for five weeks to check out the scene in 1964 and had stayed, producing hits, for seventeen more years), and the Yardbirds, a project the Rolling Stones' first manager, Giorgio Gomelsky, had put together, "For Your Love." The original invaders, the Beatles, were represented by *Beatles VI*, a mishmash of tracks from two British releases and a single or two, and they announced an August release for *Help!*

Solomon Burke's odd stab at Dylan's "Maggie's Farm" notwithstanding, black music wasn't folkswinging, either. It was getting ready for summer with some amazing slow jams: Otis Redding came out with his career-defining "I've Been Loving You Too Long," co-written with Jerry Butler; the Dells released the epic "Stay in My Corner"; Chess's Knight Brothers came out with "Temptation 'Bout to Get Me"; while their label-mate Billy Stewart gave us "Sitting in the Park," a classic vocal group sound; as was the Manhattans' "Searchin' for My Baby," backed with "I'm the One Love Forgot." Picking up the tempo was Wilson Pickett with "Midnight Hour" and the Coasters talking about "Money Honey," and Bobby Robinson's Enjoy label somehow got a hit out of Elmore James's "It Hurts Me Too," first released in 1957. There would be no tour for James, though; he'd been dead for two years. Although the track listing for *The Complete Motown Singles, Vol. 5: 1965* now looks like a greatest hits album interspersed with a few obscurities, the label managed only the Miracles' "Tracks of My Tears" and the Contours' "First I Look at the Purse" in June, although the two-sided Temptations smash "Since I Lost My Baby" backed with "You've Got to Earn It" was released on July 1. And with Jackie DeShannon's "What the World Needs Now" (what it needed was "love, sweet love") as a soundtrack, that was just June.

Summer was festival season, with folk festivals in Berkeley, Denver, Chicago, and Philadelphia, all in the shadow of the big one, Newport. The Newport Folk Festival had grown out of the Newport Jazz Festival and was where new acts, including the growing number of discovered and rediscovered traditional performers, took the stage. It was also where veterans got to bask in admiration, and provide a sense of continuity as each evening ended with a mass sing-along of young and old. This year, Elektra managed to talk the festival's foundation into allowing the Paul Butterfield Blues Band onto the program on July 22, but one of the board members, Alan Lomax, wasn't too happy with the decision, even though Michael Bloomfield was chairing a workshop on blues earlier in the day and showing his usual respectful deference to the elders. Introducing Butterfield, Lomax showed a lot of ambivalence: "Us white cats always moved in, a little bit late, but tried to catch up. I understand that this present combination has not only caught up, but passed the test. That's what I hear—I'm anxious to find out whether it's true or not . . . Anyway, this is the *new* blues from Chicago," and the band began to play. Albert Grossman, who by this time was managing the Butterfield Band, blew his top: "What the fuck kind of way is that to introduce a bunch of musicians? You should be ashamed of yourself." Lomax then offered to punch Grossman in the mouth. Blows were eventually traded while the audience looked on with a mixture of incomprehension and guarded amusement: Was electric blues *real* blues? Could white men play the blues—or *should* they? One thing was certain: they were doing a better job of it than the Rolling Stones, who would never in a million years have gotten invited to the Newport Folk Festival, although some folkies were catching on through them that there was another world out there, and anyway, wasn't "Satisfaction" a protest song?

Butterfield had been on in the afternoon, and it wasn't until later that Grossman's most controversial client, Bob Dylan, arrived at the festival grounds. Determined to play his new electric material, he had to recruit a band on the spot. He and Grossman repaired to Nethercliffe, the mansion on the festival grounds where performers hung out, and ran into Al Kooper on the way. Dylan, Grossman, and Bloomfield started putting together a band to back Dylan on Sunday night.

The Butterfield Band was scheduled to perform again on Sunday afternoon (although it was rained out and rescheduled for just before Dylan), so it was natural to have Bloomfield on guitar, Kooper and Barry Goldberg (a Chicago friend of the Butterfield crowd) on keyboards, and Jerome Arnold and Sam Lay from the Butterfield Band on bass and drums. They started rehearsing on Saturday night, and right away the rhythm section was having trouble with the music, Arnold in particular. By the next evening, though, everyone was fairly ready, and after Butterfield delivered a short set, delaying things somewhat, Peter Yarrow introduced Dylan, who was wearing a pistachio-colored shirt with big white polka dots—hardly folkie togs—and was already plugging in a guitar. The audience was clearly excited and making a variety of sounds. "Ladies and gentlemen," Yarrow intoned, "the person that's gonna come up now has a limited amount of time. His name is Bob *Dylan*!" The band launched into "Maggie's Farm," with Bloomfield playing fast and loud, the keyboardists inaudible, and Jerome Arnold still not in control of the chord changes. Nobody had ever heard anything like it, even though the next song the band played, "Like a Rolling Stone," was then all over the radio. Finally, a song from the album Dylan was currently recording, "Phantom Engineer" (titled "It Takes a Lot to Laugh, It Takes a Train to Cry" on the album), closed things out. By now, the audience was screaming and generally going nuts. There *was* booing, but those who were there maintain that it was in response not so much to Dylan's playing loud rock and roll as to the sound mix—remember, this was the era before onstage monitors—which was just unacceptable.

Backstage, Pete Seeger was about to burst a blood vessel over this invasion of electricity. Something had to be done, so even though the show was running late, Dylan went out with an acoustic guitar and played "It's All Over Now, Baby Blue" and "Mr. Tambourine Man." And with that, Bob Dylan and Michael Bloomfield left for New York to finish up the album Dylan had started, this time with a new producer named Bob Johnston—Tom Wilson had been taken off the project and was continuing work with Dion on an album called *Kickin' Child* that would remain unreleased until 2017—which would see release at the end of August as *Highway 61 Revisited*. The line drawn in the sand at Newport stretched into the future.

The top 40 immediately picked up the spirit of protest, no matter how anodyne it might have to be to get on the radio, so that *Billboard*'s front page on August 21 bore the headline "Rock + Folk + Protest = An Erupting New Sound." A week earlier, the rag had covered a "controversial" new single by Barry McGuire, "Eve of Destruction," written by P. F. Sloan, whom they described as a former surfer. Dylanesque in sound, with acoustic guitar and harmonica, the song communicated anger and frustration, although it also didn't get very specific, and fifty years later, Sloan was admitting that he had no idea what some of the words meant. The single soon drew a similarly confused right-wing answer record by "The Spokesmen," whoever they really were, called "Dawn of Correction," which bombed. More to the point was Bonnie and the Treasures' "Home of the Brave," about a boy in trouble at school for long hair; Sonny Bono's melodramatic "Laugh at Me," also about being mocked for his hair (although he offered to pray for his mockers); numerous recordings of Buffy Sainte-Marie's "Universal Soldier" (Donovan and Glen Campbell battled it out on the charts with that one); Joan Baez's pious reading of Phil Ochs's "There but for Fortune"; and the one that arguably had the biggest impact on society, the Animals' "We Gotta Get Out of This Place," written by Teen Pan Alley songwriters Barry Mann and Cynthia Weil, which was an instant hit with the increasing number of American military "advisors" being shipped to the small Southeast Asian country of Vietnam; it remained on their "charts" for several years. And as if to confirm *Billboard*'s trend spotting, there was Simon and Garfunkel. Back in 1957, these two kids from Queens, New York, calling themselves Tom and Jerry, had had a hit with "Hey, Schoolgirl," but subsequently hadn't done much. With folk suddenly appearing popular, Paul Simon went to England to hit the folk clubs with some of the songs he'd written lately. Someone from Columbia Records heard him and had him record an album there, *The Paul Simon Song Book*, but the U.S. office passed on it. Still, Simon was inspired, and when he returned, he called Art Garfunkel, who'd been going to grad school, about doing a folk act, and they got a deal with Columbia. They recorded an angsty acoustic album called *Wednesday Morning, 3 AM* that got some traction with the college crowd but not enough to base a career on. Then Tom Wilson got a flash and overdubbed one of the songs, "The Sound of Silence," with a light electric band like he'd used on *Bringing It All Back Home* and released it as a single. By the end of November, it topped the charts, and the duo forgot the anger they'd felt upon discovering Wilson's move. In fact, they let him electrify the rest of the album and released it as *Sounds of Silence* while they got busy writing another one.

When they returned to San Francisco at the end of September, the four veterans of the Red Dog Saloon found a changed pop landscape. For one thing, San Francisco seemed to have sprouted a bunch of new bands. On the same block as the Charlatans' house, a crazy bunch from the scene around Stanford University had moved in. They'd evolved from a bluegrass band into a jug band, Mother McCree's Uptown Jug Champions, consisting of banjo/guitarist Jerry Garcia; harmonica player Ron "Pigpen" McKernan, whose father had been an R&B disc jockey; and guitarists Bob Weir, who was taking lessons from Garcia, and Robert Hunter. One day, they decided that this wasn't the direction they wanted to go in, so they sidelined Hunter, added drummer Bill Kreutzmann, and plugged in. They called themselves the Warlocks and talked their way into a regular gig at Magoo's Pizza Parlor, in downtown Palo Alto, playing six nights a week, five sets a night, with Chuck Berry numbers, some adapted jug band tunes, and British Invasion material. Word got out among the local high school students that there was a cool band at Magoo's, and the Warlocks began drawing a couple of hundred people each night.

On May 8, 1965, an odd college student named Phil Lesh, a couple of years older than the Warlocks, went with some friends to see this phenomenon, and although he'd been writing avant-garde classical music, he heard something in this band that had potential. Talking to Garcia subsequently, he was surprised when Jerry said, "You should play bass with us." Suddenly, the Warlocks sounded a great deal better.

It was perhaps inevitable that the two most culturally avant-garde forces in town would find each other. Ken Kesey had written a successful novel, *One Flew Over the Cuckoo's Nest*, and with the proceeds, he and some of his other LSD-enthusiast friends, who called themselves the Merry Pranksters, bought an old school bus, painted it with colorful designs, and traveled across the country, with Jack Kerouac's road buddy Neal Cassady doing most of the driving. Upon their return, they decided to throw, not exactly a party, but an event, and posters went up all over town saying, "Can *You* Pass the Acid Test?" (Much to the annoyance of the East Coast LSD crowd, the West Coasters were calling it "acid," as in lysergic acid.) The first one was held at the compound they all shared, and the Warlocks were recruited as the band, an ideal setup for them: "Nobody came to the Acid Test to see *us*," Garcia remembered happily years later. The band could take things as far out as they wanted, to see what would happen, and they did.

Kesey's crowd also made friends with the local chapter of the Hells Angels motorcycle gang, who also enjoyed taking LSD, which by now Owsley was making in large quantities, and they and the Pranksters and the Warlocks all got to know one another. Finally, the band decided it was time to go for the big time, which in their case meant the big city, San Francisco, and another wooden Victorian house near Haight Street became inhabited by an anarchic crew of young people. They pooled money from their gigs to make a demo tape, but by the time they went into Golden State Studios in early November, they'd discovered that there was another Warlocks, on the East Coast, who had a record deal. A new name was imperative. The tape from Golden

State was labeled as being by "the Emergency Crew," but that was temporary. Shortly thereafter, someone pulled down a hefty Funk and Wagnalls dictionary from a bookshelf and opened it at random. A finger stabbed out and hit a term used in the study of mythology, in which the hero is helped in his quest by the souls of the departed who loved him: the *grateful dead*. It stuck. As Garcia explained later, "[T]hat name was just repellent enough to filter out curious onlookers."

Another new group had formed around another bunch of folkies, and they were lucky enough to own their own club in San Francisco, at the end of Fillmore Street, down by the Marina: singer-songwriter Marty Balin and a couple of friends had gotten the lease on a former pizza joint (and its liquor license) at Fillmore and Lombard and named it the Matrix. It opened in August, with Balin's band as the main attraction. Like the Grateful Dead, they were an odd collection of people: a couple of Prankster-affiliated folks, a couple of local folk stars, and a guitar-playing drummer whom Balin assigned to that chair because he thought he looked like a drummer. Their name was a folkie in-joke, riffing on country blues players' names. Bob Dylan had done this early in his career, when he appeared on other people's records as Blind Boy Grunt. This band named themselves after Blind Thomas Jefferson Airplane. As the Red Dog was for the Charlatans and Magoo's for the Dead, the Matrix was the perfect laboratory for the Jefferson Airplane to find its voice. And if you didn't have a club like the Airplane did, you could invite people to your rehearsals: two brothers named Albin were cobbling together a band with a Detroit refugee named James Gurley; and Chet Helms, an odd-looking Texan who was working with the LEMAR marijuana legalization campaign, found them a gorgeous house at 1090 Page, in the neighborhood adjacent to Haight Street, with a Victorian music room in its basement. He was soon charging fifty cents' admission to keep the crowds down, and the band began calling itself Big Brother and the Holding Company.

The Great Society was fronted by a married couple, Darby and Grace Slick, who had an interest in Indian music that they inserted into the songs they were writing, and the Mystery Trend was centered on some San Francisco Art Institute students whose pianist, Ron

Nagle, was writing some witty material. (The band was named after Nagle's mishearing of a Dylan line about a "mystery tramp.")

Across the Golden Gate Bridge, in Marin County, an electric guitarist, John Cipollina, met folkie David Freiberg, and they started jamming together. A chance meeting with two other musicians made them a band, and as they got to know one another they found they were all but one Virgos, with two even sharing a birthday, so they decided to call themselves the Quicksilver Messenger Service. Bands were coming out of the bushes, falling out of the trees: the Oxford Circle, the Final Solution, the P. H. Phactor Jug Band, the Marbles.

By the middle of October, the four Red Dog folks figured it was time for a show, so they borrowed some money and put down a deposit on Longshoreman's Hall, a union facility in the North Beach district of San Francisco. Hanging up a couple of posters and distributing a lot of handbills, they advertised a "Tribute to Dr. Strange" event for the evening of October 16, featuring the Charlatans, the Jefferson Airplane, the Marbles, and the Great Society. The promoters were calling themselves the Family Dog, and they had no idea what would come of this odd event. Alton Kelley was even nervous enough to grab a handful of tickets and stand outside the hall, selling them. As it turned out, a couple of hundred people from all over showed up, and the event was the Bay Area's equivalent of London's Royal Albert Hall poetry reading in June: a "who *are* all these people?" moment of realization that there were a lot more odd people out there than anyone had guessed. (It was at this event that Cipollina and Freiberg met the other Virgos for their band.) At the end of the evening, the crowd even picked up after itself before leaving. The next day, Ralph Gleason, jazz columnist of the *San Francisco Chronicle*, reviewed it in glowing terms. One thing nobody noticed: the event lacked a dance permit, and was thus illegal. But it would never happen again, right? Right: there's only one first time for anything, but they did it again the next weekend, with a "A Tribute to Sparkle Plenty," featuring the Charlatans again, along with the Lovin' Spoonful. The Jefferson Airplane attended but didn't perform, and the Grateful Dead's Phil Lesh walked up to Ellen Harmon and told her, "Lady, what this little séance needs is *us*!"

Besides bands, new theater groups were springing up in the Bay Area, and testing the limits of what constituted entertainment. These troupes were constantly getting threatened and arrested for obscenity. Two of the most outrageous were the Living Theater, which had been around for a while, and the San Francisco Mime Troupe, whose work was presented free in public, but whose themes (pacifism and sexual freedom) rankled the Establishment. By the end of October, the Mime Troupe was out of money and decided to put on a benefit for themselves. They rented a Cadillac and drove it around handing out leaflets for a November 6 benefit called "the Appeal." All this was being coordinated by their business manager, a scowling, abrasive man named Bill Graham. Graham had an interesting past: Born Wolfgang Grajonka in Poland, he walked across Europe with his sister after the Nazi invasion of Poland; the two eventually made their way to New York, where the newly christened Graham learned business management. Somehow he'd wound up in San Francisco, and had quit a well-paid job to work with the Mime Troupe. The Appeal pressed all Graham's organizational and publicity buttons: he got on the phone lining up acts to perform, including Allen Ginsberg and some poet friends of his from New York who had a ramshackle band called the Fugs. The Jefferson Airplane played—they could hardly refuse because they practiced in the Mime Troupe's loft, where the Appeal was to be held—and Graham wound up putting the Family Dog down as an act, when all they'd done was offer their help getting entertainers. (In the end, they presented their own show at the Longshoreman's Hall on that same night; Graham had thought they were an animal act.) The Appeal was a huge success, so much so that plans were made for another Appeal in December. This one had the best ad of all: a rather bland poster but one held up by Bob Dylan on Ralph Gleason's *Jazz Casual* television show, saying he'd like to go but wouldn't be around for it. Gleason had been instrumental in finding the location: the Fillmore Auditorium, which had been a centerpiece of San Francisco's jazz and R&B world for years—Johnny Otis discovered Etta James there in the early 1950s—but was sitting empty because its audience had moved on. It was on the edge of San Francisco's black community, easily accessible from Haight Street.

The second Appeal proved that there was a large and potentially lucrative audience for rock dances, and soon a reworked Family Dog—two of the originals had backed out, and Chet Helms had amicably stepped in—and Bill Graham were alternating weeks at the Fillmore. In the weeks to come, Graham decided to take full control of the Fillmore, and the Family Dog found an empty ballroom, the Avalon, on the corner of Post and Polk Streets. There were enough bands to fill both places every week, and more kept coming. In fact, there were plenty in the Bay Area alone who never played either place, bands from the suburbs who weren't considered very hip but who were nonetheless putting out records locally. The hot new record company in town was Autumn, born of a partnership between two disc jockeys, Tom "Big Daddy" Donahue, from top 40 KYA (and he *was* big, too, weighing in at four hundred pounds); and Sylvester Stewart, who used the name Sly Stone on KSOL, the East Bay soul powerhouse, in 1964. They had a hit right off the bat, with Bobby Freeman, a local singer who'd had a hit in 1958 with "Do You Want to Dance" and who had been working the clubs ever since. Sly wrote him a song based on a current dance craze, and suddenly Freeman was back in the top 10 with "C'mon and Swim." This gave Donahue and Stewart enough money to sign up the Beau Brummels, a band that had its origins playing Irish dances in San Mateo, and to buy a full-page ad for them in *Billboard* at the end of 1964. In the ad they are pictured wearing derbies and carrying umbrellas, and although, like the Sir Douglas Quintet, they weren't British, unlike them they *sounded* British: playing Beatles and Searchers tunes at their gigs, they internalized the sophisticated harmonies those bands were using, and guitarist Ron Elliott knocked out hit after hit for them in 1965: "Laugh Laugh," "Just a Little," "You Tell Me Why," and "Don't Talk to Strangers." In the East Bay suburbs of El Cerrito, the Golliwogs were chafing under the name that Fantasy Records, a successful jazz label looking for a Beatle-like band, had given them, but they recorded an album's worth of material and released a single the promotion of which two in the band, including chief songwriter and lead singer John Fogerty, sabotaged by joining the army. Also in the South Bay was another Autumn act, the Vejtables, whose gimmick was a singing girl drummer, Jan Errico, who eventually left for another Autumn band, the Mojo Men. Autumn penetrated the ballroom scene a bit, too, signing the Great Society and putting out a couple of 45s by them on its North Beach subsidiary.

But San Francisco wasn't a media center, and out of town, nobody was paying any attention to it except the radio stations playing the Beau Brummels' records. For one thing, those darn British kept invading: the Yardbirds were hot, with a couple of pop hits ("Heart Full of Soul" and "For Your Love") before releasing their version of Bo Diddley's "I'm a Man," which includes a section they called a "rave-up," where the band inserted a rhythmic vamp over which their new guitar player, Jeff Beck, played some hot licks. The band's founder, guitarist Eric Clapton, had quit over the pop stuff: he was interested only in blues, so he joined an obscure band called the Bluesbreakers, fronted by harmonica player John Mayall. Not all the British blues purists were so inflexible: the Pretty Things, a very early spin-off of the Rolling Stones, were trying to write pop songs but were not making a dent outside their home country. As for the Stones, after "Satisfaction" they were having it both ways, releasing pop singles and relegating the blues and R&B covers to their albums. Suddenly, they were ascending to the top of the singles chart with every new release. So, for that matter, were Herman's Hermits and even the Dave Clark Five, while Them and the Hollies both established themselves in the United States.

And the Beatles—well, they were the Beatles. Their film *Help!* came out on schedule in August, an odd affair that strived for the bright spontaneity of *A Hard Day's Night* but was mired in a semi-coherent plot revolving around a sacred ring that Ringo had been given "by an Oriental bird," which marked its wearer for human sacrifice. Incredibly racist by twenty-first-century standards, it was shot in color on location in the Alps and the Bahamas. It really wasn't very funny, but the music was good and the soundtrack album, which showed the four lads making semaphore signals with their hands (which you'd assume spelled H-E-L-P but was N-U-J-V or N-V-U-J, depending on whether you had the U.K. or U.S. version of the cover), ran up the charts, as did the title single, the album remaining glued at number one for weeks on end. In September, Capitol released a single that it hyped in a most unusual way: "Yesterday" was advertised as "Paul solo," and "Act Naturally" as "Ringo solo," which was more or less the truth. Paul's backing on his side was a string quartet, while Ringo had the rest of the group along for a cover of country singer Buck Owens's 1963 country chart-topper. (Ringo's previous bands had always indulged his love of country music when giving him a solo spot.) Then came another single by the band ("Ticket to Ride" backed with "Day Tripper") and, in December, a very unusual album called *Rubber Soul*. There was more acoustic instrumentation; the songs were more introspective; Paul had another quiet ballad, "Michelle," on which he sung a line or two in French; and there was an enigmatic song, "Norwegian Wood," with a weird twanging sound that turned out to be an Indian instrument called the sitar, which George had just picked up. Some fans were scratching their heads, but they were all buying it: released on December 6, 1965, with no fanfare, *Rubber Soul* sold 1.2 million copies in the first nine days, breaking every sales record the band had set and sorely taxing Capitol's two-million-unit pressing allocation.

Still, American bands were standing up to the Beatles: guitar bands were erupting everywhere, led by the Byrds, whose twelve-string twang went into non-Dylan folkie territory with Pete Seeger's "Turn! Turn! Turn!," and the Lovin' Spoonful, whose label was careful to avoid "folk-rock" in favor of "good time music," which made equal sense: the group's debt to jug band revivalists probably sent some of their fans to the Jim Kweskin Jug Band. The summer of 1965 saw the McCoys, from Indiana, doing "Hang On Sloopy," the latest iteration of the "Louie Louie" chords—the Stones did theirs with "Get Off of My Cloud"—and the Bobby Fuller Four with "Let Her Dance." One-shots like the Castaways ("Liar Liar"), the Newbeats ("Run Baby Run"), the Nightcrawlers ("The Little Black Egg") and the Knickerbockers (whose "Lies" was uncannily Beatle-ish) had their runs up and down the charts in the second half of the year. Guitars were so popular that Buck Owens, who wasn't even chasing pop success, had a hit with the instrumental "Buckaroo," which was at least as catchy as the T-Bones' adaptation of an Alka-Seltzer commercial, "No Matter What Shape (Your Stomach's In)." And older listeners were jolted by the Paul Butterfield Blues Band's debut on Elektra, with Michael Bloomfield's blazing guitar work inspiring a lot of folkies to go electric. On the West Coast, a different kind of vocal group seemed to be growing out of the folk era, as We Five, managed by Frank Werber (who'd masterminded the Kingston Trio), hit with "You Were on My Mind," and the final triumph of Cass Elliot's networking skills, the Mamas and the Papas, two men and two women who'd spent the summer working up their act at a resort in the Virgin Islands before moving to LA, signed to Dunhill, which had lots of dough from "Eve of Destruction; the band immediately had a hit with "California Dreamin'," which they'd written in New York. And in the last week of the year, that faux-British band, the Sir Douglas Quintet, was set up with a drug bust, orchestrated by an ambitious young lawman serving as the head of the San Antonio region of the Bureau of Narcotics, Joe Arpaio: Doug Sahm, Frank Morin, Augie Meyers, and their friend Charlie Prichard were found each to be in possession of a metal tobacco can filled with the "deadly" weed. Their lawyer suggested they leave the state for a while and not get in any more trouble. Four of them went to LA. Doug Sahm went to San Francisco.

Soul music was also beginning a golden era. Stax Records had found its way into the mainstream, now that Atlantic was distributing it, and Otis Redding was the big discovery, with "Respect," which he wrote; "I Can't Turn You Loose"; and a version of "Satisfaction" that probably had Keith Richards shaking his head in wonder: the Stax band had read his mind about the horns on the fuzztone line. The Florida duo Sam and Dave also looked like they were going places, ending out the year with "You Don't Know Like I Know," their first hit; and the Mad Lads' "Don't Have to Shop Around" showed that the South could also do vocal groups. In fact, that genre was almost indestructible, with the Jive Five chiming in with "I'm a Happy Man" and of course Motown's Temptations beating them all with "My Baby." Don Covay, a South Carolina singer signed to Atlantic who'd had his first hit, "Have Mercy," squashed by the Rolling Stones' cover version, released "Seesaw," and gave another great song, "I Don't Know What You've Got (But It's Got Me)," to his friend Little Richard, who was trying a comeback. It's a forgotten masterpiece, because of both Richard's inspired gospel performance and the two guitars of Covay and Richard's newly hired guitarist, fresh out of the air force, a lefty named James Marshall Hendrix. In fact, Covay liked him enough to use him on some of his 1966 sessions; when not on the road with Richard, Hendrix was hanging out in New York City, in Greenwich Village.

The other big news in soul music in the last half of 1965 was white folks. Phil Spector had briefly signed the Righteous Brothers, a West Coast act that had been trying for a hit for some time. He scored a number-one hit for them late in 1964 with "You've Lost That Lovin' Feeling," and then produced more hits for them throughout the year, most notably "Unchained Melody," in which they gave the kind of achingly slow performance that suited Spector's bombastic arrangements. Both records sold as well to black customers as to white. In Houston, Don Robey had signed a madman named Roy Head, whose "Treat Her Right" just hinted at the wild show he put on. A chicken farmer from Arkansas, Charlie Rich, who'd been a late arrival at Sun Records, was now on his third label, mystifying radio with his adept blend of jazz, country, and R&B; he had a mild hit with "Mohair Sam" but was too hip for most people. Atlantic was betting heavily on the Young Rascals, most of whom had been in Joey Dee's Starliters in that band's "Peppermint Twist" days and who had gone back to their New Jersey club roots until Atlantic found them there and signed them. They'd take a while to catch on with black audiences, but it would happen. Black listeners didn't get white soul vocalist Mitch Ryder, who, with his crackerjack band, the Detroit Wheels, scored a hit with "Jenny Take a Ride!," a mash-up of Little Richard's "Jenny, Jenny" and Chuck Willis's "C. C. Rider."

The real revolution in soul music was being held up in court, as James Brown's unilateral defection to Mercury Records continued to be challenged by his first label, King. Rumors were all over the place: Mercury would just plain *buy* King, with its irascible head, Sid Nathan, staying on as the head of Gem Plastics, its pressing plant. Lois Music, which had all King's publishing, would be sold. While this was playing out, Brown had a new band of youngsters and a couple of new ideas. Somehow he got to talking to Arthur "Guitar Boogie" Smith, who now owned a recording studio in Charlotte, North Carolina, and asked if he could record there. Smith said yes, and in February 1965, Brown pulled up with his band and got to work. He stepped up to the mike and shouted, "It's a HIT!" and the band started a minimalist groove, with the bass out front. The lyrics were nothing much, mostly a recitation of dances leading up to a quick strum on the guitar and Brown announcing, "Papa's Got a Brand New Bag." They worked on it for seven minutes, with a long saxophone solo by Maceo Parker, whose drummer brother, Melvin, anchored the tight stings of the brass. In July, with a brand-new contract with King, Brown edited this epic down to two minutes and six seconds, sticking the rest on the B-side, and he was back on top of the charts, even making top 10 on the pop charts. When that died down, he pulled out another session he'd done in Florida in May with more or less the same template, "I Got You (I Feel Good)." Neither record sounded like anything anyone else was doing. Miles Davis was running around playing them for his friends. It was a new bag indeed.

As 1966 dawned, there was the sound of slowly released breath at Hitsville U.S.A. It was coming off the most phenomenal year of its existence, with Motown and its associated labels (Tamla, Soul, V.I.P.) scoring five number-one pop hits, and nineteen more hitting the top 20. The Supremes, the Temptations, the Miracles—all the usual suspects were doing well, but there was a problem with one act who hadn't yet done what Berry Gordy knew he someday would: no-longer-Little Stevie Wonder's voice had changed. The chirp had morphed into more of a foghorn, albeit a soulful foghorn, and all eyes were on the performance of his new single, "Uptight." As it climbed the charts, though, Motown collectively relaxed and got back to work: 1966 would see an unprecedented 75 percent of the company's singles on one chart or another—or several. Nobody was much worried when, a little later in January, "Uptight" was knocked off the R&B chart's top slot by none other than Slim Harpo, who hadn't visited the national scene in five years, with "Baby Scratch My Back," which also got picked up by pop radio. It was kind of odd, but blues was, in fact, having a new golden era, even if much of it wasn't on the pop charts.

After fifteen years, B.B. King had wrested himself away from the Bihari brothers at Modern and joined Ray Charles on ABC, where he hoped to make some smoother records. In Chicago, a new generation was asserting itself, with the powerhouse team of Junior Wells and Buddy Guy; and young Koko Taylor growling her way through a recent Howlin' Wolf song, "Wang Dang Doodle," while veteran Sonny Boy Williamson stopped in London to cut an album backed by the Yardbirds, about whom he memorably quipped that British kids want to play the blues *so bad,* and that's what they do: play them *so bad.* Chuckle chuckle. But one part of the blues world wasn't chuckling: Vee-Jay, the veteran blues label (which had also pioneered soul music before going pop with the Four Seasons and the early Beatles album Capitol had passed on) was in serious trouble. By the end of January, it was facing bankruptcy, and by summer it'd be all but gone.

A couple of new words entered the vocabulary right around then, both misunderstood. First, there was *camp,* a complex term long used by homosexuals to mean a specific kind of irony. Popular culture decoded this as playing something serious for laughs, maybe something to do with pop art, and the new *Batman* television show, with its BIFF! POW! SOCK! captions in cartoon balloons during fight scenes, was, for now, the height of camp. The "Batman Theme," composed by Neal Hefti, was moronically simple, and joined the pantheon of TV theme songs, which included "Dragnet" and "Davy Crockett," as instantly identifiable pieces of pop culture. Of course, copycats were right around the corner, with a disastrous *Superman* Broadway show and the Green Hornet also on the scene. The other word was *psychedelic,* coined by English psychiatrist Dr. Humphry Osmond in correspondence with his friend Aldous Huxley sometime in the early years of the decade. It was in the air the day before Huxley (and President Kennedy) died because of that odd folk duo, the Holy Modal Rounders. They were in the studio doing their thing, which consisted of warping old-timey folk songs (which they did expertly), when they recorded "Hesitation Blues" with the words "Got my psychedelic feet in my psychedelic shoes / I'm leavin' lordy mama, got the psychedelic blues." Nobody paid it any mind; it was just the Rounders being the Rounders, but America was becoming vaguely aware that its children were using drugs—and, worse, singing about it. The Byrds recorded and released "Eight Miles High," their last top 20 hit, and insisted that the lyrics weren't about being high but about their plane ride to London, hence the reference to "small faces"—the band Small Faces, who toured with them, was one of the few decent British bands to make no impression on America. The Yardbirds' "Shapes of Things" also seemed druggy, as did the Who's "Substitute." The Byrds' follow-up was "5D (Fifth Dimension)," which also seemed suspicious, but Paul Revere and the Raiders, now with a vocalist, Mark Lindsay, grabbed a song from Mann and Weil, "Kicks," urging a girl in search of kicks to get straight before it was too late. The Stones hinted at drug use in "19th Nervous Breakdown" and would get more specific a year later with "Mother's Little Helper." Then along came Bob Dylan, with a riotous number, recorded in Nashville during sessions for his new album: "Rainy Day Women #12 & 35" was a romp, with Dylan seemingly making up lyrics on the spot (and cracking himself up as he did so), each verse culminating in everyone in the studio yelling, "Everybody must get stoned!" As pious moralists took to the media to explain that "everyone" knew that a *rainy day woman* was teenage slang for a "reefer," or marijuana cigarette, American teenagers took the record to number two on the pop charts. And nobody even noticed, a month later, when Ray Charles, who had an acknowledged heroin problem, recorded "Let's Go Get Stoned" by a young songwriting duo, Nickolas Ashford and Valerie Simpson. Of course, a lot of people who bought it were used to the phrase meaning what Ashford and Simpson (and Dean Martin and Frank Sinatra) meant: having a drink or two too many.

For his part, Dylan was above all this. He'd left a bunch of tracks behind from the Nashville session—he was still working with Bob Johnston as producer—and had taken off in mid-April for a grueling tour that started in Australia and New Zealand and would head to Europe at month's end for a string of dates, most of which were in Britain. With him was the Hawks, a band that had been together for some time backing Ronnie Hawkins, a madman from Arkansas who started off playing rockabilly and went straight into unhinged rock and roll. The drummer, Levon Helm, was the only U.S.-born member of the band; Hawkins had picked up the rest in Canada. After Michael Bloomfield turned down Dylan's offer to form a band, Dylan stole the Hawks, and their lead guitarist, Jaime "Robbie" Robertson, joined him in the Nashville sessions. Helm opted to sit out this tour, so Dylan took on Houston drummer Mickey Jones, and off they went, with a film crew for a movie Dylan had in his head called *Eat the Document*. The film never came out, but the tour was faithfully recorded, and bits of it leaked out, starting in July, when a new Dylan single, "I Want You," had an absolutely coruscating live version of "Just Like Tom Thumb's Blues" from the Dublin date on the B-side; being six-plus minutes long, it didn't make it onto the radio but got passed along on the collectors' circuit. Soon enough, an entire concert by this band showed up on a high-quality bootleg album. (Dylan's career was plagued by unauthorized releases, until the day he started getting his label to do them itself, as "The Bootleg Series.") Titled *Dylan Live at the Albert Hall*, it was actually from the May 17 show at the Manchester Free Trade Hall, and shows the audience in full tumult, booing and cheering the electric material until, in the pause between "Ballad of a Thin Man" and "Like a Rolling Stone," which closed out the show, a fan, later identified as Keith Butler, shouted "Judas!" Dylan, momentarily stunned (and a performer who never talked to his audience), replied, "I don't believe you. You're a *liar*," and then turned to the band and said, "Play fucking loud." They complied. Two days at the Albert Hall in London followed, after which Dylan and his new wife, Sarah Lowndes, flew to Spain to recover. Then it was back to New York for the release of his "novel," *Tarantula* (think an entire short book of the sort of abstract ramblings that had appeared as liner notes on his albums up to now, except not as good), and, in early June, a blessed retreat to his new home on Camelot Road in the Upper Byrdcliffe section of Woodstock, in upstate New York.

Judging from the length of time the song stayed on the radio and the charts, the rest of the nation may well have been California dreamin', and there was no doubt that something was stirring there. Not all of it was good: in April, Jan Berry of Jan and Dean was driving on a notorious part of Sunset Boulevard when his car spun out of control and hit a parked truck at high speed. Berry sustained severe head injuries that necessitated years of therapy to bring him back to normal functioning. But record companies had finally woken up to the fact that there was something going on in Los Angeles, and May saw Elektra taking its first tentative steps into electric music. Having missed the boat with the Beefeaters before they became the Byrds, it signed a multiracial band fronted by a guy named Arthur Lee, who'd made a couple of surf records with his friend Johnny Echols, unusual only in that both were black and from Watts. Lee was fascinated with the Byrds, who often played the emerging Sunset Strip scene. After a Byrds gig at Ciro's he began talking to one of their roadies, Bryan MacLean, who'd auditioned for the band but hadn't been invited to join. The two envisioned a band, rounded up Echols and a rhythm section, and started rehearsing. Before they knew it, they were playing the clubs, too, under the name Love. Lee, Echols, and MacLean all wrote and sang, but Elektra hedged its bets by putting out "My Little Red Book," by Burt Bacharach and Hal David (the team behind Dionne Warwick's string of hits), as Love's first single. Live, the band was made for the dancers who thronged the Sunset Strip's clubs (including the bunch who followed an eerie older guy named Vito from club to club, dancing the whole time), and like many other bands on the Strip, they did a song called "Hey Joe," about a jealous man killing his girlfriend, which had been written by Chester Powers, an abrasive songwriter who sometimes used the name Dino Valenti.

Another bunch popular with the dancers was a loose aggregation fronted by a tall, gangly Italian fellow from the high desert in Lancaster, California, with the Pop Art name Frank Zappa, who was under the wing of Herb Cohen, owner of the Unicorn coffeehouse, another Strip hangout. While still in school, Zappa and another misfit named Don Van Vliet started playing together, and soon Zappa had a string of blues bands, all racially integrated. He started hanging out at a recording studio in Cucamonga run by Paul Buff, who'd learned electronics in the service, and was soon watching intensely, learning about multitracking (building up a recording by layering musical lines instead of having them played in real time by an ensemble) and microphone placement. Eventually, he bought the studio from Buff and called it Studio Z. Right away, he got in trouble. The local sheriff's department decided that the studio was a front for pornographic films and sent an undercover agent to talk to Zappa about using multitracking to make, if not a dirty movie, then at least a dirty audiotape. Zappa and his current girlfriend, Lorraine Belcher, recorded noises such as squeaking bedsprings, and when the guy showed up to get it, he had only fifty of the three hundred dollars he'd promised. Zappa, broke, took it, and immediately found himself charged with "conspiracy to manufacture pornographic materials and suspicion of sex perversion." A trial ensued, and Zappa did ten days of a six-month sentence. The experience flipped a switch in his mind that never switched back; he perceived himself as being in opposition to nearly everything while being persecuted for it. He moved to Los Angeles, where he soon took over a band called the Muthers, which he expanded with some musician friends, and after changing the name to the Mothers, he started getting work on the Strip with help from Cohen, who immediately began looking for a record deal. One day Zappa heard that Tom Wilson, Bob Dylan's ex-producer, had left Columbia, started work with MGM Records, and was out in LA with the Animals. Zappa found Wilson in a club and whisked him down to a Mothers gig, where he watched him go nuts. Wilson immediately contacted New York. His bosses weren't sure this was what they wanted, but Wilson, lying through his teeth, told them that despite the odd name, the Mothers was a blues band, and they gave him the okay. The result, a double album entitled *Freak Out!*, by the band now called the Mothers of Invention, debuted in July. Despite its title (a common drug slang term for going nuts), Zappa was rigorously anti-drug, as he was anti-so-many-other-things.

Wilson was also producing another band in Los Angeles in the spring of 1966. Jerry Garcia and his friends had heard right: there *was* another band called the Warlocks, and they *did* have a record deal. Their manager, however, didn't like the band's name, and he was the reason MGM had signed them in the first place: *he* was Andy Warhol, Mr. Pop Art himself. Warhol had hired this bunch of oddballs, which included a contract songwriter for an exploitation label on Long Island; a Leonard Bernstein Young Composers Award winner from Wales; an English Lit major from Rochester, New York; and somebody's sister on drums, to play in his multimedia extravaganza (or what passed for an extravaganza in Warhol's chronically underfunded world), the Exploding Plastic Inevitable, in which a live band, projections, and dancers provided "sensory overload." By then, the band had changed its name to the Velvet Underground, after a sleazy paperback by one Michael Leigh (legitimized with a foreword by a real doctor!) exposing wife-swapping and other swinging sex scenes in suburbia. Warhol decided that none of the musicians had actual star appeal, and put one of his own circle, a model who'd made a couple of singles in England and had had a walk-on part in Federico Fellini's *La Dolce Vita*, up front. Born in Cologne to a prominent family of brewers, Christa Päffgen had taken the name Nico. In the same studio he'd used for the Mothers, Wilson spent some time in April 1966 recording the Velvet Underground. MGM released a single in July, "All Tomorrow's Parties," with Nico's flat monotone casting its spell—and then, perhaps mindful of other songs on the tape, such as "Waiting for the Man," "Heroin," and the almost eight-minute-long noisefest "European Son," the label sat on the album until the following March. It's not as if the single had been a hit, after all.

And what about those other Californians, the ones with a much sunnier image of California than Zappa had? Early in 1966, a single by Brian Wilson, "Caroline, No," backed with "Summer Means New Love," was noted in *Billboard*, never to darken its pages again. Instead, a new Beach Boys single, "Sloop John B," came out in March and headed up the charts. Of Bahamian origin, this rollicking staple of hootenanny bands had been slowed down and given a particularly baroque arrangement, emphasizing its inherent melancholy. Then, in May, it showed up on the latest Beach Boys album, *Pet Sounds*. This (as the single that was released simultaneously, "Wouldn't It Be Nice," demonstrated) was something else entirely. Brian Wilson had been obsessing about Phil Spector, watching him lose direction and start floundering after the magnificence of "You've Lost That Lovin'

Feeling"; and about the Beatles, whose growing complexity intrigued him. Wilson had started taking LSD (and, in fact, "California Girls," that most iconic of Beach Boys tunes, was written as he was coming down from his first trip), and he was hearing melodies that he felt came directly from God. While the rest of the band was on tour in early 1966—Brian was replaced, as usual, by another musician—he hooked up with a lyricist named Tony Asher, and together they wrote an album of material (except for "Sloop John B"). While Brian conducted orchestrations, using Phil Spector's backup musicians (who came to be known later as the Wrecking Crew) and studio (Gold Star), the rest of the band came off tour and went in to record their parts. Mike Love hated the new album, declaring that Brian was "fucking with the formula," and Capitol almost killed it by releasing *Best of the Beach Boys* virtually simultaneously, but *Pet Sounds* sold in decent quantities to the fans, sold some to people who hadn't been fans before, and seriously disturbed Paul McCartney, who rightly perceived a rock-and-roll arms race beginning. Since they couldn't tour the album with its huge orchestra, Brian kept on in the studio with another song he'd written that they *could* do live: "Good Vibrations." And he saw things beyond that opening up, big things.

One thing Brian certainly had right was Phil Spector's decline. He'd been acting odder and odder, holed up in his mansion with his girlfriend (the Ronettes' lead singer, Veronica), a virtual prisoner. The Righteous Brothers weren't actually his in the way that the Ronettes and the Crystals had been, and their previous label kept releasing their records while they were being courted by other labels. Spector had been spending time with comedian Lenny Bruce, Frank Zappa, and other odd folks at a table at Canter's Delicatessen, in Los Angeles, where the topics under discussion ranged all over the place. It was a new world, but it was time for a return to the charts! He sure picked an odd way to do it: since they were currently not recording for anyone, he grabbed Ike and Tina Turner, handed them a song he'd written with Ellie Greenwich and Jeff Barry, and announced to the world that if this didn't make it, he was quitting the music business forever. The resulting 45, "River Deep–Mountain High," was every bit as bombastic as his statement, with Tina mouthing the ridiculous lyrics with no hint of involvement (and Ike invisible as usual), the arrangement positively Wagnerian. It got to 88 after four weeks in May and vanished except in Britain, where it sold respectably. (Spector didn't exactly vanish himself: there were a few more singles on his label, Philles Records, but produced by others.) In August, he took out a half page in *Billboard* to promote an album: "LENNY BRUCE IS DEAD. He died of an overdose of police." Bruce's act had devolved into a recitation of the wrongs done against him, complete with readings from the trial proceedings after he was busted for "indecent" language, which was part of his act. Spector recorded and released one of these late shows, but what Bruce had overdosed on was heroin. The police harassment had just helped his exit.

Pet Sounds ushered in the summer of 1966. Once again, the Red Dog opened its swinging doors, and this time Big Brother and the Holding Company was the house band. The Family Dog and Bill Graham Presents were both doing weekly dance concerts, which helped not only attract out-of-town weirdo musicians like Texas's 13th Floor Elevators (who had a small hit with the frenetic "You're Gonna Miss Me") and Seattle's Daily Flash (who hit with a commercial for pot, "Acapulco Gold") but also develop the local scene's chops. Aided by a galaxy of stunning posters drawn for both promoters by original Dog Alton Kelley and his studio partner Stanley Mouse, a Detroit immigrant who'd come up in the world of hot-rod magazines; former surf cartoonist Wes Wilson; San Francisco Art Institute instructor Victor Moscoso; and others, word about San Francisco's musical paradise began to spread.

First into the studio (after the Beau Brummels, who were now signed to Warner Bros. and recording Dylan songs) was the Jefferson Airplane, who scored a deal with RCA and released a single, "Come Up the Years," in June. It got played in San Francisco and a couple of other markets, and was followed by an album, *Jefferson Airplane Takes Off,* in the fall. It didn't make sense to tour it, though; the lead singer, Signe Toly Anderson, was newly married and pregnant with her first child. Her last show with the band (which had already replaced its drummer, Skip Spence, with Spencer Dryden) was on October 15 at the Fillmore. The next day, the Airplane's new lineup had Grace Slick, who had defected from her husband's band, as the new lead vocalist. Despite the local popularity of the other bands, nobody was in any hurry to sign more of them.

Anyway, there was enough good music to go around. The Lovin' Spoonful was putting out great stuff, and "Did You Ever Have to Make Up Your Mind?" was a big summer hit, while the Turtles from LA tried to make a hit out of the Spoonful's "Younger Girl" (they didn't). The latest song rumored to be about pot was by a mild aggregation from Los Angeles, the Association, whose "Along Comes Mary" was certainly pleasant enough. The Beatles released "Paperback Writer" and "Rain," the latter with rather trippy backward tape sounds, something John Lennon had become obsessed with. For something a bit less complex—a *lot* less complex—the Troggs picked up a song a country songwriter named Chip Taylor had written for a New York discotheque's house band, "Wild Thing," and proved that the old "Louie Louie" chords still had life in them. More smooth sounds came courtesy of the Left Banke, whose "Walk Away Renée" was insanely melodic, and continuing the Baroque rock trend, Donovan, newly signed by Epic, contributed "Sunshine Superman," produced by former skiffle star Mickie Most, with guitar by British studio stalwart Jimmy Page, who was also a Yardbird. Then out came the Spoonful with the summer's theme song: "Summer in the City," and all was groovy. What was especially groovy was that there were whole albums of this stuff coming out: the new Bob Dylan album, mostly electric, enigmatically titled *Blonde on Blonde*, was a double. So was the Mothers' *Freak Out!*, although it didn't match Dylan's sales. As the Beatles started their latest tour, their next real album came out: *Revolver* was, um, psychedelic! Literally so: beyond the obligatory McCartney ballad-with-strings ("Eleanor Rigby") lay a bunch of new sounds, from "Taxman"'s manipulated guitars, the exuberant "Got to Get You into My Life," George's Indian-inflected "I Want to Tell You," and the final track, "Tomorrow Never Knows," which quotes directly from *The Psychedelic Experience*, a "manual" for the use of LSD (or one man's vision of it), by Dr. Timothy Leary, former head of the Harvard LSD experimenters, now turned into a showbiz guru proselytizing for its use.

Revolver was a "real" album because all along, Capitol had been leaving tracks off Beatles albums it had issued in the United States. Because of differences between British and American royalty structures, there were generally more tracks on a British album than on its American counterpart. This held true for not only the Beatles but also the Stones, the Kinks, the Who, and other groups. Their U.S. labels would put out a shortened version and then collect nonalbum singles and songs released on the EPs many bands did between albums, and release them on an anthology album. Capitol had done a catch-up of recent British Beatle product in June, with an album called *Yesterday . . . and Today* and ignited a controversy: the cover showed the lovable mop tops in blood-spattered butcher smocks with pieces of raw meat and chopped-up baby dolls. Horrified, Capitol tried pasting an alternate cover on the record just to get it out the door, but the darker original cover showed through, so they recalled and destroyed a quarter of a million covers. Hell, it was the Beatles: the cost was charged against their earnings, and they could afford it. Somewhat more worrying was the fact that just before the release of *Revolver* and the new tour, John Lennon had shot his mouth off to Maureen Cleave, who was writing a piece for the London *Evening Standard*. "We're more popular than Jesus now," he told her. "I don't know which will go first—rock and roll or Christianity." While the quote went mostly unnoticed in Britain as more pop star hyperbole, in the United States it spread all over the place, causing denunciations, anti-Beatle sermons, and, in Alabama and Texas, Beatle record bonfires. (The one that radio station KLUE, in Longview, Texas, sponsored might not have been to God's liking, though: it was held on August 13, and the KLUE tower was hit by lightning the next day, taking the station off the air.) When the band arrived in Chicago to start their tour, they held a press conference in which an unhappy John tried to walk the quote back, but it followed them around the country. Even the pope denounced the Beatles, and in Washington, DC, the Ku Klux Klan not only threatened them, but also picketed the show in full regalia. The September 3 issue of *Billboard* had an article on the beginning of the tour that fairly dripped with schadenfreude: the group had drawn only 45,000 to New York's Shea Stadium, a venue that held 55,000. The band, the magazine said, was finally declining in popularity.

In July, Elektra had released an album called *What's Shakin'*, featuring a quartet of groups: the Lovin' Spoonful, the Paul Butterfield Blues Band, Al Kooper, and Eric Clapton and the Powerhouse. This last group consisted of Jack Bruce, Paul Jones, Peter York, and Stevie Winwood; Winwood, who was only fifteen, was on loan from the Spencer Davis Group, who'd had a small hit with "Keep On Running." Between the Butterfield tracks (from their first sessions, before Newport) and the Clapton tracks, a trend was emerging: white blues bands with virtuosic lead guitars, something that hadn't really been in the picture with contemporary music until now. Bloomfield and Bishop, and Eric Clapton, the former Yardbird (and current Bluesbreaker), played accessible, complicated lines as they soloed above their groups. Then the Butterfield Band released its second album, *East-West*, and the gauntlet was thrown down. The album featured regular Chicago blues, but its centerpiece was the two long tracks on each side, the title song and a version of Cannonball Adderley's "Work Song," which provided room for everyone in the band to solo at length. They were certainly up to it. The song "East-West" was credited to Nick Gravenites (who was mostly a vocalist) because it had its origin in his song "It's About Time," but its execution hinged on the discoveries Bloomfield and Bishop had made about modality and Indian music, which, as virtuosi, they understood far deeper than George Harrison or the other British musicians who treated it as a seasoning, not a dish. And yes, the breakthrough had come about earlier in the year, when the two guitarists took LSD together. As for Clapton, he was searching for something new, but based in hard-core blues and under the influence of Ginger Baker, a drummer who was also in search of better things, he added Manfred Mann's bassist, Jack Bruce, to form a band. They were the cream of the London blues scene, so that's what they called themselves: Cream. They started rehearsals, and graffiti reading CLAPTON IS GOD started to appear on London walls.

On the other side of the spectrum, at summer's end, teaser ads started appearing in *Billboard* for something called the Monkees. This was producer Don Kirshner's next triumph. Kirshner and his partner,

Al Nevins, had sold their firm Aldon Music, with its roster of teenage songwriters, to Columbia Pictures in 1963, and now Kirshner had an entrée into film and television via Columbia's publishing company, Screen Gems–Columbia. With his Teen Pan Alley songwriters writing hits for new groups like the Byrds, Paul Revere and the Raiders, and the Animals, Kirshner decided that with the success of the Beatles' films, a made-up group with a weekly television show would be a perfect outlet for his writers' material, so in 1965 he put an ad in *The Hollywood Reporter* and *Daily Variety* seeking "Folk & Roll Musicians-Singers for acting roles in new TV series. Running Parts for 4 insane boys, age 17–21. Want spirited Ben Frank's [a Sunset Strip hangout] types. Have courage to work. Must come down for interview." Of course there were loads of teen hopefuls in Hollywood, 437 of whom showed up; four were chosen: Davy Jones, star of Broadway's *Oliver!*, who'd appeared on Ed Sullivan's show the same night at the Beatles' debut; Michael Nesmith, a Texan who'd been performing around town as Michael Blessing; Micky Dolenz, from a showbiz family; and Peter Tork, a New York folkie who'd washed up in Hollywood. They got busy filming the show and learning the songs they were handed, while Kirshner saw this as a golden moment: developing a band from the ground up, he'd have control over their image, and by premiering on television, they'd have a built-in weekly audience. Also, younger teens who'd missed the Beatles and found themselves confused by all the psychedelic noise around them would get good, clean-cut (but wacky) kids doing pop material created by proven craftsmen. The show hit the airwaves on September 12, 1966, and was an instant hit. The Monkees' first single, "Last Train to Clarksville," rocketed to number one, as did their album when it came out a few weeks later.

In all the hype and noise over the "pre-fab four," nobody seemed to notice that "Last Train to Clarksville," written and produced by Tommy Boyce and Bobby Hart, could be taken as an antiwar song sung by a guy who wants one more night with his girlfriend because he's not sure he's "ever coming back." For all the innovation and creative energy young people were producing, there was also a darkness looming. America had stepped up its military involvement in Vietnam, and once a young man was eighteen, he was eligible to be drafted and, perhaps, to be sent there to fight and, perhaps, die. Robin Cook had written a novel, *The Green Berets*, which was very gung-ho about the situation, and in an odd move, RCA decided to release a song based on it, cowritten by Cook and an actual Green Beret, Staff Sergeant Barry Sadler, who'd mustered out of the army after a serious injury. They hyped the record to death, and 1966 started with it at the top of the charts, provoking many another pro-war song, predominantly by country performers, none of whom had seen actual combat, and none of which disturbed the pop charts overly. Not many songs protesting the war got airplay, either, unless they were as nebulous as Buffy Sainte-Marie's "Universal Soldier." No, things were still groovy, what with Ringo singing about living in a yellow submarine and the Kinks facing disaster with a nice cuppa on a "Sunny Afternoon."

And much as some people complained about the Monkees, they were merely being up-front about their factory production of hits. Motown had been practicing it for some time, and 1966 was the year that it really paid off. The reason was down to three young men who had become an unstoppable writing/production team (one of whom had sung a couple of mild hits for the label a couple of years earlier): Eddie Holland, Brian Holland, and Lamont Dozier, collectively known as Holland–Dozier–Holland, or HDH for short, were behind the year's incredible run of hits. Not all of them—Smokey Robinson was also reaching for the heights with the Temptations, who'd been knocking out hits he'd penned, filling two great 1965 albums, *The Temptations Sing Smokey* and *Temptin' Temptations*. But it was HDH who were responsible for the former "no-hit Supremes" finally having hit after hit; who helped Jr. Walker & The All Stars find their way back after some not-so-spectacular follow-ups to their freak instrumental hit "Shotgun" in 1965 by writing "(I'm a) Road Runner"; and especially, who guided the Four Tops in finding an identity—they'd been on the midwestern supper club circuit forever prior to signing with Motown—by placing vocalist Levi Stubbs up front and then writing hits starting with 1964's "Baby I Need Your Loving," on into 1965's "I Can't Help Myself" and "It's the Same Old Song," and culminating in the most revolutionary record Motown had put out so far,

"Reach Out I'll Be There." The group was mystified by this last song at first, and Smokey Robinson hated it and didn't want to put it out. But Berry Gordy heard something: an oboe, some Arabic drums someone had lying around clattering away, and the shouted Dylan-esque vocal on the verses. "The phrasing for 'I'll Be There' came from listening to the way [Dylan] sang," Lamont Dozier admitted. "He'd do that thing . . . where he'd drag a phrase out, that I liked." Well into the song, Stubbs shouts, "Just look over your shoulder!" and in that moment, one of the great Motown records gets even greater. It veers perilously close to being actual soul music, which Gordy tried to avoid, but as he said when Robinson objected, "It's . . . different than anything out there in the street." It sure was.

Mr. Dylan was unavailable for comment, however. In fact, where was he? His influence was suddenly everywhere, with younger song-writers feeling free to write abstract, literate, personal lyrics whose meaning, if any, only they knew. He'd been announced, with Joan Baez, for a festival somewhere, but that didn't happen. After coming off tour in the spring, he'd gone back to Woodstock and seemingly vanished. During the summer, rumors began to spread that he was dead, or that he'd been badly hurt, at minimum, in a motorcycle ac-cident. The good news was he wasn't dead. He wasn't in great shape, however. His manager, Albert Grossman, wanted a fall tour; Mac-millan wanted him to promote his book, *Tarantula;* and ABC wanted its television program from the last tour.

One night in Woodstock, Dylan later told rock journalist Ben Fong-Torres, he looked up at the sky and heard a voice in his head saying, "Something's gotta change." And it did. On the afternoon of July 29, Dylan was heading home from the Grossmans' house to his own, driving his Triumph motorcycle. Apparently blinded by the sun, he panicked and hit the brake, locking the rear wheel and being thrown from the bike. Fortunately, his wife, Sara, was behind him in the family station wagon, and she picked him up and drove him back to the Grossman home, where Sally Grossman, who was on the phone with her husband, conveyed the news. Apparently, Albert told her to take Dylan to Dr. Ed Thaler, in nearby Middletown, who treated some of Grossman's other clients.

Although the injuries from the motorcycle accident weren't serious, Dylan had apparently had a total physical and mental collapse and stayed with the Thalers for at least ten days. By the time he was back in Woodstock, Grossman had canceled the tour and kept ABC and Macmillan at bay. The Hawks, Dylan's band, were now under Grossman's wing and hanging out in New York waiting for orders for the tour. Once it was canceled, Dylan, awash in a box of books Allen Ginsberg had trucked up to him, invited the band to upstate New York, and they discovered they loved it: it was like the rural Ontario they'd grown up in. Three of them, Garth Hudson, Rick Danko, and Richard Manuel, wound up going in on the rent for a large pink house in nearby West Saugerties. Dylan was recovering slowly and discovering he loved being away from pressure and out in public. Far from dying, he was coming back to life.

In other Canadian rock-and-roll news, a Canadian businessman named John Eaton approached Motown with the Mynah Birds, a band he thought they might like to record, and Berry Gordy was intrigued. For one thing, they were interracial, and the black lead singer, Ricky Mathews, really had something. The backup band was also pretty tight, so Gordy put them in the studio and was very happy with the results. They were on the verge of releasing a single, "It's My Time," backed with "Go On and Cry," when their manager made a confession to Gordy: Ricky had joined the U.S. Navy at fifteen. Suddenly scared by what he'd done, he went AWOL and, when he discovered that military police were looking for him, fled to Canada. It would ruin everything if he got arrested, so Gordy took the kid aside, told him to turn himself in and do the time, and when he got out, he'd have a home at Motown. He did so, and spent a year in a naval correctional facility in Brooklyn.

The Mynah Birds had recruited a star of the Toronto folk scene, Neil Young, as lead guitarist, and now Young decided it was time to go to Los Angeles and look for another folkie, Steve Stills, whom he'd met on the folk circuit in New York. Apparently Stills had gone West to hang out at the Troubadour bar, and had auditioned for (and been rejected by) the Monkees. Commandeering the Mynah Birds' hearse,

Young and bassist Bruce Palmer headed off and spent several days searching for Stills, to no avail. Frustrated, and with the hearse on its last legs, they decided that San Francisco might hold better opportunities, so they started driving down Sunset Boulevard toward the freeway, praying the vehicle would last. Going the other way on Sunset was a white van that held two songwriters, Richie Furay and . . . Steve Stills! Somehow the van managed a U-turn right there on Sunset and overtook the hearse. Pulling into Ben Frank's parking lot, they caught up on things. By the end of the summer, they'd acquired a drummer, Dewey Martin, from Vancouver, a production/management team (the same one Sonny and Cher had!), a deal with Atco Records, and a name: Buffalo Springfield. Their first single, "Nowadays Clancy Can't Even Sing," a song Young had taught Stills in New York, came out and stalled at 110 on the charts. They'd be back.

And, finally, while Berry Gordy may have perfected The Sound Of Young America®, 1966 was the year when more down-home soul music, masterpiece after masterpiece, also caught the ears of white American teens. In Memphis, Stax added to its roster of stars with former Motown singer Mable John's "Your Good Thing (Is About to End)," with its menacing horn chart; Carla Thomas came into her own with "Comfort Me," "Let Me Be Good to You," and the biggest hit of her career, "B-A-B-Y"; Sam and Dave had a remarkable run of hits, from "Hold On! I'm Comin'" through "You Got Me Hummin'"; Eddie Floyd hit with "Things Get Better" and "Knock on Wood"; and even Chicago-based blues guitarist Albert King hit with "Laundromat Blues" and "Crosscut Saw" on the R&B charts. Atlantic was taking full advantage of the (mostly white) crew in Muscle Shoals, Alabama, with Percy Sledge recording "When a Man Loves a Woman," "It Tears Me Up," and "Warm and Tender Love" there; and Wilson Pickett, taking a break from recording at Stax, cut "Mustang Sally" at nearby Fame Studios. New Orleans unleashed a new sound with Aaron Neville's "Tell It Like It Is"; and Lee Dorsey, produced by Allen Toussaint and backed by a band including some of Aaron's brothers and relatives, had a string of crossover hits with "Get Out of My Life, Woman," "Working in the Coal Mine," and "Holy Cow."

Philadelphia was bitten by the Motown bug, with a small label called Arctic trying to figure out a formula for its talented signing Kenny Gamble, and failing—at which point he started the Gamble label.

A young white songwriter/producer, Jerry Ragovoy, with close ties to Teen Pan Alley in his past, was having better luck with a former gospel singer, Howard Tate, who kicked off his career with "Ain't Nobody Home" and "Look at Granny Run Run." Ragovoy was also trying to help Warner Bros. get its soul act together in its New York office, and was busy writing material for another former gospel singer that Warners had signed, Lorraine Ellison, when he got a phone call from his boss telling him Frank Sinatra had canceled a session scheduled for July 22, seventy-two hours away. There was a large orchestra booked for the session that, by union rules, would have to be paid whether Sinatra showed up or not, so Ragovoy leapt at the chance, picked up one song he and cowriter David Weiss had finished, "Stay with Me," and wrote out the arrangements by hand. Staggering into the studio after having not slept since the call, he passed out the sheet music—the orchestra was still expecting Frank—and four minutes later the record that did everything that Phil Spector's "River Deep–Mountain High" failed to do was born—a live first take except for the first eight bars, where Ellison had flubbed the lyrics. It almost made it into the R&B top 10, stalling at 11, a titanic masterpiece of soul that, with its big backup and virtuosic vocal, pointed the way to the future.

That fall, Congress decided it was time to halt the drug menace threatening America's teenagers, and on October 6, they added LSD to the list of Class A narcotics, joining marijuana, heroin, and cocaine in the rolls of felonious intoxicants. Except for increasing the penalties for possessors and users, most of whom were already smoking pot, it made little difference: Owsley was still producing, the word *psychedelic* was being used to describe all sorts of things, and, it was feared, hordes were just waiting for next summer so they could descend on the Haight-Ashbury.

So ended the eighteen-month annus mirabilis, rock and roll's second and the one that began cementing it as the world's default popular music. Christmas and its retail season beckoned, the record business stood to make an unprecedented amount of money, and as various articles in *Billboard* contemplated the future of the stereo tape cartridge—wasn't this cassette thing from Philips, now being sold in America, easier to use? Or do we go with four-track cartridges? Or eight-track?—a small photo wedged into the December 3 issue at the last minute showed a smiling Jerry Wexler signing Columbia's failed jazz/supper club singer Aretha Franklin to Atlantic, something he'd wanted to do for a long, long time. She looks pretty happy in the picture, as does her manager/husband, Ted White. Jerry told Franklin to find some material, while he looked, too. Well, that was no problem; she was even writing stuff herself now. But while she was riding from the airport home to Detroit for the holidays, the car radio played a local hit by the Rationals, one of the city's better rock-and-roll bands. Like the Stones, whom they modeled themselves after, they liked to cover soul tunes. Their latest hit, a cover of Otis Redding's "Respect," which hadn't been much of a pop hit in 1965, caught her ear. Aretha was ready.

chapter three

THIS IS THE
LOVE CROWD, RIGHT?

Rock festival audience (Woodstock)
(Photo © Baron Wolman)

S omething was happening, but the record business, like Bob Dylan's hapless Mr. Jones, didn't know what it was. It was time to put its best minds on the case. First up was a study of college radio stations with the shocking news that rock and roll was no longer limited to teenagers: an analysis of airplay showed that it had taken over from folk as the number-one music programmed on campus. "The idea and styles of teenagers is [*sic*] influencing both adults and young adults . . . The age gap is closing musically," an unnamed Columbia Records executive told *Billboard,* ungrammatically. Shortly thereafter, a survey of college record stores pretty much confirmed this. There was a "pop music confab" in San Francisco in April (probably sponsored by the magazine, which was readying a special section on the city), featuring Tom Donahue, who'd dissolved Autumn Records and was now working for Warner Bros.; Ralph Gleason, the jazz and (now) local rock music columnist in the *San Francisco Chronicle;* Phil Spector, who'd stopped producing records; and Bill Graham, who, besides booking the Fillmore Auditorium, was now managing the Jefferson Airplane. As *Billboard* reported, "The speakers agreed that the young are in control of the industry and that, having once heard the amplified music and poetic lyricism of the Beatles, Bob Dylan, Donovan, and the Rolling Stones, [they] are now wide open for any music that can stimulate them."

Well, it sort of depended on what *kind* of stimulation, apparently. A few pages later, Gordon McLendon, owner of the McLendon group of radio stations and one of the early adopters of the top 40 format, placed a full-page ad stating his disgust with the music his program directors were being offered. "In the past month," he thundered, "six records which were on the national charts far *overstepped* the boundaries of good taste, and we were forced to ban them." His solution was to require every record serviced to a McLendon station to come with a lyric sheet, or it would not be considered. Effective immediately. On the one hand, it was like your dad telling you to turn down that awful racket. On the other hand, getting added to the McLendon group was a mighty kick in the pants in terms of airplay and sales. Letters of support came in—telegrams, too. One station owner thanked McLendon but noted that there was still a problem: why, his station had added a record on which "the British slang term for LSD" appeared. (It's hard to figure what this was, although Eric Burdon had just put out a B-side titled "A Girl Named Sandoz," though the song was so awful it's hard to imagine anyone playing it. Sandoz, of course, was the Swiss firm that manufactured the legit stuff.) Acknowledging that it was hard to keep up with slang, McLendon then announced that because he was still inundated by filth, he would set up a panel of "prostitutes, ex-prostitutes, junkies, and ex-addicts" to screen submitted lyrics. Paul Revere, whose Raiders had just lost their gig as house band of Dick Clark's *Where the Action Is* TV show, opined dourly that only "crud" groups wrote song lyrics pushing drugs. He'd recorded a song, "Kicks," that was strongly antidrug. Oh, and it was on the newly released *Paul Revere and the Raiders Greatest Hits* album.

There was a point here, however boneheadedly expressed. The Rolling Stones' recent hit "Ruby Tuesday" had risen to the top of the charts because there was widespread disapproval among radio programmers over the intended A-side, "Let's Spend the Night Together," which, however great a song it was, certainly wasn't at all subtle. (The Stones, however, caved when they did Ed Sullivan, a performance notable for both the last-minute lyric change to "Let's spend some time together" and the mammoth bandage around Brian Jones's head due to an encounter with a studio door.) Mitch Ryder had a barn burner of a single called "Sock It to Me, Baby" that had a line, "Every time you kiss me / Feels just like a punch," where the last word was mumbled, although its vowel sound wasn't. Tommy James and the Shondells' "I Think We're Alone Now" was a bit suggestive, but its album cover featured some footprints that seemed up to some hanky-panky (which, come to think of it, was the title of James's first single). As for dope, there were a few wink-wink, nudge-nudge songs out there, as well as such blatant encodings as Simon and Garfunkel's "59th St. Bridge Song (Feelin' Groovy)," which was about smoking a joint across the street from New York's current hip club, Steve Paul's Scene, where the Young Rascals, who'd just released "Groovin'," were the house band. Simon and Garfunkel stuck "59th Street Bridge" on a B-side, but Harpers Bizarre, a soft-rock vocal group from Santa Cruz featuring a former Beau Brummel and Ted Templeman, soon to become an important Warner Bros. producer, took it high in the charts. (The less said about *The Velvet Underground and Nico,* with its semi-obscene "peel slowly and see" cover—peeling back the banana skin revealed a sick pink fruit—and its songs "Heroin" and "Venus in Furs," the better, although the album was also impossible to find because the first run of covers was recalled due to an unauthorized picture of Warhol associate Eric Emerson in a light show shot; but at least it had finally come out.)

Yes, indeed, something was happening and it was incumbent on the record industry to corral and control it as soon as possible. Old-style singers still sold albums, but suddenly so did some of the new acts: the Mamas and the Papas, for one, seemed to be selling as many albums as singles, although their singles were doing very well (and of course you could say the same about the Beatles and the Stones). Trends were eagerly chased: a freak hit by the New Vaudeville Band, from England, "Winchester Cathedral," sounded like an old 78, thanks to the use of modern studio techniques, and ignited a slew of weirdo do-wacka-do records. The one that did best was from California's Dr. West's Medicine Show and Junk Band, "The Eggplant That Ate Chicago," and they followed it up with an album crammed with dope slang and hideous puns ("How Lew Sin Ate," about a hungry Chinese guy).

Given that America hadn't been without a trumpet star since Louis Armstrong, and with Al Hirt's appeal fading, along came Herb Alpert and the Tijuana Brass, whose gimmick was a mariachi-style ensemble that may have been mostly Alpert (a rare record executive who was also a skilled musician), overdubbing himself at first, set to a snappier, somewhat rock-y beat. Alpert added to his A&M (Alpert and Moss) Records stable with Sergio Mendes & Brasil '66 and Julius Wechter and the Baja Marimba Band, all of whom sold singles and albums, as well as the Sandpipers, a soft vocal group who slowed down popular songs and had a hit with "Guantanamera" and (gasp) "Louie Louie." So, a kind of new MOR (middle of the road, a new category that *Billboard* had introduced) was one way to go. Another was to hold your nose and leap into the mass of crazy kids thronging the clubs and ballrooms in California and the late British Invasion bands who, inspired by the Beatles and Stones, were headed to directions unknown.

The latter choice had yet to really pay off. Elektra had bravely done a second album with Love, *Da Capo*, but its second side was an unfocused jam called "Revelation," the result, producer Paul Rothchild later confessed, of his giving the band acid and telling them to let go, afraid he'd never get another song out of them. He'd also signed an odd band that was drawing crowds on the Strip, largely because of its charismatic lead singer: the Doors were a bunch of UCLA film students who named themselves after Aldous Huxley's book on his LSD experiences, *The Doors of Perception*. They lacked a bass player, but keyboardist Ray Manzarek had bass pedals he used in performance; and lead singer Jim Morrison wasn't the poet he thought he was, but he had the girls mesmerized.

Elsewhere on the Strip, another charismatic front man, who called himself Sky Saxon, led the Seeds, who were snapped up by LA jazz producer Gene Norman for his GNP Crescendo label, and had a minor hit with "Pushin' Too Hard," followed by several more singles and albums, before the public snapped that they actually knew only two chords. (Three, you could get away with: the Kingsmen were still putting out records, after all.) The Strip was still recovering from the "riot" of the previous November, when the Pandora's Box club was in the way of what the city considered necessary road widening and traffic control, and a demonstration turned violent, resulting in the mass arrest of three hundred people. There was much fussing and fuming about "the Man," and a rather awful exploitation film followed, called *Riot on Sunset Strip*, with a soundtrack album of surf bands disguised as motorcycle bands and a theme song by the Standells, but the incident birthed a hit, finally, for Buffalo Springfield, "For What It's Worth," written by Stephen Stills, with lyrics that may have been a bit strident but were catchy enough to take the song to the national top 10.

You could also try what RCA tried with the id—groovy! All lowercase!—who came out of nowhere and were touted as a "new switched-on group with a psyched-out sound that bends the mind and makes things happen," possibly setting a new record for cliché density in a record-company ad; having come out of nowhere, they remained there. You could grab your town's favorite Beatle-y band, as Epic did with Boston's Remains, one of America's great lost bands from this era, who were good enough to open for the Beatles on tour but not capable of standing out among the crowd. Or, you could be totally honest, like Warner Bros. president Joe Smith, and sign the Grateful Dead while admitting, years later, that "we knew there was this scene up there [in San Francisco] and we had to make contact with it—not that we understood the lifestyle." RCA at least had the intelligence to try again with the Jefferson Airplane and record a second album in Los Angeles, which was given the switched-on psyched-out title *Surrealistic Pillow*. Its first single underlined the fact that this was a *California* sound: "My Best Friend" sounded as close to the Mamas and the Papas as the Airplane would get, and had been written by their former drummer, Skip Spence. The second single, "Somebody to Love," which new singer Grace Slick had brought from her previous group, the Great Society, would do somewhat better.

In England, the interesting stuff seemed to be coming from the divide between the Mods, who were in decline, and the dopers, many of whom were former Mods. The Mods, a youth tribe who'd been around for a while, centered on fashion, amphetamines, rhythm and blues, frenetic dancing, and not much else. The Mod bands who made the charts were the Who (who were a bit artier than the average Mod and who were putting out very odd records indeed at the moment) and the Small Faces, who were the happy face of the movement, dressing impeccably and racking up hit after hit, but not in America, where, for some reason, no record company would touch them initially. Other Mod bands kept trying, but their culture was on the way out: March 1967 saw a brief blip on the British charts by John's Children, led by a fey-looking young man named Marc Bolan, who was insanely ambitious. But most Mod bands saw, like the Who, that things were changing: the Kinks were heading into an odd territory marked by a chipper, very British domesticity with a dark undercurrent, as in their semi-hit in America, "Sunny Afternoon," as well as barbed social commentary like "Dead End Street" and "Big Black Smoke." Another band that seemed to match the Who's arty explorations, the bass-heavy Move, from Birmingham, showed up on the British charts with what seemed to be explicit songs about acid trips, "Night of Fear" and "I Can Hear the Grass Grow." The Creation, more art-school dropouts who dressed Mod, liked to do action painting or destroy television sets during the course of a performance. More weirdness came from Pink Floyd, who despite being named for a couple of Georgia bluesmen, Pink Anderson and Floyd Council, purveyed a hard-to-pin-down but murky sound on their debut single, "Arnold Layne."

All this was going on while some of the original wave were changing or falling apart. The Yardbirds seemed to be in a constant state of flux with their guitarists: first they lost Eric Clapton, and next was Jeff Beck, his replacement, who left to front his own group, with ex-folkie Rod Stewart on lead vocals. Jimmy Page, former teenage wunderkind and first-call electric guitar studio man, was now the sole guitarist in the band. The Animals were increasingly uneasy about their records suddenly appearing as "by Eric Burdon and the Animals." First to leave was keyboard player Alan Price, whose band it had originally been, and he set about organizing the Alan Price Set, which had hits like "Simon Smith and his Amazing Dancing Bear" and "The Biggest Night of Her Life," both written by a professional LA songwriter, Randy Newman. Bassist Chas Chandler also quit, and went to New York to plot his next move. Snooping around the Village, he heard about a phenomenal guitarist who'd been playing around, most recently with John Hammond Jr., and had his own gig at the Cafe Wha?, on MacDougal Street, with a so-so band. Finally, curious, he went there to check him out: it was the guitarist from Little Richard's band, Jimmy Hendrix, and yes, he was everything Chandler had heard. He also fit in with Chandler's long-range plans: to reenter the music business as a manager and record producer. He stepped right up and offered Hendrix a deal: come to England, let me give you a rhythm section, we'll get a record deal, and you'll be famous. After all, Clapton was making hit singles with his band Cream; the time was right. And that's what happened. By the start of 1967, the Jimi Hendrix Experience had a deal with Track, the label started by the Who's management, and singles (that old workhorse "Hey Joe" and a Hendrix-written tune, "Purple Haze") on the English charts. Across the water, Frank Sinatra's Warners-affiliated label, Reprise, picked him up, advertising "Hey Joe" as a soul single. Bad move but not irreparable.

There was another clue to the new phenomenon that the record business was missing. Sometime in late 1966, the *Village Voice,* a contrarian publication founded in 1955 by novelist Norman Mailer and two of his friends to cover Greenwich Village, printed an item in Howard Smith's "Scenes" column that began "Behind a door on 6th Avenue, an 18-year-old ego burns." This was by way of mocking Paul Williams, a skinny, nervous kid with thick glasses and an unruly shock of blond hair. Williams had moved to New York from Cambridge, Massachusetts, because it was the obvious place for him to continue publishing his magazine, *Crawdaddy!,* the first issue of which had come out in late March 1966. Williams had come from science-fiction fandom, which had a long tradition of "fanzines," mimeographed magazines of criticism and news, dating back to the 1930s. He felt, along with some of his friends, that there was serious music being made at the moment that deserved the respect that jazz got from its fans in *Downbeat* and other magazines. By the end of January 1967, he was commanding a staff of three, getting drop-ins from performers like the Blues Project (Al Kooper's latest band), and being asked to consult with Paul Rothchild on whether Elektra should release an entire album by the Doors. (It did, and in a situation reminiscent of Dylan's "Like a Rolling Stone," the seven-minute second single off it, "Light My Fire," topped the charts that summer.) Mock they might, but the *Voice* soon started printing serious articles, too, at the hands of Richard Goldstein and others, and *Esquire* initiated a column called "Secular Music," written by a Long Island journalist named Robert Christgau. Even the *New Yorker* had a regular column, by noted feminist and essayist Ellen Willis. And *Crawdaddy!*'s vacuum was soon filled in Boston by *Fusion*, using some of its predecessors' contributors, such as Jon Landau. (The *Village Voice*, too, had started having descendants, with the *Los Angeles Free Press* appearing in 1964, the *Berkeley Barb* starting up in 1965, and New York's *East Village Other* in 1966, beginning the "underground press" movement that covered alternative politics and culture.)

What was going on here was beginning to dawn: the rat had entered the snake, an inelegant image but as good a way as any to think about it, the bulk of the rat causing a bump in the snake's profile as it was slowly digested. After World War II ended in 1945, loads of American men returned from battle. Most of them either had or got wives; government projects helped them find jobs, housing, and education; and along in there a lot of babies got born, because the booming economy meant you could support them without your wife having to work, too. You could even afford to have more than one or two kids. By the time the Beatles and the Stones and the Beach Boys were starting to show up on the radio, these babies were teenagers, who heard kids a little older than them making this music and, it seemed, making it for them. And they, in turn, made some. The reason the music business paid attention was that there were so many potential customers out there: as these kids got older, found easily available jobs, and went to college, they consumed music (usually one of the proliferating varieties of folk or rock and roll) that their peers were making. You could try feeding them Frankie Avalon or the New Vaudeville

Band or the id—for a while. They'd bite, but they wouldn't take another bite unless it tasted good.

There were very few of these people in the record business at first. Phil Spector had stood out because of his age and his success, but not many were like him. Then, suddenly, there were: Brian Epstein was only a couple of years older than the Beatles, and Andrew Loog Oldham was younger than most of the Stones. The audience was on the stage in places like the Avalon Ballroom or the Whisky a Go Go on the Sunset Strip. These people spoke your language, took your drugs, wore your clothes (or clothes you might aspire to wear), and seemed like your partners and friends as well as entertainers. And except for the occasional genius like Bill Graham (who turned thirty-six in 1967, to Chet Helms's twenty-five), nobody in the music business much older than their mid-twenties had any idea how to speak to this age cohort. Smart record executives like Elektra's Jac Holzman and Paul Rothchild, Track's Kit Lambert and Chris Stamp, and Warner Bros.'s Joe Smith knew this, but they also knew they were driving blind in search of a destination they'd never seen before (as, of course, was the audience). It was an exciting and terrifying time to be in the business. The potential stakes were high, but let's face it, the risks were fairly small: there was always another group. There were suddenly loads and loads of young people.

Of course, that fact had its darker side: at the age of eighteen, American boys were required to register for the draft, which, during the postwar era, had been a drag but no big deal: you went in and endured being asked to do silly things like march around and salute and stuff, but maybe you'd do it in a far-off, exotic place like Japan or Germany, where Elvis had gone, or maybe Louisiana or California, and you might pick up a useful trade like auto mechanics or electronics. Then you came home and married your girlfriend. But, increasingly, there was the specter of the undeclared war in Vietnam, where nobody spoke your language; there was a dense, impenetrable jungle to fight in; and the chances of death were very high. There was resistance to this, starting with the folkies, and soul music was also beginning to respond, since initially a disproportionate number of

American soldiers in Vietnam were black. Some of the records weren't hard protest—the Monitors' "Greetings (This is Uncle Sam)," on the Motown subsidiary V.I.P., for instance—but increasingly, songs flying under the national radar, such as the Mighty Hannibal's "Hymn No. 5," sung by a soldier in Vietnam who doesn't seem to think he's coming back, showed up on jukeboxes, if not the radio.

Another problem with reaching this new "youth market" was that it was integrated and regional. White kids were listening to a lot of soul music (and not just the tidy Motown productions, although these were selling by the truckload) and, inspired by the British blues bands, were helping prop up the fading careers of electric bluesmen. But Southern soul had also begun to reach the mainstream: Stax was an early pioneer of this, with Otis Redding, Carla Thomas, Eddie Floyd, Booker T. and the M.G.'s, and Sam and Dave selling in quantities that clearly signaled that it wasn't just the black teenagers across the nation responding to this stuff. Again, they were all peers, with Redding, for instance, being twenty-six and Thomas twenty-five in 1967. But that was just on a national level. In major cities, and especially all through the South, white kids were responding to locally produced records on long-forgotten local soul labels (Frisco, Cash, Murco, Silver Fox, Arctic) that would keep record collectors exploring into the next millennium. On many of these records, the musicians were also integrated: half the M.G.s were white, as was most of the house band at Fame and, later, Muscle Shoals Sound, and Otis Redding had been managed by a white teenager named Phil Walden since the start of his career. This was music they'd grown up with, and the idea of doing country music would never have occurred to most of them. And then there was the biggest new soul phenomenon of 1967: Aretha Franklin. How were you going to explain her?

Freed from the gentility she'd been obliged to display at Columbia, Aretha had exploded at the start of 1967. Her first single, "I Never Loved a Man (The Way I Love You)," had a contentious road to release, but the recording session remained stamped in the memories of everyone concerned. Wexler, Ted White, and Aretha may already have had their bags packed when that *Billboard* picture was taken: they arrived at Fame Studios in late January and found the Fame Gang, the studio band, ready to go. The song didn't sound like much to them, and they were curious what was going to happen. Aretha sat down at the piano and played a chord (its makeup lost to history), and Spooner Oldham, who'd been assigned that chair on the session, immediately begged to let her replace him. He sat down at a Fender Rhodes electric piano instead, as everyone tried to work up an arrangement. Finally, Oldham played what sounded like a tentative line on the Fender Rhodes, the band fell into the groove, and Aretha, as they say, "had church." Whether to work on the tune further was moot, although they still needed to overdub background vocals. By this time, much whiskey had been consumed, and tempers were raw. Some sort of confrontation between Rick Hall, whose studio it was, Ted White, and a trumpet player led to Ted and Aretha stomping out; a further confrontation between White and Hall happened back at the hotel; and Wexler grabbed the tape and headed back to New York. There was a problem: there was only the one song, plus the beginnings of one for the B-side: "Do Right Woman–Do Right Man," a Dan Penn/Chips Moman collaboration. Wexler had to fly most of the Fame Gang up to New York to complete the session and—just for fun—record a bunch more, to fill out not only the single but also an album, over the next couple of weeks. When Rick Hall found out his talent had been kidnapped, even for a few days, he went ballistic: he'd never work with Wexler again. But the reaction on the part of America's record buyers was just as intense: "I Never Loved a Man" unsurprisingly zoomed to the top of the R&B chart, but it also went high on the pop charts. That such an uncompromisingly intense performance, partaking of the deepest emotional resources of the black church, sung by a woman, would strike a chord with young white record buyers seemed astonishing. Berry Gordy, who scrupulously minimized (but didn't eliminate) that element in the performances Motown released, was undoubtedly caught up short. And Aretha did it again, with "Respect" going number-one pop. (In probably their most chickenshit move of all, the McLendon "clean lyrics" campaign forced Atlantic to edit "Respect" to eliminate the background singers chanting, "Sock it to me." The lyric wasn't on the version in the stores, but radio stations could ask the Atlantic promo guy for "clean" copies.) Franklin's second album, out that summer, was called *Aretha Arrives*. Misnomer: she already had.

Around the same time as Aretha was arriving, another sea change took place in rock and roll, although it wouldn't mean much in America for another decade. The Beatles had just turned down a million dollars from producer Sid Bernstein do to two shows at Shea Stadium in New York, probably for the very good reason that the music they were making (most of the tracks on *Revolver*, for instance) couldn't be performed live, which was what their fans would be expecting. They were about to release two more songs, not on an album yet, in February, and they knew they'd be hits. The problem was the most popular pop music broadcast in England, BBC Television's *Top of the Pops*. Every Thursday night, British teens would sit in front of the television as the announcer declared, "The weekend starts here!" and the countdown of the top songs in the nation, featuring the bands themselves lip-synching their records, would begin. Of late, some performers hadn't been taking this too seriously: the lead guitarist would mime his solo on a tuba or something equally ridiculous. The Beatles were above that. They would of course provide the songs, but in a new way: two experimental films by Swedish television director Peter Goldmann, recommended by the band's Hamburg friend Klaus Voormann, who'd drawn the cover of *Revolver*. "Penny Lane" was somewhat straightforward, given that it's a Liverpool street with a bus terminus on it, so there are shots of double-decker buses with "Penny Lane" as the destination. Although, at the end, the Beatles, riding horses, arrive at a place where there's a bandstand set up, no performance happens; the boys enjoy a cuppa, then overturn the table. "Strawberry Fields Forever" was even more avant-garde: the Beatles are scampering around a field in which kettledrums are scattered, focused on a large dead tree with a ruined piano in front of it, its strings attached to the tree. The time varies from day to night, Beatle faces are shown, and at one point, Paul's in the tree, adjusting what seem to be light bulbs, while the rest of the band paints the piano. Again, there's no performance; nor, unlike "Penny Lane," is there any depiction of Strawberry Fields, a Salvation Army children's home near John Lennon's childhood house. British teens must have been mystified at first—they'd get to see it a couple of more times as the single ascended the charts, although it was the first Beatles single not to reach number one there—but not as mystified as American viewers, who got to see the films once, as the Beatles fulfilled their contract with Ed Sullivan. They'd have to wait for the advent of home videotape to have any hope of seeing them again.

In May, Dunhill Records, the Mamas and the Papas' label (and the label that had released "Eve of Destruction"), made a bid for a summertime hit with "San Francisco (Be Sure to Wear Flowers in Your Hair)," by Scott McKenzie, a former singing partner of Papa John Phillips, who'd written the song. It painted an idyllic picture of the city that was at increasing odds with the reality. By the summer of 1967, many of the cultural leaders of what the media had dubbed the "hippies" had abandoned the city, the Haight-Ashbury neighborhood in particular.

On January 14, 1967, various community forces had gathered for a "Human Be-In," an event with an unspecified purpose and no particular schedule. A stage was built in Golden Gate Park's Polo Field, and a bevy of culture heroes—Allen Ginsberg, poet Gary Snyder, Timothy Leary, Lenore Kandel (a poet whose collection of erotic poetry, *The Love Book,* had gotten a Haight Street merchant busted for selling obscene literature), philosopher Alan Watts, and others—presided over this "gathering of the tribes." Bands set up and played, Quicksilver Messenger Service, the Grateful Dead, the Jefferson Airplane, and Big Brother and the Holding Company among them; Owsley's people distributed LSD; the Hells Angels sat peacefully, tripping their brains out; and at the end, some people made their way to the beach, while others, under Allen Ginsberg's direction, picked up the trash. All in all, a peaceful, groovy day in the park, but residents of the Haight-Ashbury returned to a mass arrest for blocking traffic as they flooded the streets. It was a neighborhood in crisis. Community leaders were very much aware that when schools let out midyear there would be a flood of kids coming to the city in search of what it had to offer; there'd been a steady trickle of runaways for months. After word of the Be-In got out, the trickle grew, and the meager resources that countercultural organizations such as the Diggers provided (free clothes, free meals) would come under increasing stress. No wonder the Grateful Dead had already decamped to Marin County, and the Jefferson Airplane to a mansion on Fulton Street. McKenzie's hit "San Francisco (Be Sure to Wear Flowers in Your Hair)"—and it was a hit, going to number four—was not popular with San Franciscans.

Not that this was going to stop anybody. Already Phillips and Dunhill's head, Lou Adler, had heard an idea floated by former Beatles publicist Derek Taylor: how about a *pop* music festival? There was already an important jazz festival in Monterey, a city halfway between Los Angeles and San Francisco, and a venue to present a festival in, and there were all these bands that deserved to be popular in both cities. The Jefferson Airplane had played last year's Monterey Jazz Festival, and of course there was Dylan at Newport, which was a folk festival. What if this music had its own festival? Lord knows, Adler had contacts, as did Phillips, so in May they announced the First Monterey International Pop Festival, run by a nonprofit foundation headed by the two men, with a board of directors that they claimed included Donovan, Mick Jagger, Paul McCartney, Jim McGuinn, record producer Terry Melcher, Andrew Loog Oldham, Johnny Rivers, Smokey Robinson, Paul Simon, and Brian Wilson. Proceeds would go to a charity to be named later. Some of this was wishful thinking: a few of those listed claimed they were never contacted, but Phillips and Adler pressed on and announced that the festival would take place the weekend of June 16–18, at the fairground site of the jazz festival.

Up in San Francisco, Ralph Gleason was skeptical that the plastic pop machinery–created LA bands could compete with the organic, community-supported bands from his city, but he pitched in to help anyway, and got an assignment from the left-wing San Francisco magazine *Ramparts* to cover the event. To defray expenses, the organizers let D. A. Pennebaker, who'd made Bob Dylan's about-to-be-released documentary film, do one on Monterey. The lineup kept changing, and a lot of unsigned bands were on the bill, which made it exciting for record companies and managers looking to make deals. Among the buzz bands were Big Brother and the Holding Company, with their new lead singer, Janis Joplin, an old friend of Chet Helms's from Texas who'd gotten disillusioned with the folk scene in Austin and had been biding her time back in Port Arthur, her hometown, when he showed up to take her West; Country Joe and the Fish, a Berkeley jug band with left-wing politics that had plugged in and taken acid; Quicksilver Messenger Service; Buffalo Springfield; and Michael Bloomfield's new project, the Electric Flag, an "American music band" with a big horn section and a mammoth black teenage drummer/vocalist, Buddy Miles, who'd been wooed away from Wilson Pickett. Britain, due to the expense of travel for a one-shot appearance, wasn't all that well represented, but the Who was going to play, since they'd planned to be in the country anyway, as was a returning American, Jimi Hendrix, and Eric Burdon and his new collection of Animals. Jazz would be represented by South African trumpeter Hugh Masekela. Soul music's sole ambassador to the festival, after Dionne Warwick and the Impressions had to drop out at the last minute, would be the much-anticipated Otis Redding. The last day would be devoted to a full performance by Ravi Shankar, whose star was rising because George Harrison's patronage was causing a spurt of sales of his albums. The Beach Boys canceled late in the planning, and it's uncertain whether Smokey Robinson and the Miracles were ever booked—or whether Smokey ever did anything as a director of the festival. The audience was neatly summed up by a stoned young woman in the resultant film who explained, "Like, you kinda have to wait for a whole new wave to come and then a whole new set of rock and roll bands comes with it, which creates all the other"—and here she pauses to find the right word—"bullshit."

Bullshit or not, the show went on. Pennebaker's camera crew included renowned still photographer Barry Feinstein, future documentarian Albert Maysles, and Joan Baez's brother-in-law, painter Brice Marden, while the stage manager was another painter and Dylan insider, Bob Neuwirth. There wasn't enough film to shoot everyone, nor was there even enough to film entire sets. Bands that were filmed but left out of the eventual movie included the Association, the Blues Project, Buffalo Springfield, the Paul Butterfield Blues Band, the Electric

Flag, and Laura Nyro. The "Ungrateful" Dead, as they were referred to during the weekend, not only refused to be filmed but kept threatening to do their own festival in competition with the plastic LA vampires. Some indelible performances did make it into the movie, though: Janis Joplin singing with an intensity that caused Cass Elliot, watching, to mouth, "Oh, wow," in wonder; Pete Townshend destroying his guitar at the end of the Who's set; Jimi Hendrix exploding onto the stage, not to be outdone, and, at the end of his performance, dousing his guitar with lighter fluid and burning it as he knelt and bid it farewell; and Otis Redding, in full command in front of a whole new audience catching his breath after his opening number, Sam Cooke's "Shake," to say, "This is the love crowd, right?" and getting a titanic roar out of the audience. "We all love each other, right?" Another roar as he lit into his current hit, "I've Been Loving You Too Long." As unforgettable as all this was, it wasn't mere cynicism for veteran jazz photographer Jim Marshall, who was covering the festival, to say years later that "There was a lot of action on the stage at Monterey, but the real action was backstage in the bar, where record executives were fighting over who would sign who." Columbia had three top executives, including president Goddard Lieberson and the ambitious young lawyer Clive Davis, on hand; RCA had a top guy there; and Jerry Wexler was representing Atlantic and Stax. Bill Graham was also on hand; and producers Andrew Loog Oldham, John Simon, and Tom Wilson were watching closely. The crowd of 175,000 left with their memories, and Columbia left with contracts for Big Brother and the Electric Flag and an option on Laura Nyro. Five hundred thousand dollars was raised at the gate. Not bad.

The top 10 that month showed that the new generation was definitely making itself felt: The Association's "Windy"; the Young Rascals' "Groovin'"; the Music Explosion's "Little Bit O' Soul"; McKenzie's "San Francisco"; "She'd Rather Be with Me," by the Turtles; Aretha's "Respect"; "Can't Take My Eyes Off of You," by the Four Seasons; "Let's Live for Today," by the Grass Roots; "Come On Down to My Boat," by Every Mother's Son; and "Don't Sleep in the Subway," by Petula Clark. It was a week without the Monkees, for a change (but they'd be back), and the only fake groups on list were the Grass Roots, who existed (but with shifting personnel) as a showcase for Steve Barri and P. F. Sloan's songs; and Every Mother's Son, one-hit wonders partially assembled by their label, MGM. The album charts were more conservative, but then, albums weren't on the teen radar yet. Only the Monkees' *Headquarters* and *More Of* albums, Aretha Franklin's first album, and *Surrealistic Pillow* were in the top 10. Oh, and something called *Sgt. Pepper's Lonely Hearts Club Band,* by the Beatles, was comfortably ensconced at the top, where it had sat practically since the day it was released a couple of weeks back.

Brian Epstein had been heard muttering about how "Penny Lane" and "Strawberry Fields Forever" were very good, but that the Beatles' new album would prove that they were the best band in the world. Now it could be heard blasting from the window of every college dormitory, every high school student's bedroom, up and down King's Road in London, MacDougal Street in New York, and of course Haight Street in San Francisco. In retrospect, the album was of a piece with *Rubber Soul* and *Revolver*: some John Lennon songs, a Ringo vocal, a Paul ballad with strings, a bit of curried exotica from George, and several more songs all sequenced very neatly, with a long, enigmatically somber song at the end, "A Day in the Life," featuring the tagline "I'd love to turn you on," and some avant-garde orchestral writing. The engineering was superb, the sounds the boys had come up with in partnership with producer George Martin were unprecedented, and perhaps most important, the album came out at exactly the right moment: summer, post-Monterey, on the heels of a great single, right at a time when young people were taking to pot and LSD in larger numbers than ever. Whimsically packaged, with the real Beatles dressed in military band costumes posing in front of an array of famous and less-than-famous people's pictures and the wax Beatles from Madame Tussauds, and an insert with "memorabilia" of the Edwardian (but fictional) band of the title. For a moment, the war in Vietnam, the race riots in Detroit and Newark, and all the other bad news could step aside.

What, some people were wondering, would the Beach Boys, the Rolling Stones, or Bob Dylan come up with in response? The answer to that was complicated. The Rolling Stones, well, they'd had a party.

Hardly unusual: they were selling tons of records and touring like crazy. Come February, they were kicking back. Several had bought stately homes, away from ever-swinging London, and in them, they swung. On February 11, 1967, Mick Jagger; Keith Richards; Jagger's girlfriend, singer Marianne Faithfull; and assorted others were at Richards's new house, Redlands, south of London in Sussex, taking a new batch of LSD that someone had brought from America and then getting into some cars and going to the beach. After a few hours of this, the partiers were tired and went back to the house. In the early morning hours of February 12, Faithfull went upstairs to take a bath, while downstairs, however, someone noticed some people gathering outside the house. This was no acid hallucination (although Richards remembers thinking at first that the trespassers were dwarves): the tabloids had been harassing the band, as they do in England, and finally the *News of the World* had gone too far, ascribing some incoherent talk about drugs by Brian Jones to Jagger, who'd called his lawyer and hit them with a writ. It was as good as a declaration of war: the men outside Redlands that day were a combination of West Sussex Constabulary and *News of the World* reporters, who'd been alerted by a mysterious phone call from Redlands at 3:00 a.m. The police were separating the men into groups to be searched when, all of a sudden, down came Marianne, wrapped in a fur rug, to see what the commotion was. She found out, all right. Various pills (notably some amphetamines Jagger had bought legally in Italy, but also heroin for one of the guests who was a registered addict) and brownish lumps were confiscated for analysis, along with candles, souvenir hotel soaps, medication for diabetes and asthma, cigarette butts, and some packets of mustard that had come from someone's take-out food order. A trial was set for June, and although the amounts of drugs directly traced to the Stones (cannabis residue for the most part) were minuscule, Jagger and Richards were both jailed. The uproar was immediate: there were spontaneous demonstrations in front of the *News of the World* offices, and the Who announced that, in sympathy, they'd be recording two Jagger/Richards tunes, which they released forty-eight hours later. In any event, the lawyers did their bit, an appeal was filed, and the two were released on bond. The London *Times* editor, William Rees-

Mogg, wrote an editorial headlined, "Who Breaks a Butterfly on a Wheel?" which was reprinted by several other papers. As a way of thanking their fans, the Stones trooped into Olympic Studios and recorded a single, "Dandelion," backed with "We Love You," the latter complete with the sound of a prison door slamming and a warden's footsteps, not to mention backing vocals from John Lennon and Paul McCartney. (It pretty much stiffed.) The bust, along with Brian Jones's faltering sanity and failing physical health (not to mention his own recent drug bust, which wasn't as highly publicized), was delaying the new album, but the Stones kept on Rolling.

Not so the Beach Boys. There had been silence from them since the previous fall's triumphal "Good Vibrations," and rumor had it that Brian was living in the studio working on an album, entitled *Smile* (or *SMiLE,* as it's now known), that would be a "teenage symphony to God," He'd been working with a new lyricist, Van Dyke Parks, a diminutive Southerner who'd been kicking around the LA scene for a while and who was writing some evocative but rather outré lyrics. The Beach Boys and Capitol Records were locked in a lawsuit over their new contract, and late in July came a press release stating that Capitol had agreed to distribute a new label, Brother, that the Beach Boys would administer. Then, a new Beach Boys single, a teaser for the *Smile* album, entitled "Heroes and Villains," came out and promptly showed what the more conservative members of the group (notably Mike Love) were saying: too complex, not "fun" enough. Parks's lyrics certainly were mysterious, although they were evocative (and not nearly as opaque as those of "Surf's Up," which Brian had played on a Leonard Bernstein TV special—just what did "columnated ruins domino" mean?) and the single barely squeaked up to number 12. Brian at this point was writing an instrumental suite about the elements (earth, wind, fire, and water) for the album, and he made the studio musicians put on kids' plastic fireman's helmets while they recorded "Fire," after which a nearby building burned during the night and Brian, overworked, and chasing something he just couldn't find, collapsed and retreated to his house with *Smile* unfinished; he'd reemerge in 1976. *Smile,* meticulously reconstructed from the original tapes, came out in 2011.

Retreat was very much on Bob Dylan's mind, too. He had his house in Woodstock; he and his wife, Sara, were getting to know each other better; and his band had settled in around town, most notably at that large pink house in West Saugerties. Like a suburbanite going to the office, Dylan started dropping in over there, enjoying jamming with the band in various combinations on folk songs, Johnny Cash songs, and whatever they felt like. Eventually, keyboardist Garth Hudson brought his Wollensak tape recorder down to the basement and let the tape roll. Dylan started coming in with some new songs he'd written, and some of the other guys, including Rick Danko, helped shape a couple of them. In October, Albert Grossman asked Hudson to compile what he felt were the ten best songs from these informal sessions so he could send out a demo to various performers who might cut them and bring in a bit of publishing money. It would be a while before these songs started getting professionally recorded, though, and many never were.

While *Sgt. Pepper* had been a groundbreaking album, generating lots of media attention, a groundbreaking single had been released on almost the same day. The Paramounts were a band from Southend, a seaside town in Essex, due east of London, where there were lots of venues for bands, mostly playing cover versions of American R&B songs, to hone their chops. The Paramounts' attempts to move farther up the ladder—a record deal, for instance—were stymied, so the band split. But their pianist, Gary Brooker, wasn't about to give up, especially after finding Keith Reid, who wrote odd lyrics that appealed to him, so he put an ad in *Melody Maker* for musicians, and soon found some. Going into the studio with Brooker's old friend Denny Cordell as manager/producer, they recorded what they thought was the best of the songs they'd come up with, "A Whiter Shade of Pale," and issued it under the name Procol Harum. (Nobody seems to know what the name means or where it came from, whether from the pedigree papers of someone's cat or a garbling of the Latin for "far from these things," which perhaps someone thought was "far out" in Latin.) Reid's lyrics were just mysterious enough, and Brooker's adaptation of a chord progression from Bach's third orchestral suite provided a stately feel, carried by Matthew Fisher's classical-sounding organ line, which, with the slow tempo, rendered it unforgettable. Its release was also perfectly timed: the song rose on the charts, especially in the United States, slowly enough to serve as the summer's slow-dance back-to-school hit. Although nobody knew it at the time, it ushered in a new genre of music, which would also rise slowly in the years to come and would eventually answer to the name "progressive rock." You couldn't dance to much of it (especially not slow-dance), but it was going to be a big deal. As for Procol Harum, they released an album, a follow-up single ("Homburg," which did fairly well), and started a career that lasted ten years and was revived in the early 1990s.

If the audience was making the hits, it was also unmaking hit makers. In June, guitarist Zal Yanovsky quit the Lovin' Spoonful, which had just had its eighth top 10 hit. This would, in short order, destroy one of America's most popular bands. What apparently happened was that Yanovsky and bassist Steve Boone had been busted for pot in San Francisco sometime in 1966. The narcotics officers who nabbed them had an offer: reveal who had sold them the dope, and they'd let them off. When the two hesitated at that, they were asked to buy some from anyone they could find and turn them in. And so, they went to a friend of a friend, bought some weed, and turned it and his name in to the cops. According to Ralph Gleason, an envelope with $2,500 was delivered to this guy for his defense, and he slipped some copies of the agreement between the band and the cops to the press. Someone bought a full-page ad in the *Los Angeles Free Press* calling for a boycott of the Spoonful, their records, their concerts, and, for the girls, their bodies. Boone, racked with guilt, filed an affidavit admitting what they'd done, and Yanovsky signed a similar one, hoping to get the dealer off, but Zal was a Canadian citizen and was afraid he'd be deported. The boycott worked: the band was over, despite John Sebastian's hiring LA folkie Jerry Yester to replace Zal. A Yanovsky solo record failed to sell, and soon Sebastian walked away from the group, which filled out its commitment to MGM/Kama Sutra with what was essentially drummer Joe Butler and studio musicians posing as the band. A while later, *John B. Sebastian*, a solo album, came out on both MGM and Warner Bros.—the exact same album. Nobody made money off of it but the lawyers.

Not that you needed musicians making bad decisions to sink a worthy band: record companies and managers were perfectly capable of doing it themselves. One of the more popular new bands in the San Francisco ballrooms in 1967 was Moby Grape, an interesting bunch of guys who included the Jefferson Airplane's late drummer, Skip Spence, and three guitarists. All five band members wrote wonderful songs in a variety of styles. They played the ballrooms a lot, as well as Monterey (although they'd already been snapped up by Columbia by then). Blessed with more material than they could record, they banged out an album in no time. By early June, everything was ready to go. Columbia, hearing lots of hits, spared no expense: it rented the Avalon Ballroom on June 6 and decorated it in all purple; the caterers even prepared purple food. The press got copies of the album, titled *Moby Grape*, and then . . . everything fell apart. After the party, in the wee hours of the morning, police found Peter Lewis, Skip Spence, and Jerry Miller smoking dope in the back of a van with three underage teenage girls. The next day, Columbia did something unprecedentedly stupid: along with the album, it released five singles at once. Hey, it was a way of showing that there were five songwriters in the group! Never mind that radio programmers weren't going to wade through ten songs to find one to push, or, if they did, agree on which one. Oh, and look at that album cover, and the poster that came with the album, showing it even bigger! Look at Peter Lewis's finger! Gonna have to recall all the albums out there and airbrush *that* out! Incredibly enough, that was only the beginning of the band's disastrous career, which would feature drugs, violence, Skip Spence vanishing into a series of mental hospitals (and reemerging in 1969 with one of the weirdest albums ever, *Oar*), breakups, reunions, fake Moby Grapes touring the country, and much more. Despite all the drama, they put out some great music, especially that first album.

Compared to the riotous world of the hippies, soul music was an island of sanity, with what came to be called "deep soul" in the ascendant, led by Aretha Franklin, Otis Redding, Sam and Dave, Percy Sledge, and others on small labels such as the Parliaments, a group that had driven from northern New Jersey, where they'd formed in the back room of a Bergenfield barbershop, to Detroit, where they'd parked their ramshackle bus in front of the offices of Hitsville U.S.A. in the hope of getting an audition. They got one, at last, and were told they weren't wanted, so they took their best song, "(I Wanna) Testify," to Revilot, one of the several Detroit labels catching the overflow from Berry Gordy's operation. Like all deep soul, it partook of the church, both in performance and lyrics. A follow-up, "All Your Goodies Are Gone," was a little stranger, but it, too, sold. Then Revilot disappeared, and in the course of its bankruptcy, the band lost the rights to its name. They'd be back.

Despite the unquestionable dominance of deep soul, there were a couple of other things happening on the black charts. James Brown had been working on a new band, although he held Maceo Parker over from his last one, adding him to a horn section that included Richard "Kush" Griffith, Fred Wesley, "Pee Wee" Ellis, and St. Clair Pinckney. Getting the rhythm section right was crucial. He stole John "Jabo" Starks, Bobby Bland's drummer, and then incorporated a much younger drummer, Clyde Stubblefield, into a second drummer's seat. Stubblefield would be Brown's primary recording drummer, but the two playing together fueled Brown's live show. Brown would record long jams for singles and cut them down, releasing the full-length version on an album, and 1967 was the year of "Cold Sweat," a song with a stop-start structure; it went to number one on the R&B charts and top 10 pop.

An even more radical band evolved in Phoenix, Arizona, not previously known as a soul capital. The O'Jays were a veteran vocal group from Ohio who'd been around since the early '60s, successful enough on the road but not quite meshing with the public with a record. They'd settled in Phoenix, which is where they changed their name to reflect their sponsor, local deejay Eddie O'Jay, who had somehow heard of a group in Buffalo, Carl LaRue and the Crew. He invited them to come to Phoenix, which had more soul fans than bands, to back up the O'Jays, but LaRue didn't like the place, and left. The O'Jays, as their act improved and they began to tour, decided to move, too. The remaining Crew renamed themselves the Three Blazers and walked

Phoenix's version of the Stroll, Broadway, until they found a club that wanted to book them. In gratitude, they wrote a song, "Funky Broadway," which dancers loved, despite the fact that it had rudimentary lyrics and only one chord. What made up for that was the incredible rhythm section of bassist Alvin Battle and drummer Willie Earl (who helped stretch the song out for up to ten minutes) and the gasped, barked vocal of their former bassist, now lead singer, Arlester "Dyke" Christian. Heaven only knows how Art Laboe, the man who'd made a fortune with his series of *Oldies but Goodies* albums, heard them, or why he decided that this was the next big thing, but in the summer of 1967, "Funky Broadway" was split into two parts, slapped onto a single on Original Sound, Laboe's label, and began its ascent on the charts. It would surely have done better than it did, but Wilson Pickett heard it and recorded it, and with Atlantic's much more sophisticated promotion machine working for him, he took it to the top of the R&B chart and the top 10 in the pop charts. The Blazers, though, were expert constructors of grooves, and the thirty-three tracks they left behind (including bigger hits like "We Got More Soul" and "Let a Woman Be a Woman—Let a Man Be a Man") were listened to avidly by dancers and musicians. There was something new going on here. Even James Brown, who considered Dyke a threat onstage, was impressed, and among those almost certainly listening with interest was Sly Stone, Tom Donahue's former partner in Autumn Records, who had inhaled enough of San Francisco's hippie spirit to put together a gender-mixed interracial band he called the Family Stone, who put out their first album, *A Whole New Thing*, on Epic in the fall. Who knows what might have happened had Dyke not been shot to death over a drug deal on Broadway in 1971, aged only twenty-eight.

New things were even appearing in the conservative, slumbering world of country music. Like the other branches of popular music, it had had its infusion of younger performers, but the tight Nashville machine had smothered a lot of creativity. (Not just in country, either: MGM had bought Roy Orbison's contract in 1965, and put out another dud single on him every three weeks while he lived in his bus, touring the country.) But spearheaded by the wacky crossover songwriter/singer Roger Miller, some new blood was coming into the industry. Willie Nelson stopped making albums of the hits he'd written for other people and signed a contract with RCA in 1965, and while not exactly burning up the country charts, he was making a name for himself with stark, depressing songs like "One in a Row" and "The Party's Over." He, too, did a lot of touring, always with his Mephistophelian drummer, Paul English (commemorated in Nelson's classic song "Me and Paul"), and often with bassist Bee Spears. He headlined sometimes; sometimes he opened for friends like Ray Price (whose band he and Roger Miller had been in); and he caused a bit of a stir when his shows were opened by a new talent he was championing, a singer who performed fairly generic country tunes (good ones, but not striking): Country Charley Pride. The "country" bit was necessary because Pride was . . . black. Nelson was among those who agitated to get him signed to RCA, for whom he'd make millions of dollars after "Does My Ring Hurt Your Finger" scored in 1967, starting a career that would produce an amazing run of number-one country hits through the early 1980s.

Billboard ran a trend story in October 1967 headlined, "Crisis Hits C&W as Young Acts Head for Rock Hills." It mentioned Dave Dudley, who'd ignited a new subgenre of truck-driving hits; Waylon Jennings, a Buddy Holly protégé who gave up his seat on the fatal plane ride and was now covering Nashville soul (Joe Simon's "The Chokin' Kind"), folkies (Gordon Lightfoot's "That's What You Get for Lovin' Me"), and some harder songs by Nashville types (Mel Tillis's "Mental Revenge"), but who was still not accepted in Texaphobic Nashville. Another young talent, Merle Haggard, who'd come up in the tough honky-tonk scene in Bakersfield, California, after a stint in San Quentin, wrote autobiographical tunes of rebellion such as "Branded Man" and "Sing Me Back Home," and didn't much care what Nashville thought about him because he was recording for Capitol in LA. The article noted that Nashville had "kicked out" Johnny Cash and Jerry Lee Lewis and thus missed out on a single called "Golden Idol," by a former Rhodes Scholar who was working as a janitor when Cash heard a couple of the songs he was writing and got him a deal: Kris Kristofferson.

Nineteen sixty-seven's biggest country crossover, however, was

Bobbie Gentry, "The Hippie from Mississippi," whose self-written, utterly enigmatic "Ode to Billie Joe," a masterpiece of storytelling that she refused to explain, tantalized listeners years after it rode the top of the pop charts for most of the summer. This narrative approach to songwriting also fueled the career of Tom T. Hall, who put out his first single in 1967, but would find his stride the next year with "The Ballad of Forty Dollars," which began a run of mostly narrative songs that lasted twenty years.

The old ways in Nashville did, however, manage to birth a star, although her rise wouldn't happen right away. It was a tradition for a major male star to carry a girl singer in his show; they'd perform duets, and he'd hand over the spotlight to her for a few solo numbers, which she'd be recording in the hope of having a hit. Porter Wagoner had been working with Norma Jean, but she wasn't getting much traction, so RCA's new signing, Dolly Parton, who'd had a semi-hit with "Dumb Blonde" at the start of the year after a string of dull records on Monument—her career had actually started in 1959, when she was thirteen, with the out-of-tune "Puppy Love"—joined him, starting a duet and solo career that went on for over a decade, until her star eclipsed his.

On August 27, the Beatles' world—and, indeed, the whole pop world in Britain—was shocked by the news that Beatles manager Brian Epstein had been found dead in his home. This came at a very odd time in the foursome's career: under the influence of George Harrison's wife, Patti, they'd gotten interested in an Indian guru, Maharishi Mahesh Yogi, who was selling a popularized version of Hinduism that he'd branded Transcendental Meditation. One took instruction, at the end of which one was given a short phrase, or mantra, to use to achieve certain things. Most Hindus looked down on it for its commercialism (although there was something to the Maharishi's belief that Westerners wouldn't value enlightenment that didn't cost them money), but thanks to his followers' business acumen, celebrities went to his sales lectures and spread the word that TM worked, at least for them. A few weeks before Epstein's death, the Beatles had attended a lecture in London and signed on immediately. In preparation for receiving their mantras, they went to a camp in North Wales, where

Patti gave their London office the number of the only telephone in the dormitory where everyone was staying, in case something came up. The group was initiated, and they were trying to figure out how to make the new meditation technique work when the telephone rang with the news.

Just what had happened is subject to some question. Brian Epstein had never been a particularly cheerful man. He had a secret that those closest to him, including the Beatles, knew: he was gay. Homosexuality in Britain at the time was both a big presence (especially toward the top of the economic scale and in show business) and a big secret that had to be kept, especially when, as was Epstein's case, one had a taste for rough trade and rent boys, and because it was totally illegal and punishable by jail. The guilt and stress constantly ate at Epstein, and as he added new clients to his roster at his management firm, NEMS and as the Beatles changed from a touring band to a recording-only one; and as Epstein's empire grew (as it had recently when he brought on another partner, Robert Stigwood, whose clients included the rising stars Cream and a trio of brothers from Australia, the Bee Gees), the stress only increased. Epstein had first attempted suicide a year earlier, but friends had found him in time, and by keeping him out of the hospital, they'd also kept him out of the papers. He'd left a note, so despite his claim that he'd just accidentally taken one pill too many, insiders knew that wasn't true. This time was different. He'd invited a couple of friends out to his country house for the weekend, and they noted that he was acting distracted, but that was nothing new. He'd tried to round up some rent boys for a party but was too late: it was a holiday weekend, and the discreet agencies he used were booked up. At some point after dinner and quite a bit of wine, he announced that he was going to take a drive, leaving his friends to hang out, and when he didn't come back after a while, his guests got concerned. They called his London flat and were told by his butler, Antonio, that he'd arrived there and headed straight up to bed and was now asleep. On Saturday afternoon, Epstein called and said he was driving back; he sounded groggy, and his guests suggested that he take the train. He agreed. He never showed up, and by the next day they had gotten worried and sounded the alarm, telling Brian's secretary not to call his personal doctor but another doctor who lived closer. His bedroom doors, made of thick oak, were locked, and when the doctor arrived, he and Antonio knocked them in. Brian was on the bed, dead of what was eventually revealed to be a cumulative overdose of carbatrol, a chemical in his sleeping pills that can build up in the body until a fatal quantity is present.

Someone found the number Patti had left and called it. Paul was the one who got the news first, and he was also told that the press had somehow found out, so beware. The four had a private session with the Maharishi, who assured them that Brian's death was only physical and handed them flowers, which he instructed them to crush to see that life is only water and a physical structure. They then walked out and met the press, to whom they gave dull quotes about what a shock it was, except for George, who recycled some cant about death not being real. What was real, although they weren't dealing with it, was that the Beatles no longer had a manager. In New York, an accountant named Allen Klein knew the moment he'd been waiting for all his life had just come. He was driving across the George Washington Bridge with a friend when he heard the news on the radio; he snapped his fingers, saying, "I've got 'em!"

Klein was on a roll. Born in 1931, he'd become known as a fearless guy who could uncover unpaid royalties and get you paid, then write a deal as a manager that'd get you a million dollars. He'd faced down Morris Levy, the Mob-connected head of Roulette Records, and gotten his client's money; and in 1963 he added his first big star to his clientele: Sam Cooke, whose affairs with RCA Records he sorted out. He then became not only Cooke's accountant but his manager, and the executor of his estate after his death. Next up was the Dave Clark Five, a relationship that educated Klein in the British tax code, a messy affair he handled with aplomb. Having mastered that, he moved on to the Animals. By 1965, the Rolling Stones' manager, Andrew Loog Oldham, was getting tired of his partner, Eric Easton, and looking for someone to advise the Stones, who'd leapt into stardom with "Satisfaction." Klein was the man. He scrutinized their contract, saw a bunch of holes, and went to work. When the dust had cleared, the Stones were well on their way to becoming millionaires. Paul McCartney went with the details to Brian and asked why they didn't have a similar agreement; they'd make even more than the Stones, with the number of records they were selling. Klein was like a steamroller, brokering deals for the Kinks, Donovan, Mickie Most, and the Who, using his transatlantic knowledge to make money for the artists (and, of course, himself) but never taking his eyes off of the big prize, the Beatles. With Brian Epstein's death, NEMS fell into the lap of Brian's brother, Clive, who was more interested in keeping it alive than participating in the tax-saving scheme called Apple that the band's financial advisors had set up. But among the adjectives applied to Klein—*ruthless, bloodthirsty, amoral, arrogant, abrasive, thuggish*—one would reluctantly have to add *patient.* He (almost) had 'em, all right, but how to go about it? He bided his time.

Fall was coming, and fall means the end of summer. In later years, the summer of 1967 would be marketed as the Summer of Love, with nostalgic pictures of the street signs at the junction of Haight and Ashbury, hippies with their faces painted, ecstatic dancing at the Fillmore and Avalon, and similar hogwash. The reality was quite different: the Haight-Ashbury was still a place to score and take drugs, but methamphetamine and heroin were just as easy to find as pot and acid, and alcohol, especially cheap wine-based products, was also very much in the mix. The most important storefront in the neighborhood was not a groovy boutique, but the Haight-Ashbury Free Clinic, which had opened just in time on June 7, started by an idealistic young medical student named David Smith, who'd interned at San Francisco General Hospital up the hill. It had thirty doctors on call, and uncounted volunteers. The Free Clinic alone couldn't do much about the sources of the overdoses, rapes, and freak-outs it treated, but it did a great deal of harm reduction.

Still, bands were continuing to arrive in San Francisco: The Steve Miller Blues Band was started by a young Dallasite whose doctor father had treated musicians, including T-Bone Walker and Les Paul, at reduced rates, with Paul paying off some of his bill by tutoring young Miller on guitar. Miller had come to San Francisco via Chicago, where he'd had a short-lived band with Barry Goldberg, and soon was re-united with his childhood friend William "Boz" Scaggs. Shortly after his arrival in California they got swept up in Capitol Records's sign-ing mania, with what was reportedly the largest advance ever given a rock band, plenty enough to get them to drop the "Blues" from their name. Their first album had a cover by underground cartoonist and poster artist (and San Francisco Art Institute teacher) Victor Moscoso.

Another Texan who came to town was Doug Sahm, late of the Sir Douglas Quintet, whose 1966 pot bust had fractured the original band. Sahm went for San Francisco, where he recorded with a new band, gigged around the state with them, and made friends with the Grateful Dead. And whether Mother Earth can be said to have ar-rived or just coalesced, it was a band of Californians and Texans fea-turing Tracy Nelson, a powerful former folk singer whose alto proved capable of country and blues. Another band, Mad River, had come together at Antioch College, in Ohio, and moved West in time to get swept up in Capitol's enthusiasm after making a homemade EP, and soon had a fan in hippie poet Richard Brautigan, who also got a Cap-itol deal. The Youngbloods, a band based around Boston folkies Jesse Colin Young, Jerry Corbitt, and Lowell "Banana" Levinger, began making albums for RCA that seemed to be more popular in Califor-nia than at home, and decided to move to Marin County. This didn't sit well with Corbitt, who opted for a solo career. The band's blan-dishments failed to move a couple of members of another band made up of Boston folkies in New York (also with an RCA album out), Auto-salvage, led by Rick Turner and Tom Danaher, who were all for it but couldn't talk their rhythm section into the move. Their album is one of the lost classics of the era, and Turner eventually went to Califor-nia, producing high-end guitars for the Grateful Dead and others. Michael Bloomfield's Electric Flag first produced the soundtrack for Roger Corman's exploitation film *The Trip*, starring Peter Fonda as an ad executive who starts to question his life (the Flag's contribution was mostly blues jamming), and then their long-awaited LP, *A Long Time Comin'*, which failed to catch fire with its first single, "Groovin' Is Easy." By the time a tour would have happened, the band was riven with drug problems, and theirs remains a sad tale of wasted potential.

And Big Brother and the Holding Company saw a self-titled album come out on the Mainstream label. It was recorded when the band was touring and got stuck in Chicago, and the local label had them churn out a dozen sides in exchange for enough money to get back to San Francisco. It was coolly received.

Elsewhere in California, the Mamas and the Papas announced a yearlong sabbatical and released a greatest hits album called *Farewell to the First Golden Era,* which wasn't technically a swan song but felt like one, and the Doors put out a second album, *Strange Days,* that entered *Billboard*'s album chart at 100 and went to four the next week. The Beach Boys had a major problem: Brian Wilson was sequestered in his house, sleeping a lot, and had had his piano set up in a sandbox, so he could feel the beach as he played. Meanwhile, the label Capitol had given them, Brother Records, wasn't delivering product. In August, they'd put out one of the few completed pieces of *Smile,* a wonderfully complex song called "Heroes and Villains," as Brother catalogue number 1001, which got to number 12. In September, they joined up some more fragments of this much-anticipated album as *Smiley Smile,* a commercial flop, as Brother 9001. Realizing that Brian wasn't doing much, the other guys seized the initiative and suspended Brother, went back to Capitol, and announced that they were now being influenced by soul music. "Wild Honey" sure didn't sound like soul music, but it was a Mike Love/Brian Wilson cowrite, as was its successor, "Darlin'." Neither did very well, although the *Wild Honey* album got to 24. Some rethinking was in order, and the band fell off the radar for a while.

The Monkees were now insisting on playing their own instruments, and put out a year-end album, *Pisces, Aquarius, Capricorn and Jones,* with a Neil Diamond–penned hit, "Daydream Believer." All they had to do was get their TV contract renewed, and with the upcoming season featuring cameos from avant-folkie Tim Buckley and Frank Zappa, that would be no problem. One of LA's best bands, Buffalo Springfield, released *Again,* this time displaying the full spectrum of their talents, including Stephen Stills's near-hit "Rock 'n' Roll Woman" and a couple of Neil Young tunes arranged by Phil Spector's arranger Jack Nitzsche, "Broken Arrow" and "Expecting to Fly."

On October 3, 1967, Woody Guthrie finally succumbed to the neurological disease that had sidetracked him for a decade, aged fifty-five, and at the end of the month, his son Arlo released his first album, *Alice's Restaurant,* the title track of which was a side-long comic song about how Guthrie had avoided the draft by becoming a criminal—for littering. At nineteen minutes, it wasn't a single, but it was a hit on FM radio, which was getting stranger and stranger, not only in San Francisco, but in New York, where the venerable WOR had experimented with free-form programming with considerable success on its FM band. Featuring old-school AM jocks like Murray "the K" Kaufman and Scott Muni, WOR made a star out of a black jock who called himself Rosko, who'd soothe late-night stoners with readings from Kahlil Gibran's *The Prophet.* A nervous management pulled the plug at year's end, and the format was picked up by WNEW-FM. *Billboard* was now printing weekly lists of "progressive" stations so that record companies would know where and to whom they should send their odder releases.

The South, too, seemed to be getting weird: one of the year's surprise hits was "Judy in Disguise (With Glasses)," by John Fred and His Playboy Band, which not only riffed on the Beatles' "Lucy in the Skies with Diamonds" but also raised its makers out of the southern Louisiana/East Texas showband circuit to national stardom as it rose to number one. The Box Tops, another showband, were led by seventeen-year-old Alex Chilton, son of a prominent Memphis family, and scored another number-one hit with "The Letter," which took more than thirty takes to get right, according to producer Dan Penn. It was worth it. And from Florida came a kind of psychedelic band on the Liberty label, the Hour Glass, formerly the Allman Joys, fronted by two brothers of that name who'd played Trude Heller's, a nightclub in New York, to some acclaim. The album, however, stiffed.

On October 6, a solemn parade went down Haight Street, carrying an oversize coffin containing love beads and other paraphernalia. It was the celebration of the Death of Hippie, a sort of spontaneous demonstration by community members marking the end of the hippie dream and the first anniversary of the illegalization of LSD. A number of community organizations participated, including the Free

Clinic (whose medical section was now closed), the Switchboard (the housing and communications organization, a thousand dollars in debt due to embezzlement and no income), the Psychedelic Shop (a whopping six grand in debt, mostly in legal fees), and even the Diggers' free store, Trip Without a Ticket, which had been served with a housing code violation for a broken door from when some geniuses had kicked it in to rob the place. The funeral was mocked by others in the community, but that the original utopian impulse was dead was undeniable. Of course, nobody told the music industry.

In England, Robert Stigwood was still keeping NEMS alive. His latest signing, the Bee Gees, were writing enigmatic songs that were charting in both England and America; the Kinks were putting out excellent singles; Cream was even having single hits with tight pop songs like "Sunshine of Your Love," which allowed for Eric Clapton to solo in performance while being perfectly edited for airplay; and the Who did a true Pop Art stunt with their album *The Who Sell Out*. Its cover showed the band members "endorsing" products like Heinz Baked Beans and Odorono deodorant (who sued); the album interspersed the songs with fake commercials (recorded by a jingle company in Dallas) and station IDs for Radio London (a pirate station that also sued); and it contained their first U.S. top 10 hit, "I Can See for Miles." Van Morrison had quit Them and signed with Bert Berns's Bang label, quickly producing a major hit in "Brown Eyed Girl" and a very strange album called *Blowin' Your Mind!*, whose centerpiece was a ten-minute bit of rambling about a dying friend, "T. B. Sheets." Donovan was cheerier, with songs like "Wear Your Love Like Heaven" and record company ads in the trades saying, "A Donovan record is an experience—emotional and profitable." The Beatles put out a couple of enigmatic songs, "Hello Goodbye," backed with "I Am the Walrus," as teasers for a film they'd made themselves, *Magical Mystery Tour*, which they promised for mid-December. And the Rolling Stones delivered their answer to *Sgt. Pepper* with *Their Satanic Majesties Request*, featuring a lenticular photo on the cover, simulating 3-D (albeit out-of-focus 3-D), a few decent songs, and lots of aimless jamming on "Sing This All Together (See What Happens)" and the nadir of their career so far, a percussion freak-out entitled "Gomper." The album was widely derided at the time as not being as good as *Sgt. Pepper*, but when the Beatles finally got *Magical Mystery Tour* out, it was evident that they, too, were fallible, as it was jaw-droppingly amateurish.

Soul music had had a banner year, with lots of pop crossover, especially for Southern soul, which still tended to sell regionally; Motown's output—although it included Gladys Knight and the Pips' breakout "I Heard It Through the Grapevine," Marvin Gaye and Tammi Terrell's "Ain't No Mountain High Enough," the Four Tops' "Bernadette," Stevie Wonder's "I Was Born to Love Her," and the Temptations' "I Wish It Would Rain"—wasn't nearly as strong as it had been in '66. Probably the label's most brag-worthy feat was knocking *Sgt. Pepper* off the top album slot after nineteen weeks with the Supremes' *Greatest Hits*. Aretha was claiming hit after hit; Jackie Wilson returned from nowhere with "Higher and Higher"; Joe Tex, who'd been toiling in Nashville on the verge of making it with his half-sermon, half-song records finally scored with "Skinny Legs and All"; Etta James had her career-defining hit with "Tell Mama"; and outside Stax, Memphis delivered with new talent, including James Carr, an eccentric former gospel singer. A Detroiter, Al Green, made his debut with a record called "Back Up Train" that went into the R&B top 10, and he went on tour, where he heard Memphis bandleader Willie Mitchell and his band perform. The next night he asked if he could do a song with them to raise fifty dollars to get back home, and Mitchell was impressed. "Why don't you come back with us to Memphis? I can make you a star," Mitchell said. "How long will it take?" Green asked. "Eighteen months," Mitchell told him. "Man, I don't have that much time," Green replied. But he got on Mitchell's bus and rode to Memphis, then borrowed fifteen hundred dollars from Mitchell to buy his way out of his contract, and vanished. Mitchell wasn't happy about that.

Meanwhile, Otis Redding and his manager, Phil Walden, had been thinking over Redding's breakthrough at Monterey. It was obviously his time, but the initial attack on the pop charts had to be done just right. Otis spent some time developing his songwriting, and one day, staying on a friend's houseboat in Sausalito, California, he came up with a song that he thought would work. As soon as he got off tour, he called Steve Cropper to tell him he was coming into the studio. Cropper was happy: Otis had been touring so much they hadn't seen much of him, and an operation on his vocal cords that summer had changed his voice a bit. Hauling out his little acoustic guitar, Redding played the new song for Cropper, who helped him write a bridge for it, and they laid it down. "The day we recorded 'Dock of the Bay,'" Cropper told Robert Gordon, "we looked at each other and said, 'This is our hit. We got it.'" It was completely unlike any other song Redding had done: mid-tempo, introspective, featuring an acoustic guitar—a stone smash for the pop charts. It took six takes to get it, with Cropper making seagull noises on the first take to indicate where he wanted sound effects and then totally blowing the little whistled melody at the end, cracking everyone up, with Otis warning him "You're not going to make it as a whistler." They went over it a bunch more, and then on Friday, December 8, Otis had to do some dates with the Bar-Kays, a rising young Stax band, backing him. Three dates: Nashville, Cleveland, and Madison, Wisconsin, then back to the studio. Cropper was mixing some overdubs, and Redding said, "See ya on Monday." They were the last words Otis Redding would speak to his friend and mentor Steve Cropper. Something went wrong with the small plane that he, his valet, and some of the Bar-Kays (two of them were on a different flight) were flying in as it approached the Madison airport, and it went down in Lake Monona, killing everyone but trumpeter Ben Cauley. The Bar-Kays were all between eighteen and nineteen years old. Matthew Kelly, Redding's valet, was seventeen. Otis Redding was twenty-six.

The "Summer of Love" notwithstanding, between Vietnam and the summer race riots, the year had been turning dark for some time. Redding's death just put the cap on it. There was more to come.

chapter four
IT'S 1969, OKAY

Iggy Pop *(Photo © Baron Wolman)*

In late October 1967, Garrett Press, a print shop at 746 Brannan Street, in an industrial part of San Francisco, with a ship's chandlery across the street, rolled off the first copies of a newspaper-like magazine whose editorial offices were upstairs by the typesetters. It was called *Rolling Stone,* and it was the brainchild of Jann S. Wenner, an ambitious former UC Berkeley student and columnist for the student newspaper who'd helped publicist Derek Taylor at the Monterey Pop Festival earlier that year. Wenner had not only enjoyed the music that weekend but had also wished he could report the event as news. *Newsweek* had run a big article by Michael Lydon, but it had been longer on criticism than on reportage. Wenner also read *Crawdaddy!,* but it didn't really print news, either, and it had a rather lofty tone, although not as mandarin as Boston's *Fusion.* The emerging audience— the one Wenner could see outside his window and on weekends at the Fillmore—wanted news as well as criticism: things were happening that involved the stars they cared about. The first issue of *Rolling Stone,* for instance, had John Lennon on the cover dressed as a World War I soldier; he was then filming Richard Lester's *How I Won the War.* The second issue had an investigative feature by Lydon on where the Monterey money had gone—there was still a lot unaccounted for, and Ravi Shankar was as yet the only performer who'd been paid— and floated the theory, later proven correct, that the bookkeeper they'd hired, one Sandra Beebe had embezzled $52,000; also in that issue was the news that the Byrds had thrown David Crosby out of the band. The next issue added to that story with the news that Jim McGuinn had asked Gene Clark to leave, too. A&M Records had bought the old Chaplin Studios complex, and Boston's Youngbloods, a local ballroom favorite, were moving from Boston to San Francisco. None of this was being covered anywhere else. Distribution of the new magazine was patchy, confined largely to record stores and head shops in San Francisco, with some distribution in LA, but it was clear that Wenner expected it to be taken seriously by fans and the industry. *Billboard*'s March 9, 1968, issue had a full-page ad with a photo of Steve Miller by *Rolling Stone*'s photographer Baron Wolman with the confrontational headline "Capitol Records Paid Him $50,000 and You Probably Don't Know Who He Is." The body copy was just as strong: "Every other professional art has had a journal for its members, followers, and fans, yet rock and roll—the most popular of them all— until now has not had one . . . [W]hat is most important about *Rolling Stone* is the intangible way in which it reflects—in fact, is *part of*— the changes in rock and roll since the Beatles . . . It may be what's happening."

It was a shot across the bow of an industry that was already changing. Warner Bros.–Seven Arts had announced in October that it was going to buy Atlantic Records, probably in large part because Ahmet Ertegun was now balancing his partner Jerry Wexler's soul expertise with a similarly savvy nose for rock-and-roll talent, signing Cream and watching them take off and then, closer to home, finding acts like Iron Butterfly and Vanilla Fudge, while his brother Nesuhi was continuing Atlantic's jazz program, which balanced art jazz performers like Charles Mingus and Ornette Coleman with more popular stuff from the likes of Herbie Mann. A month later, Warner Bros. took advantage of a puff piece in *Billboard* to note that the new market had set it on a hunt for "a new breed of music man" to sign and sell it, which its Reprise subsidiary was already doing with the Kinks, the Jim Kweskin Jug Band, the Electric Prunes, Jimi Hendrix, and Arlo Guthrie, while the main label tried to figure ways to sell the Grateful Dead and Brian Wilson's *Smile* collaborator Van Dyke Parks, whose ambitious *Song Cycle* ushered in the new year and would result in 1969's "How we lost $35,509.50 on 'The Album of the Year' (Dammit)" ad. RCA had its "Groupquake" campaign, focusing on bands instead of individual artists (a new concept, believe it or not), hyping the Youngbloods, the Loading Zone, Autosalvage, and others, while snagging the rights to an odd piece of hippiesploitation called *Hair*. The musical had opened at New York City's Cheetah discotheque in October, gone Off-Broadway, and then moved to Broadway, where it was a sudden smash—and not just because of the scene where the cast took off their clothes and ran through the audience. The music was mostly ersatz rock, but as with any good musical, there were hits to be mined in the soundtrack. In March, *Billboard* noted that "Labels' Promotional Spending Blankets Underground Press," noting the rise of alternative publications such as *Crawdaddy!* and *Rolling Stone*, the *Berkeley Barb*, San Francisco's *Oracle*, the *Los Angeles Free Press*, the Houston *Rag*, Chicago's *Seed*, Milwaukee's *Kaleidoscope*, the *East Village Other*, the Boston *Avatar*, and the *Washington Free Press*. For these and many other alternative publications, record company advertising would be a lifeline to survival, as long as they covered the records and shows and, of course, helped hip the music men in New York and Los Angeles as to what was happening, baby, in their own hometowns. Not that this necessarily worked: MGM was so insistent that Boston had a hearty, thriving rock scene that it announced the "Bosstown Sound" promotional campaign in January, featuring the Beacon Street Union, Orphan, and the Ultimate Spinach, three bands that nobody in Boston itself had ever heard of. (The wily manager who'd conned MGM into signing his three clients eventually left town, and in *Rolling Stone* a polite Jon Landau proclaimed the hype "extremely premature.")

The new music was big business: advances were rising; the Fifth Dimension, a kind of black MOR version of the Mamas and the Papas, had gotten a $40,000 advance from the new Soul City label, partially owned by singer Johnny Rivers, and Warners had paid a reported $80,000 for the Association. The Jefferson Airplane had the gall to demand more studio time after they told RCA they'd finished their new album, *After Bathing at Baxter's*, because they felt it wasn't right and that bits of it needed further fixing—and they got it. An unnamed A&R man told *Billboard*, "One sound leads to another; they have to hear themselves in playback. Many times this sound they're after exists only at the time of creation." As obvious as this sounds today, it was news back then. No longer were hit makers going into the studio, doing their three-hour session on a number the A&R guy had found them, and getting ready for the next day's tune. Sessions ran long, and there was, as this guy implied, jazz-like experimentation and improvisation involved in the creation of the actual song: if this resulted in something the kids wanted, well, it was worth the extra time and money. Of course there was pushback: a representative of the discount chain E. J. Korvette whined that the cover art that artists demanded on some of the new releases was "putting off older consumers." Well, of course. Lacking any guidance of the sort the underground press and *Rolling Stone* were developing, with "progressive" FM stations nonexistent in most markets, loads of kids bought albums just because their covers looked interesting. They also seemed to have pretty good intuition about this, which is maybe why Audio Fidelity Records didn't do so well with *How to Blow Your Mind and Have a Freak-Out Party.* (You needed an album for this?)

Even the records themselves were changing. Spurred by the ubiquity of portable transistor radios, Philco introduced Hip Pocket Records, one-sided flexible records of current hits that played on a device scarcely bigger than a transistor radio and, protected by a sleeve, could in fact be carried in your pocket—or you could wear up to twenty on each ear with a big round earring of spring steel, like a large paper clip, which Philco made available to dealers. What Philco didn't reckon with, of course, was that by the time a record had proved worthy of pressing as a Hip Pocket, consumers had moved on. More consequential was a raging war over the death of the mono album—and maybe the mono single. This wasn't just about high fidelity, though; it was about having to replace cartridges and needles on home rigs and jukeboxes, although more consumers now owned stereo reproduction equipment, even if it didn't have both channels, but mixed them together. This battle was mirrored by the so-called "tape CARtridge" battles, which had grown out of the makers of Learjets. Realizing that in-flight sound was impossible with records, it came up with a boxy plastic cartridge with a tape loop inside that played for a certain amount of time and then switched to another channel after a pause, delivering an entire album. These were available in four- and eight-track formats, but in order to make the music fit on each channel, they often rearranged the playing order of an album, which made the cartridges useless for classical music and for the growing number of pop fans who expected to hear an album's songs in a given order and, of course, the longer songs heard uninterrupted. The cartridges fit well into a car, though, and players integrated into the dashboard were offered as options on some models. Patiently waiting in the wings was a much better format, Philips's cassette, which had only two sides, which you could flip over just like an album. It suffered from poor fidelity and a much thinner, more fragile tape, but it could play up to sixty minutes and had already been adopted to some extent in Europe. By mid-1968, tape sales of recorded product were a full 10 percent of the market.

Whatever. Pop fans were still buying 45 rpm singles and 33⅓ rpm albums, and the dollar extra that one paid for stereo LPs over mono wasn't really an issue. And there were some spectacular albums appearing at the start of 1968. Love, the band Paul Rothchild had feared he'd never get a second side out of when they recorded their second album, released a third album. Leader Arthur Lee had spent the summer of 1967 holed up in a remote part of Laurel Canyon, convinced, at age twenty-six, that he was dying. Rothchild was impressed enough with the resulting collection of songs that he allowed a production budget for strings and horns, and although no hits came out of it, *Forever Changes* is one of the landmark achievements of its era. It also destroyed the band: unable (or unwilling) to tour, and torn apart by alcohol, acid, and heroin, they vanished into history, although Lee kept the Love brand functioning for some years, and even convinced Jimi Hendrix to play on a couple of tracks on one of the later albums.

Another enigmatic black Angeleno rocker was Taj Mahal, formerly of the Rising Sons, who'd recorded an unreleased album for Columbia. Now playing LA clubs with a new interracial band that included another virtuosic guitarist, Jesse Ed Davis (an American Indian), he made enough waves that Columbia exercised its option and released *Taj Mahal,* an album full of Mahal's laid-back folkie takes on electric blues seasoned with blazing guitar work. It, too, wasn't a hit. Nor was the Electric Prunes' *Mass in F Minor*, composed for them by former Cannonball Adderley arranger David Axelrod, which, Reprise reported, had sold fifteen thousand albums with zero airplay, probably because it actually was a Mass and, as such, sung entirely in Latin. ("Drivel," opined *Rolling Stone*.)

Also on Reprise was a second Jimi Hendrix album, *Axis: Bold as Love*, which sold even better than his first despite the lack of a hit single, and *Something Else by the Kinks*, their finest album yet, also with no hits, although it ended with "Waterloo Sunset," perhaps Ray Davies's most moving song. Other labels' notable releases included *Gris-Gris*, by Dr. John, the Night Tripper, which was actually Mac Rebennack and the AFO All-Stars, the crew that had emigrated from New Orleans at the end of 1963 to become fantastically successful studio musicians in LA; the first album by Spirit, an odd, jazzy group fronted by a middle-aged jazz drummer with a shaved head and his adopted guitarist son; the first album by Steppenwolf, a Canadian group formerly known as the Sparrow who'd played the San Francisco ballrooms, purveying loud hard rock with a single, "Born to Be Wild," a hit with bikers and would-be bikers; *Journey to the Center of the Mind*, by Detroit's Amboy Dukes, with flamboyant lead guitarist Ted Nugent; *10 Years After*, the debut from a British band attempting blues with an even more flamboyant lead guitarist, Alvin Lee; *White Light/White Heat*, a second album by the Velvet Underground, more cohesive but no less outrageous than their first; an album by Canadian novelist and poet Leonard Cohen; an album by the International Submarine Band, featuring the Byrds' new guitarist/songwriter, Gram Parsons, which disappeared almost immediately under a welter of lawsuits; and *Days of Future Passed*, by the Moody Blues, British Invaders who'd scored a top 10 hit with a cover of Bessie Banks's obscure "Go Now," in 1965, and returned with a string-soaked album (courtesy of the "London Festival Orchestra," whatever that was) following up on their hit single, "Nights in White Satin."

This onslaught of releases was just beginning, but it was interesting how little of this music showed up on the Hot 100. A bifurcation was taking place, much of it driven by one small label that seemed to have appeared out of nowhere. Buddah Records (the misspelling was one of its trademarks) had come up with a new take on rock and roll that resonated with much younger record buyers who were put off by psychedelic stuff. Eventually dubbed "bubblegum music," it featured simple melodies, no guitar solos, basic (sometimes even moronic) lyrics, and a chugging rhythm. Popularized by productions by Jerry Kasenetz and Jeff Katz (although foreseen by acts like Tommy James and the Shondells and Tommy Roe), it was squarely aimed at the preteen audience that Kasenetz, Katz, and Buddah president Neil Bogart saw as underserved. The first hits were "Green Tambourine," by the Lemon Pipers (an actual band from Ohio), and "Yummy Yummy Yummy," by the Ohio Express (who may or may not have been a real act), both of whom submitted to K-K contract songwriters for future releases: the Lemon Pipers' follow-ups were "Rice Is Nice" and "Jelly Jungle (Of Orange Marmalade)." Much more of this was on its way, serving to drive young adults away from AM radio and into the groovier arms of FM. And it would land the Monkees in an odd position: having fought to be recognized as musicians and playing their own instruments on their TV show and records, they were losing their target demographic to the new sound. No such worries haunted Don Kirshner, who, seeing what had happened with the Monkees, hooked up with an animated Saturday morning cartoon based on a popular comic and, using Teen Pan Alley stalwart Jeff Barry and a new writer, Andy Kim, eventually started having hits in 1969 with the Archies. "Sugar, Sugar," the best of them, topped the charts in 1969, and Wilson Pickett, of all people, recorded it and proved it wasn't such a bad tune after all.

There were plenty of performers who knew the pains of a waning audience, though; not just the dinner-jacketed and ball-gowned relics of the supper club and Vegas circuits—they were still putting out records and selling to older adults, over forty—but the original rock-and-rollers. After charting more than a hundred records, Fats Domino was without a contract in 1968. Little Richard had recorded a remarkable Don Covay song, "I Don't Know What You've Got but It's Got Me," in 1965, with Jimi Hendrix on guitar, but it had gone down with his label, Vee-Jay, and he'd signed with a revived OKeh label, who'd decided to create the "Angel Town Sound" under the guidance of Johnny "Guitar" Watson and Larry Williams—talk about handing the henhouse to the foxes!—and making some good records that vanished there. Richard, too, was at liberty. Ray Charles, sunk deep in heroin addiction, was still putting out records that people bought when they were Beatles covers ("Yesterday" and "Eleanor Rigby") and not so much when they weren't. Carl Perkins was still opening for Johnny Cash, and Elvis was still around, grinding out movies with soundtracks and showing up in trade magazine ads every few months announcing the latest single from the latest movie with a kind of deer-in-the-headlights look in his photographs. The single would enter the lower regions of the charts and then vanish in a couple of weeks. In January, Colonel Tom Parker, Elvis's manager, announced there would be a Christmas television special at the end of 1968, sponsored by Singer sewing machines, of all companies. Only Jerry Lee Lewis seemed to be showing signs of life. After unsuccessfully trying a one-man rock-and-roll revival, he appeared as Iago in a rock musical adaptation of *Othello* called *Rock My Soul,* to favorable notices, but his recording career was stuck until March, when, perhaps remembering Sam Phillips's faith in him as a country artist, he hooked up with Mercury's hottest young Nashville producer, Jerry Kennedy, and recorded "Another Place, Another Time," which went to 97 on the pop charts but zoomed to four on the country charts, his first showing there for four years. The follow-up, "What's Made Milwaukee Famous (Has Made a Loser out of Me)," went to number two, as did its follow-up, "She Still Comes Around (To Love What's Left of Me)." To hell with the pop charts! The Killer was back!

Hotshot producer Bert Berns, who'd always known he had a chronic heart condition that would kill him, died at age thirty-eight in December. This meant the end of the Bang label he'd set up with Jerry Wexler and the Ertegun brothers, thus freeing his two biggest artists to move on. Van Morrison was being courted by Warners, and Neil Diamond lost no time in signing with Uni, a pop label developed by Universal Studios in Hollywood. Another significant death early in 1968 was King Records's Syd Nathan, sixty-four, whose retirement didn't last long, and after the dust cleared, his sole remaining successful artist, James Brown, announced that his organization would be helping with the transition to King's future. In practice, for the rest of its existence, King would be James Brown.

In February, a who's who of the folk world gathered in Carnegie Hall for a Woody Guthrie memorial concert to benefit research into ALS, the disease that had killed him. The surprise of the evening was a short-haired, bearded Bob Dylan coming out to do a few songs, his first appearance in public since his "motorcycle accident." Almost simultaneously, one of the songs written in that big pink house in West Saugerties came out, performed by Albert Grossman clients Peter, Paul and Mary (much as they'd done to expose Dylan initially with "Blowin' in the Wind"), but "Too Much of Nothing" failed to make a dent.

San Francisco seemed to be the place where the richest lode of talent lay. Albert Grossman undertook to untangle Big Brother and the Holding Company's Mainstream Records mess, and took the band under his powerful management wing. He was ultimately looking to separate Janis Joplin from the band, but for the moment, it was enough to do what he could to suppress the early album and sign them to Columbia so that a mass audience could hear what everyone was talking about in the wake of Monterey. As for other local bands, the good news for Moby Grape was that the two members found with the underage girls after the record release party were cleared of pot and delinquency charges—the girls were merely interviewing the band for their high school newspaper, we were told—and then continued on its kamikaze course by releasing a second album, *Wow*, which was packaged with a second LP entitled *Grape Jam*, in which the band wasted its time in free-form jamming with the likes of Al Kooper and Michael Bloomfield. It also had a track featuring Arthur Godfrey singing a song that had to be played at 78 rpm. Despite all that, it managed to hit 20 on *Billboard*'s LP chart. And Columbia managed to cash in on Grace Slick's popularity with the Jefferson Airplane by releasing two LPs of recordings by her former band, the Great Society, which weren't bad at all.

The news of Otis Redding's death had killed the best soul Christmas record in some time, "Every Day Will Be Like a Holiday," by William Bell on Stax, but soul and even blues were still going strong:

B.B. King, his name being recognized by more and more white fans (thanks to Eric Clapton's self-effacing interviews, in which he suggested that his fans, before praising his guitar work, listen to B.B. and Albert King) did very well with "Sweet Sixteen" and "Paying the Cost to Be the Boss," the latter of which was an enormous soul hit, now that he was on a major label. Vocal groups showed they could still be relevant, as Philadelphia's Delfonics scored with "La La Means I Love You" and another Philly group, the Intruders, scored with "Cowboys to Girls," produced by the hot young team of Kenny Gamble and Leon Huff, themselves vocal-group veterans. Percy Sledge showed ballad power with "Cover Me" and "Take Time to Know Her," and Archie Bell and the Drells—"from Houston, Texas, and we dance just as good as we want"—had a smash crossover in "Tighten Up," frustrating Bell, who'd been drafted before the record was even released and was in an army hospital in Germany recovering from a leg wound on the day it went to number one. Fortunately, the group didn't lose momentum. They picked up Gamble and Huff as producers, and continued to help folks dance as good as they were able to after Bell's release. Aretha Franklin's backup singers, the Sweet Inspirations, hit the charts with "Sweet Inspiration"; and as for Aretha herself, *Billboard* found it newsworthy in April to report that she'd just scored her fifth gold record in a row, something no "girl singer" had ever done before. James Brown was still putting out records that didn't sound like anyone else, and reaping the rewards when a gauntlet was thrown down: Sly and the Family Stone had finally found their groove and put out an album titled *Dance to the Music*, after its first single and opening track. The second track was "I Want to Take You Higher." A star was born and would shine, albeit briefly.

The problem with soul music, though, was its very inconsistency. Aretha aside, high-earning, long-term careers didn't appear to be happening there, which is why Atlantic's new owners were mollified by the rock end of the label's acquisitions and the fact that this hot "girl singer" seemed to be the exception to the rule. Despite the overwhelming success of "Dock of the Bay," Stax hadn't generated a consistent star, and now with the one who was a star on his way, and with the Bar-Kays, who seemed like they'd be the second big winner, both dead (although the two surviving Bar-Kays kept the name alive and successful for a couple of decades), its future looked shaky. To top it off, the Warners/Atlantic deal turned out to be the end of the road for the Atlantic-Stax partnership. Jim Stewart discovered, to his horror, that despite all the hits Stax had delivered to Atlantic, it didn't own the master tapes. Furthermore, the Warners sale meant that the clause in Stewart's contract with Jerry Wexler that called for renegotiation if Wexler gave up his Atlantic stock (which he had just done) clicked in, and now Stewart had six months to find a new business partner. To twist the knife further, Wexler announced that Atlantic was signing Sam and Dave, whose hits had been bigger than Otis Redding's, directly to Atlantic. This turned out to be a terrible decision: without the Stax production and songwriting team behind them, Sam and Dave were lost. Wexler took them to Muscle Shoals to record, but they never had another real hit. How could things get worse for Stax? All it took was a second: on April 4, an assassin took out Martin Luther King Jr., who'd come to Memphis to cool tensions over a garbagemen's strike, as he stood on a balcony at the Lorraine Motel, a popular lodging for black travelers, with a coffee shop where Stax had regular meetings and where Steve Cropper and Eddie Floyd had written "Knock on Wood." The black community in Memphis erupted. Businesses were burned, windows were smashed. Stax artists took to the radio to plead for calm, while Jim Stewart and his sister, Stax cofounder Estelle Axton, loaded their tapes into a car and took them to safety. The record shop and studio closed for a week. The laundry across the street from Stax was burned, as was one of the next-door buildings. Stax put a cyclone fence around its building and parking lot. Satellite Records was closed for good.

Stax was untouched, physically, but its family was shaken. Stewart had brought a new man into the company, Al Bell, a polymathic, charismatic young black Memphian who had studied with Dr. King and had given up a promising radio career in Detroit to get even more involved with the city and music he loved. Bell realized that the time had come for black empowerment through the only thing the white establishment understood: money. And he was smart enough to know that the talk of integration in most of the country was just that, talk,

even though he was now neck-deep in a company that had been integrated from the beginning. Still, he wasn't the only person in Memphis who sought black empowerment through money, although the
most imminent danger was from young men who didn't have Bell's
intellectual capacity and who were robbing Stax talent in the parking
lot they used. Bell told the M.G.s' bassist, Duck Dunn, to buy a gun.
A new employee was brought in, Johnny Baylor, an old friend of Bell's
from Harlem, who'd worked with boxers and served with the Army
Rangers. He became security for Stax, and was scary enough that the
trouble backed off. Bell invoked another old friendship, and suddenly
Stax had an offer from Gulf + Western, a giant conglomerate that had
bought Paramount Pictures the previous year. It paid $4 million for
Stax, some of it in cash, most of it in stock and other financial instruments. But in the wake of the riots around the country that Dr. King's
assassination had set off, the easy cooperation between black and white
in the record business began to crumble, and a virulent black anti-
Semitism entered the picture. The most famous story is of Jerry Wexler at the 1968 convention of the National Association of Radio and
Television Announcers (NATRA) in Miami, where there were several unconfirmed stories later about white executives being threatened,
pistol-whipped, and hung in effigy. Wexler was on the dais waiting
to get an award when saxophonist King Curtis came up to him and
told him, "You're out of here right now," and the two left the building. Curtis had heard what he considered a credible assassination threat
and had very likely saved Wexler's life.

Another soul institution who was permanently affected by the King
assassination was James Brown. He and his band had just returned
from their first tour of Africa, and had been in Abidjan, Ivory Coast,
just a day earlier, but as cities across the United States erupted, it
dawned on Brown that they had a date in Boston to play the following night. The venue, the fourteen-thousand-seat Boston Garden, had
already canceled the show, but some tickets to it had been sold. The
local promoter and a black city councilman went to Boston mayor
Kevin White and painted a scenario of thousands of black youth de-
scending on downtown Boston that night only to find a canceled show
and nowhere else to go. White (who was white) had never even heard

of James Brown, but he saw the problem. He suggested that the show
go on as scheduled, and arranged for a local TV station to broadcast
it live, tape it, and when it was over, to continue to broadcast it through
the night, until the threat of violence had dissipated. Brown was no
fan of Dr. King's, and had refused to align himself with him, aware
that some of the harder young black politicians considered King an
Uncle Tom, but he had no way out of this. The show would, after some
financial negotiations were completed, go on. What would happen,
nobody knew. At the start of the evening, James took the mike and announced that this show would be a tribute to Dr. King, and then he
brought Mayor White onto the stage to introduce him, calling him
"a swingin' cat. The man is together!" There were only about two thousand people in the Garden—black shows were usually marked by
last-minute walk-up ticket sales, but only those who'd already laid out
the money were daring downtown Boston that night—and after a few
more remarks, the James Brown Revue swung into full action, the
band doing its steps, go-go dancers in place, and James performing
hit after hit. As the show gathered momentum, the Boston cops lining both sides of the stage—all, needless to say, white: Boston was
still very segregated in 1968—watched the audience. As James built
up to his cape routine toward the end, a bunch of kids jumped onto
the stage and grabbed him. Whoomp! In came the cops. The band
stopped playing, and the house lights came up. White cops, black
youth, live TV. James grabbed the mike: "Let me finish the show!
We're all black. Let's respect ourselves. Are we together or are we
ain't?" "We are!" the audience yelled back. James told the drummer
to hit it, he hit it, and the show went on to its conclusion. There was
no riot in Boston that night.

But that's not to say there wasn't a revolution. It occurred not only
among the many thousands of black households in the area, but in
the suburbs and middle-class white homes where kids who wouldn't
have dared expose themselves to the live show that night sat in front
of their televisions having their minds blown by James Brown. And
when it was over, they got to see the tape again. Among the thousands watching was a college kid with a radio program on which he
played blues and soul. Peter Blankfield, who'd been playing in a band

called the Hallucinations, saw a way forward for them, and the band's leader, Jerome Geils, agreed. Shortly thereafter, the J. Geils Blues Band was formed, a newly rechristened Peter Wolf on lead vocals, and there really *was* a Bosstown Sound. As for James Brown, his national profile was raised among politicians, who saw the Boston concert as proof that someone they'd never heard of could actually reach the black youth they had no idea how to communicate with; he even got invited to the White House. Still, as he had with Dr. King, he didn't get too close. In September, he released his next number-one record, "Say It Loud, I'm Black and I'm Proud." He was still James Brown.

It would be unfair to credit Brown with the political or social revolutionary content of the music that was bubbling up at this point, but he'd definitely touched something in the zeitgeist. Overt protest music wasn't on the charts, and the best hope for writing it, Bob Dylan, whose comeback album, *John Wesley Harding,* had come out after last Christmas, showed that he was still writing enigmatic songs, but his latest album, *Nashville Skyline,* which came out a few days after the King shooting, comprised country-inflected love songs. Country Joe and the Fish, being from Berkeley, were trying their best to stay political. But the Marxist principle of having the workers take over the means of production was certainly in the air when, recovering from their latest non-number-one American single, "Lady Madonna," an odd Fats Domino tribute (which Fats himself would cover later in the year for his first hit in some time) backed with "The Inner Light," another vegetarian curry from George, the Beatles announced the creation of Apple Corps in May. It was a label! It was a film-and-television production company! It was a boutique! It was a publishing company! It was an electronics company (mainly due to a maniac who went by the name of Magic Alex who, John Lennon had found, was working on, um, some groovy stuff)! Most of all, it was a successor to NEMS! They bought a building on Savile Row, in London, and would be open for business any day now.

Not long afterward, the Stones, as always pivoting away from the Beatles' sometimes cloying grooviness, hit a completely different nerve with their new single. "Street Fighting Man" announced itself with another patented Keith Richards guitar attack, as former London

School of Economics student Mick Jagger announced his (maybe) commitment to the revolution that was probably just around the corner—although, to be honest, he found "sleepy London town" an inappropriate place for his bad new street-fighting self. What on earth did they think they were doing? Selling records, of course, and it worked very nicely. Playing with fire, too? Maybe, but it was a nice reminder that rock and roll could still be dangerous. The Beatles, though, were quite serious about Apple, despite the boutique closing at the end of the summer, resulting in their giving away all the remaining stock. But they kept the label as a place for other artists: contracts were already being negotiated. (Oh, and *Rolling Stone* reported that the four were through with the Maharishi.)

Between urban riots and an escalating war in Vietnam, America was being shaken, so perhaps it's no surprise that the confrontational mood was also hitting country music: a change had even reached conservative old Nashville. Certainly, Loretta Lynn was speaking out, following her top 10 country hit "What Kind of Girl (Do You Think I Am?)" with a warning to another woman that if she messes with her man she's going to go to "Fist City"; the song resonated with enough people to ride the number-one country slot for weeks. But Lynn's guy wasn't safe, either: after that came "Your Squaw Is on the Warpath," a far cry from newcomer Tammy Wynette's "Stand By Your Man." Waylon Jennings suddenly hit on an idea that would eventually work wonders for him, and came out with "Only Daddy That'll Walk the Line," a tough, stomping rocker that pop radio didn't touch. Although Jennings would later say that "I couldn't go pop with a mouthful of firecrackers," this sort of thing was getting heard by people beyond the country audience. Some folkie influence had also invaded Nashville, where it had always been on the periphery. Besides the highly literate songwriting of Tom T. Hall, who was also writing hits for Bobby Bare, a young man named Mickey Newbury was circulating songs that were getting covered, but he bucked the local biz by signing with Elektra.

In Los Angeles, the Troubadour bar was humming with gossip and rumor. Jim McGuinn had reconfigured the Byrds, releasing *The Notorious Byrd Brothers* in February, with only three Byrds and a horse's rear end (rumored to represent the fired David Crosby—and denied by all concerned) on the front cover. It was good-bye to the first period of the Byrds, and new guitarist-singer Gram Parsons and drummer Kevin Kelley joined McGuinn in Nashville, where they cut a reported twenty-two songs. (Some of this activity was probably McGuinn rerecording songs they'd cut with Parsons singing lead: when LHI, Lee Hazlewood's label, caught wind of it, it sued, claiming that Parsons was still a member of the International Submarine Band, whose album LHI had put out. Columbia, the Byrds' label, was certain it would prevail, as it did; meanwhile, it wanted a new Byrds album, and got *The Notorious Byrd Brothers*.)

Other Troubadour denizens had banded together to form the Stone Poneys, a country-ish, folk-ish band fronted by Linda Ronstadt, an Arizonan who'd been attracting attention on the LA folk circuit for a couple of years. Capitol signed them and, in May, put out a single, "Some of Shelley's Blues," that was nice but didn't attract attention. The writer was Michael Nesmith, who'd started doing projects independently of his fellow Monkees, including an odd orchestral album called *The Wichita Train Whistle Sings*, and it was rumored that he, too, had spent time in Nashville studios cutting some tracks. When the Monkees' TV show was canceled in June, Nesmith still had dates to play with them, but far more time to work on a post-Monkees solo career. And another band in this burgeoning country-rock style was Hearts and Flowers, who'd been signed to Capitol by the same producer, Nik Venet, who'd signed the Stone Poneys. Hearts and Flowers was there first, releasing an album in 1967 that was totally ignored but that today is acknowledged as the real beginning of the LA country-rock scene. Their second album, *Of Horses, Kids and Forgotten Women*, featured a new guitarist, Bernie Leadon, but that didn't help, and the band faded away. The Nitty Gritty Dirt Band, the Dillards, and various former Byrds, too, were trying combinations—the Dillards being a family bluegrass group that eschewed the mainstream bluegrass scene and was electric-friendly, and the Dirt Band a bunch of Coloradans who initially tried the do-wacka-do shtick with no luck but who were signed to Liberty, who wanted them to fulfill their contract. This, far more than what was happening on the Sunset Strip, would, for better or worse, birth the future of the LA music scene.

The New York/Boston folk axis was still around, most notably Simon and Garfunkel, who'd discovered success in setting undergraduate angst to music—they actually titled a tune "A Simple Desultory Philippic"—with hits like "I Am a Rock," "The Dangling Conversation," and "A Hazy Shade of Winter." One of the big film hits of 1968 was *The Graduate,* starring Dustin Hoffman as a guy just out of college facing the future, and someone had the bright idea of asking Simon and Garfunkel to contribute a song to the soundtrack. "Mrs. Robinson" sent the soundtrack album; the duo's latest album, *Old Friends/Bookends;* and the single itself all to gold status, and was named Song of the Year in the 1969 Grammys—which were getting hipper: although "Up, Up and Away," by the 5th Dimension, won Record of the Year for 1967 in the '68 Grammys, *Sgt. Pepper* won Album of the Year, Aretha Franklin took Best Female R&B Solo Vocal Performance, while Best R&B Recording was awarded to "Respect," and Sam and Dave won Best R&B Group Performance for "Soul Man.")

Another veteran of the New York folk scene who shocked everyone by becoming a star was Tiny Tim, the stage name for Herbert Khaury, a lank-haired thirty-eight-year-old Lebanese American eccentric who'd been opening shows forever playing his ukulele and singing popular songs from the teens and twenties in a quavering falsetto. He'd helped a young Bob Dylan get started in New York, and was quite beloved among showbizzers, which got him onto a wacky TV program called *Rowan and Martin's Laugh-In,* resulting in a top 10 album on Reprise and a quite unexpected top 20 hit with "Tip-Toe Thru' the Tulips." Nobody was more New York than Dion, who had a smash with "Abraham, Martin and John," his tribute to Lincoln, King, and Kennedy, which showed a hitherto unknown side of his talent.

And from upstate New York came a most unusual album, its cover featuring a weird but not unskillful, semi-abstract oil painting of some musicians. One sat on the floor with what looked like a huge coffee cup on his head, playing what might have been a sitar. A headdress-bedecked Indian played a misshapen double bass, another guy helped a second lean over the back of a piano so he could play it, and way in the back was a drummer. Oh, and there was an elephant. The back showed an undistinguished pink house, and huge letters announced MUSIC FROM BIG PINK. No artist was listed. When the gatefold sleeve was opened, there was a photo, captioned "Next of Kin," of a bunch of people of all ages standing in a yard, a picture of five guys standing in a field, and another picture of that pink house. "A pink house seated in the sun of Overlook Mountain in West Saugerties, New York," that caption read. "Big Pink bore this music and these songs along its way. It's the first witness of this album that's been thought and composed right there inside its walls." The musicians were listed as Jaime "Rob-bie" Robertson, Rick Danko, Richard Manuel, Garth Hudson, and Levon Helm, along with producer John Simon. On the record label itself, one could see that these people did, indeed, write most of the songs, but two were cowritten, and one solely, by . . . Bob Dylan. He'd done the painting, too, it turned out; maybe he was the elephant in the room. But here at last was more evidence of what he'd been up to. This was the band he'd toured with, whose songwriting was as enig-matic as his. The cowrites ("Tears of Rage," with Richard Manuel, and "This Wheel's on Fire," with Rick Danko) and the album closer, Dylan's "I Shall Be Released," held their own with Robertson's "In a Station" and "The Weight" and Manuel's "We Can Talk." There was also an organ instrumental by Hudson, "Chest Fever," that probably scared Procol Harum silly. "The Weight" came out as a single from the album to no great effect, and a London jazz group, Brian Auger, Julie Driscoll, and the Trinity, released a single of "This Wheel's on Fire" that didn't disturb the charts at the time (although it became the theme song for the cult TV show *Absolutely Fabulous* many years later). In March, Manfred Mann, British Invaders who'd had a big hit with "Do Wah Diddy" a few years back, hit with "The Mighty Quinn (Quinn the Eskimo)," another of the songs Grossman had cir-culated from Hudson's tapes, and the Byrds failed to do much by "You Ain't Goin' Nowhere," which seemed, on the basis of Dylan's original demo, to have been written for them. Dylan was sort of back, although he made it clear he wasn't planning to tour. He did an interview for *Sing Out!*, the folkies' version of *Rolling Stone*, with the New Lost City Ramblers' John Cohen asking the questions; the piece was properly inscrutable, and the magazine put another of Dylan's paintings on the cover. What did this band call itself, anyway? *Rolling Stone* referred to them initially as Big Pink but put them on the cover in August as "The Band," and so they became.

Things were so hot in America, in fact, that the Brits were pretty much absent, save for superstars like the Beatles and the Stones and newcomers Led Zeppelin. There was an interesting strain of experimentation happening there, though. Steve Winwood had left the Spencer Davis Group to hole up in the country with a couple of guys who called themselves Traffic, and they put out an album, *Mr. Fantasy*, that didn't really sound like anything else. Folkier still was the Incredible String Band, two girls, two boys, with music very much tinged with Anglo-Irish folk tunes and acid, whose debut, *The Hangman's Beautiful Daughter*, produced by former Boston folkie and current London resident Joe Boyd, was a success, while coming at tradition from another angle was the acoustic Pentangle, featuring folk guitar stars John Renbourn and Bert Jansch, along with jazz bassist Danny Thompson and vocalist Jacqui McPhee. Another folkie band, Fairport Convention, formed around Ashley Hutchings and Simon Nicol, from a band called the Ethnic Shuffle Orchestra, and teenage guitar wizard Richard Thompson, with vocalists Judy Dyble (formerly a librarian) and Ian Matthews added to the mix, and it became Boyd's next discovery. Fairport was an immediate hit, thanks to their wide range of songs, including the first of Joni Mitchell's to be recorded in Britain, but Dyble left early on, and a woman from the traditional English folk circuit, Sandy Denny, joined them. The new lineup went into the studio at the end of 1968 to make a second album, *What We Did on Our Holidays*, which contained another previously unheard song from Bob Dylan's recent output, "Million Dollar Bash." (They also covered "If You Gotta Go, Go Now," a very early song of his, in French, for unknown reasons). The combination of English roots and electric instruments was to make them leaders in the nascent British folk-rock movement.

Unfortunately, the folk tradition that most new bands in England were attempting was American blues. Heartened by the transatlantic success of Eric Clapton's trio Cream, blues-ish bands were springing up all over England, causing some people to recall Sonny Boy Williamson's remark about the Yardbirds wanting to play blues so *bad*. One exception to this was Fleetwood Mac, a blues band with a couple of fairly restrained and tasteful guitarists, Peter Green and Jeremy Spencer, who recorded an album with some of the Chicago guys in 1969 while also writing blues-tinged pop tunes like "Black Magic Woman." More typical, perhaps, was Ten Years After, who, like many of the other British blues bands, substituted speed and volume for any attempt to actually understand blues and who, of course, became quite popular. Eric Clapton, distraught over what he'd wrought—again, the first time was when he'd left the Yardbirds for John Mayall—and despondent over bad reviews of Cream's albums in *Rolling Stone*, announced that after one more album and a tour, they were calling it quits. No, British rock was better off being what it was, as the Crazy World of Arthur Brown proved by evolving from a so-so blues band to an eccentric stage spectacular that culminated with Mr. Brown declaiming, "I am the god of hellfire," and igniting a helmet he was wearing. In a year when Tiny Tim could hit the top 10, it wasn't surprising that Brown's "Fire" went to number two in the United States.

Nineteen sixty-eight was a transitional year for soul music, not just stylistically, with the emergence of Sly and the Family Stone and James Brown's ongoing experiments, but in a business sense. Stax's sale to Paramount and the ascendance of Al Bell as the man whom people listened to meant a widening of the label's vision. In his deejay career, Bell had been a Memphis guy at a Detroit station, and while he knew very well that Stax wasn't Motown, he did realize that there was commercial wisdom in expanding past the blues-based sound of the records the label had been putting out, especially as that sound was being challenged by Fame Studios and the Muscle Shoals crew. He wanted to build on what the label had already achieved, in the hope of selling more records on a national, not just regional, level. To that end, he brought in a former Motowner who'd left Hitsville to open his own studio, Don Davis. Davis was producing records in Detroit but was open to freelance opportunities, and Bell approached him about coming down and working for Stax. His first project was Carla Thomas, and sure enough, "Pick Up the Pieces," his first record with her, returned her to the R&B top 20. Next was Johnnie Taylor, who, like Sam Cooke, had sung with the gospel Soul Stirrers and recorded secular material for Cooke's SAR label. Davis found a young songwriter, Bettye Crutcher, who'd had some success at Stax, and she came up with "Who's Making Love," which chided men for stepping out on their women and asked outright if maybe there was someone else taking care of them while they were tomcatting around. The forthright lyric and punchy arrangement took Taylor to the top of the R&B charts and even the pop top 10. This was more like it!

Over at Motown there was a host of problems. The Temptations had fired one of their key members, David Ruffin, who'd blown off a gig to go on a date, and given that it wasn't the first time he'd done that, they'd had it with him. It took until the end of the year to work his replacement, Dennis Edwards, into the act, but there was another serious problem that was affecting all the label's artists: Holland–Dozier–Holland, the unstoppable songwriting and production team that had been knocking out hit after hit, flat out refused to work for Motown anymore until some issues concerning royalties and bonuses were worked out. Berry Gordy, who was busy moving the business end of Motown into what he felt, after the 1967 Detroit riots, was a safer building, on Woodward Avenue (leaving the studios back at Hitsville, of course), countered by suing them. Into the courts the dispute went, and suddenly Motown had a crisis. It wasn't just that it had alienated HDH, but Berry had been spending a lot of time in Las Vegas and at Motown's West Coast offices on the Sunset Strip. He wasn't around Hitsville as much as he had been, and it had to be called to his attention that the three men had stopped working. This wasn't the old hands-on Gordy by any means. There was a constant falling away of people who'd helped him get started. Not only artists—Mary Wells was long gone; Kim Weston, a rising star who'd recorded duets with

Marvin Gaye, was on her way to another label; and Florence Ballard of the almighty Supremes finally clarified the question of why Cindy Birdsong was now performing with the group by showing up at ABC Records: she'd been quietly fired. But Mickey Stevenson, who'd been around forever, asked Gordy for stock in the company and was turned down, so he left for MGM, taking with him Clarence Paul, Stevie Wonder's early mentor. Harvey Fuqua, Gordy's brother-in-law (and formerly of the Moonglows), divorced his wife, Berry's sister Gwen, and moved to RCA, where he'd bring modern soul to the label. Even the legendary vaudeville vet Cholly Atkins, whose choreography had helped every Motown act he worked with wow audiences with amazing dancing that set them apart from other soul acts, left for Las Vegas, where he got to pick and choose the artists he worked with—some of whom, but not all, were Motown acts.

The odd thing was, none of this was necessarily because Motown wasn't changing with the times: HDH had been churning out top 10 material until the day they stopped. A raft of new producers and songwriters got to work on filling the void the three men had left. Of them, the only one who was based in Detroit instead of LA was Norman Whitfield, a brash young man who knew how to grab trends when they started. George Clinton, leader of the Parliaments, had finally been signed to Jobete as a songwriter, but until he hit with something for them (which he never did), he still had his own group to look out for. Clinton had added LSD to the pot he'd been smoking since his youth, and had been attending shows at the Grande Ballroom, Detroit's answer (right down to Gary Grimshaw's posters) to the Fillmore, to see local bands such as the Up!, Froot, Teegarden and Van Winkle, the Stooges, and the MC5. Inspired, he added a couple of instrumentalists, including a demon lead guitarist, Eddie Hazel, to the Parliaments' singers, and they started playing the clubs as Funkadelic. Black college students in particular went wild for them. "Norman Whitfield used to come see us all the time," Clinton said a decade later. "He wasn't even sneaky: he had a big-ass tape recorder and set it up on a table right up front of us, grinning the whole time." Clinton's claim that Whitfield copied him isn't as provable as the fact that when the next Temptations record, "Cloud Nine," came out, written and produced by Whitfield, it sure sounded different. From the wah-wah guitars, to the lyrics about ghetto life, to the break where the Tempts sang a cappella over a couple of conga drums, to the "boom-boom-booms" at the end—if anyone could sue for plagiarism, it was Sly Stone: the ending was a direct rip from his current hit, "Dance to the Music"—this sure didn't sound like a bunch of guys in tuxedos executing a Cholly Atkins routine. The changes seemed to be working: by the end of 1968, Motown had four of the top 10 singles on the R&B charts.

In other label news, it appeared that the Beatles' Apple label, unlike various other ventures under that umbrella, was a go. The first thing released on it was, of course, a Beatles record: "Hey Jude," backed with "Revolution." The A-side was a smooth McCartney midtempo number he'd written, supposedly, for John's son, Julian, with comforting if nonspecific lyrics and a group chant at the end that lasted a lot longer than would be expected; the entire song clocks in at a monster 7:11. The other side of the record seemed to be John's riposte to the Stones' "Street Fighting Man," again registering dissatisfaction with current events, but also seemingly criticizing the way the self-proclaimed young revolutionaries were going about changing things. It had been preceded by the latest Beatles film, which avoided some of the pitfalls of *Magical Mystery Tour* by being animated, based on the song "Yellow Submarine." The actual Beatles didn't voice their characters, and the film's soundtrack had only four new songs in it, and they weren't actually new but, rather, leftovers from previous sessions plus the title tune and "All You Need Is Love," which the band premiered during a global telecast back in July 1967. The *Yellow Submarine* soundtrack LP was held back, though, so that the latest Beatles album could be released on the fifth anniversary of their first album. The latter didn't seem to have a title, and it had two discs. The words "The BEATLES" were embossed on the cover, along with (at least on early copies) a serial number. There were thirty songs, and included in the package were rather serious-looking headshots of each Beatle, each on its own sheet of paper, and a big poster/collage with the lyrics printed on the back. In retrospect, it seems significant that there were no group shots; everyone seemed to be working on his own material.

Most radical was John's new stuff. He'd married the artist Yoko Ono, long a fixture of New York's downtown avant-garde, after meeting her at her solo exhibition at the Indica Gallery in London, and had come under her spell. Thus, there was not only a new version of "Revolution" on the record (retitled "Revolution I") but also "Revolution 9," a bizarre attempt at musique concrète that was the subject of much stoned inquiry among fans as they watched the white apple—the B-side of the label showed a cut apple; the A-side, its green skin—revolve on the turntable. (Did John really say, "I buried Paul"?) But there was certainly enough Beatle music, enigmatic though it might be, to keep the fans, who have long called it the White Album, happy, and it sold and sold. Next up for Apple was going to be a John-and-Yoko solo album, *Two Virgins*, and the two newlyweds posed totally naked for the cover: front and back. Capitol, which was distributing Apple, balked at the idea, and the record wound up on Tetragrammaton, a label partially owned by Bill Cosby, clad in a brown-paper wrapper that showed only the two heads peeking out from the cover. The album cover caused *Two Virgins* to be shunned by numerous department store chains; when *Rolling Stone* published a copy of the photo before the album's release, the issue was banned from newsstands; and a couple of poor guys with a head shop in Chicago got arrested for displaying the album in their window. In the controversy, it was barely noted that the contents were a bunch of self-indulgent pseudo-arty meanderings.

The Rolling Stones, too, dutifully got their next album cover banned. It showed a filthy gas station bathroom, its walls covered by graffiti, some of which were the song titles on the cover's back. Entitled *Beggars Banquet*, it outraged London Records in the United States, which demanded a new cover, and got a boring white one with the band's name and the album title in copperplate script, as if on a dinner invitation. The inside spread showed the band lolling around a table with the remains of a feast in front of them. The music, though, showed a big recovery from their previous effort, containing not only the "Street Fighting Man" single, but also a song, "Sympathy for the Devil," that became their theme song from there on out. In it, Jagger seems to equate himself with none other than Old Scratch, posing questions such as "Who killed the Kennedys?"—they had originally recorded "Who killed Kennedy," and changed it after Robert Kennedy's death hit the news—and stating that "after all, it was you and me." It was an audacious song and would be echoed in the months to come by events musical and nonmusical. Wisely, they didn't release it as a single.

In all this apocalyptic confusion, pity poor Elvis Presley. He'd spent the first half of 1968 dreading the television special he was doing at Christmastime on NBC. Was he just going to sing Christmas songs on a set? What on earth did the Colonel have in mind for him? MGM had lost so much money on Presley's movies that they were thinking of not renewing his contract. Elvis's life had been up and down for a number of years. On the one hand, he'd moved his teenage girlfriend, Priscilla, into Graceland, and according to her they'd been having nonpenetrative sex as they waited for her to reach the age of consent. Finally, in 1967, they'd gotten married in Las Vegas, and shortly after that, they had a daughter, whom they named Lisa Marie. For the most part, Priscilla stayed away from Los Angeles when Elvis was working on a film, but her ears were always attuned to the rumors about what went on during shoots, and there were tensions between the two from the start. After filming wrapped on *The Trouble with Girls (And How to Get into It)* in May, it was time to get real about the Christmas special. Elvis was determined to make a good showing, as RCA was going to release the soundtrack. The Colonel had chosen Steve Binder, of *T.A.M.I. Show* fame, to direct. Binder wasn't sure he wanted to get involved; he'd just joined forces with a hot record producer, Bones Howe, and Elvis—well, Elvis's last gold record had been in 1960 (eight years ago), he was making all these turkey films and dud singles and even worse albums, and he hadn't played live in a long time. But the Colonel had Binder and Howe over for a meeting, at which he declared "We're not going to tell you boys what to do creatively, because that's what we hired you for, but if you get out of line, we're going to let you know about it." Then he said something that blew them away: "We don't care what material you submit for the show. If Mr. Presley likes it, Mr. Presley will do it. However, Mr. Presley must be the publisher of the material or else we must communicate with the publisher and arrangements must be made." It sounded tough but actually was a major concession: one reason Elvis's music had suffered all the years he'd been making films was that the soundtrack numbers had been lazily chosen from songs the Colonel got kickbacks on, and few major songwriters had wanted to work under those conditions. Also, the Beatles and the rising stars in the country field notwithstanding, Elvis wasn't writing his own material. He never had, and he wasn't about to start now.

Soon it was time for Binder and Howe to meet Elvis. Binder pitched Elvis on the freedom he'd have in shaping the show, the chance to demonstrate who Elvis Presley was now. Bones had been present at some sessions Elvis had done much earlier in his career, where the hits had been made in an organic fashion, with everyone, including Elvis, participating, and he now reminded Elvis of that. Binder emphasized that the only person who could do this show was Elvis: how'd he feel about that? "Scared to death," Elvis said, half-jokingly. A few days later, he and Priscilla went to Hawaii for a vacation, and everyone got to work when they returned. Shortly afterward, Bobby Kennedy was killed in Los Angeles, and Elvis couldn't stop talking about conspiracies and how awful that that year's other assassination, that of Martin Luther King Jr., had happened in his hometown of Memphis, which made the city look awful. He knew better. Binder suggested that the special could show the world that this son of Memphis was as unprejudiced as they came. What did Elvis think about doing some songs by contemporary songwriters? Sure! On another occasion, they went downstairs from the production office and hung out on the Sunset Strip. The crowds just walked by: Elvis's presence didn't register for them at all. Presley may have realized then what was at stake: he'd never been invisible before. Okay. He'd take care of that.

Assembling the show was a huge job, not made easier by the various factions involved. On the one hand, there was NBC and the record company it owned, RCA, which in turn owed a lot of its success to its fading star, Elvis Presley, and his manager, the Colonel, and his interlocking business workings. Then there was the actual production staff, with a very nervous Steve Binder at the top. The concept for the show was to take the Jerry Reed song "Guitar Man" and weave it though the show as a motif, to take the audience from one production piece to another. Rehearsals started; Elvis did his bit, clearly enjoying himself; and at the end of every day, some of the Memphis Mafia joined him in the dressing room as they ran through songs and stories, winding Elvis down from the day's work. Binder sat on the sidelines for these sessions, watching his star and listening to the goings-on afterward, the repartee as much as the songs. Binder was also caught in a jam: Elvis had his own orchestrator and arranger, a guy named Billy Strange, who wasn't showing up. Also on hand was another Billy, Billy Goldenberg, whose main experience was in Broadway shows. Binder had asked him to be there, although Goldenberg had no idea what he was supposed to do. The time when the eighty-piece orchestra had to have actual arrangements to play was getting closer, and finally Binder put Goldenberg on the case. He was reluctant, but he and Elvis formed a bond during their first rehearsal together, over Beethoven's *Moonlight* Sonata, of all things: Elvis had been playing it on the piano when Goldenberg walked in. Elvis stopped playing, not remembering the rest of the piece. "You know this?" he asked. Goldenberg admitted that he did, and showed Presley where it went from there. Elvis snapped immediately, and started playing it again. "We spent the better part of our first rehearsal period learning the first movement of the *Moonlight* Sonata," Goldenberg said later.

From then on, work flowed. Now they had everything but the finale. Binder feared a custom-written Christmas song from the Colonel's tame songwriters, and so, truth be told, did Elvis. The Colonel was adamant, however, that there would be no original material: the run-throughs of Elvis's hits were going just swell, so there was no need, right? Binder took Earl Brown, who was doing vocal arrangements, aside and told him that they needed a song that would sum up the whole situation they were in: "I've got Elvis Presley, Colonel Parker, Confederate flags, a black choreographer, a Puerto Rican choreographer and a Jewish director! Everything in the show was integrated—behind the scenes . . ." Could Brown write a song, pretty much immediately, summing that all up, one that Elvis could sing for the finale? Brown went home and at seven the next morning called Binder, saying he had something. They met in the studio, and Brown played the song: "If I Can Dream," it was called, a hope for peace and harmony between countries and races. Binder was convinced: this was it. Now to convince Elvis, because playing it for the Colonel was a no-go. Elvis listened to it over and over, six or seven times, and then looked up and said, "We're doing it." The Colonel could hardly object now, so he didn't, especially after someone ran the lead sheet over to his music publisher and copped 100 percent of the publishing for him. And then, a few days later, after watching the post-rehearsal jam/bull sessions, Binder got another brilliant idea: what if part of the program were just Elvis and some buddies—maybe they could fly in Scotty Moore and D. J. Fontana, his original guitarist and drummer!—recreating this in an intimate group in front of an audience? Elvis was all for it, so it was scheduled. A small audience of a couple of hundred folks was assembled, the best-looking women up front (the Colonel's idea), arranged around the square stage. Elvis saw Scotty and D.J. for the first time in years. Nervous? You could see his hand shake. Dressed in a suit of supple black leather that costume designer Bill Belew had run up, and thinner than he'd been in a while, Elvis, bantering with the guys, slid into "Lawdy Miss Clawdy" and started to relax. After a couple of numbers, he said to no one in particular, "Been a long time, baby." The nervousness hadn't quite left when he ad-libbed that there'd been a lot of changes in the music field since he'd performed these songs last, "but I like a lot of new groups—the Beatles, the, uh, the beards . . ." Then the show, as presented, cut to some choreography and a short gospel section, with two gospel songs, "Where Could I Go but to the Lord" and "Up above My Head," and finished off with LaVern Baker's 1961 Leiber/Stoller hit "Saved," which is more than a bit tongue in cheek. Then back to the small square stage, where he performed, among other things, Rufus Thomas's "Tiger Man," which he'd apparently wanted to record for ages; and finished off, in the dark, with "Memories," a Mac Davis/Billy Strange ballad. The "stand-up" part of the show followed, with Elvis in fine shape, though challenged by Goldenberg's sometimes screechy arrangements, as he danced through a bizarre series of stages of the "Guitar Man"'s life, fighting off the "Big Boss Man," serenading his girlfriend, being abducted by floozies, and performing next to a belly dancer. He got to show off some moves he'd learned via his newest passion, karate, but finally the show switched back to the square stage, where Elvis, in a new outfit, sang "If I Can Dream," and the show was over. It was an unprecedented event in rock and roll: the comeback of a former star, in full command of his faculties and able to do to an audience what he'd done at the start—only, this time with close-ups on nationwide television at a time when more people were watching than during the rest of the year. On the one hand, it's not so surprising: he was only thirty-three, after all. At the end of the taping, he announced, "Tell the Colonel I want to talk to him," and the old man walked into the room at his star's command. Elvis told him, "I want to tour again. I want to go out and work with a live audience." And he would. At this time of triumph and renewal, nobody could guess that he'd be dead before ten years had passed.

And as one career from the early days of rock and roll came alive, another shut down, albeit with a fine finale. Writing groups such as the Beatles and the Stones, and the many American groups that emulated them, reduced the need for Teen Pan Alley's services, and although the writers continued to write, they went into eclipse. Gerry Goffin and his wife, Carole King, were the last to do visible work: their song "Wasn't Born to Follow" showed up on *The Notorious Byrd Brothers* in 1968, and the fact that Goffin told interviewers years later that he'd written it at Big Sur after coming down from an acid trip with his girlfriend indicated that things weren't so happy in the marriage of Teen Pan Alley's First Couple. However, they got a call they couldn't ignore. With the Monkees' TV show canceled, the band, with their producer, Bob Rafelson, decided to go out in a big way, with a wacky

Beatlesesque film that exposed the hypocrisy of the whole Monkee world. Rafelson got his buddy Jack Nicholson involved, and soon enough filming started on a thing called *Head*. It's a very strange film indeed, a lot weirder than, say, *The Trip* or the other Hollywood freak-out films. It was also teeth-gratingly self-referential, with the band singing a parody of their TV theme song, declaring themselves "a manufactured image / With no philosophies." Other oddities in the film include the full NBC News footage of Vietnamese general Nguyen Ngoc Loan executing a Vietcong spy in broad daylight, Frank Zappa walking a cow through the backlot of the studio, and Davy Jones slugging a waitress in its canteen, only to jump up and complain to the director that the fans would never go for that and that it's not fair, only to get talked into doing it again, so hard that her wig falls off and she's revealed to be a portly, bald stuntman. What most people seem to remember from the film, though, is the beginning and end, when first Mickey Dolenz and, finally, the three other Monkees jump off a bridge. The subsequent shots of them floating around are accompanied by "The Porpoise Song," a beautiful 7/4 piece of psychedelia arranged by Jack Nitzsche that got to only 62 when it was released as a single, the last new Goffin/King song to hit the charts. The song-writing couple divorced the same year, and 1969 saw Carole with a new boyfriend, bassist Charles Larkey, and a band, the City, with an album on Lou Adler's new Ode Records label. It stiffed.

There were other signs of change in the air: Van Morrison, free from his Bang contract, did an album of long, introspective songs backed by jazz bassist Richard Davis and drummer Connie Kay of the Modern Jazz Quartet (who were now signed to Apple), *Astral Weeks;* the Everly Brothers released a wonderful album, *Roots,* on Warners, featuring clips of their family radio show from their childhood and songs by Merle Haggard that went virtually unnoticed. Atlantic Records, heartened by its success with Cream, spent $200,000 to sign Jimmy Page's New Yardbirds, on a tip Ahmet Ertegun got from Dusty Springfield. To avoid problems with the old band's management, they were redubbed Led Zeppelin. (*Billboard* also announced another six-figure Atlantic signing, the Cartoone, a Scottish band on whose first album Page played, but whose second, Page-less album the label refused to release.)

Another important record, although it didn't sell at the time, came out of the Byrds, who had just released an album six months earlier: *Sweetheart of the Rodeo* caught everyone by surprise. It was the result of the sessions they'd done in Nashville, and was framed by two of the Dylan basement songs, "You Ain't Goin' Nowhere" and "Nothing Was Delivered," between which were songs by the Louvin Brothers (precursors to the Everlys in the great country brother tradition), Woody Guthrie, Cindy Walker, and Merle Haggard, as well as Gram Parsons and Stax soul singer William Bell ("You Don't Miss Your Water"). The basic Byrds (McGuinn, who'd changed his first name to Roger; Chris Hillman; Parsons; and drummer Kevin Kelley) were supplemented by some of the brighter new studio musicians in Nashville and Bakersfield, such as steel guitarists Lloyd Green and JayDee Maness, John Hartford, Earl P. Ball, and electric guitarist Clarence White. Several of the songs had featured lead vocals by Parsons and had to be rerecorded with McGuinn due to the LHI suit and to a reported power struggle between McGuinn and Parsons. After playing the Grand Ole Opry to a fairly hostile reception, the band left for a short tour of England, during which they met Mick Jagger and Keith Richards, who advised them not to do a planned tour of South Africa, which was rigidly segregated. The band came home, Columbia released *Sweetheart of the Rodeo*, and a couple of days later Gram Parsons, the only actual Southerner in the band, announced that he wouldn't join them for their South African dates and quit the band entirely. McGuinn hurriedly recruited Clarence White, and the tour went on. Between the bad publicity the band got from an increasingly politicized audience, the loss of the charismatic Parsons, and the strong dose of hard country, *Sweetheart* got to only 77 on the *Billboard* charts, but its influence turned out to be immense: country was, if not the Next Big Thing, then at least a major component of it.

The major trend at the end of the 1960s was the splintering and breakup of bands. By the end of 1968, they were dissolving everywhere: Buffalo Springfield, despite lauded albums, were beset by management and interpersonal problems, and split at the end of the year. Neil Young had already left the band and was readying a solo album with input from Jack Nitzsche for Reprise, while Jim Messina and Richie Furay sorted through tracks in the can for an album titled *Last Time Around*. Cream did their farewell concerts and released *Goodbye*. In September, with their debut Columbia album, *Cheap Thrills,* topping the charts, Big Brother and the Holding Company learned that Janis Joplin was leaving and, under the guidance of her manager, Albert Grossman, forming a new band; they did their last gig together on December 1. Michael Bloomfield had left the Electric Flag, which continued under Buddy Miles's leadership long enough to put out a second album, and had agreed to do an album with Al Kooper, where they'd jam together. Bloomfield blew off the second day's session, leaving Kooper to call in Stephen Stills for the remainder of the album. Released as *Super Session,* it sold like mad, and Kooper managed to talk Bloomfield into a couple of nights at the Fillmore West (Bill Graham's new place, formerly the Carousel Ballroom, which he'd leased after losing the Fillmore), the recordings for which were released in 1969 as *The Live Adventures of Mike Bloomfield and Al Kooper,* with a Norman Rockwell double portrait for its cover, but Bloomfield was becoming increasingly reclusive. Graham Nash announced he was leaving the Hollies, and Steve Winwood announced that Traffic was over after two critically lauded but commercially tepid albums. It was even down to the personal level: in December, Aretha Franklin announced that she'd separated from her husband/manager Ted White.

And from these shards came new groups. Given that Cream had pioneered the concept of the "supergroup," Eric Clapton was the one everybody was watching, but the first out of the gate was Crosby, Stills, and Nash, who were label shopping in January 1969 and who had their first album (for Atlantic) ready shortly thereafter. At about the same time, Richie Furay and Jim Messina rose from the ashes of Buffalo Springfield with bassist Randy Meisner to form Poco, a country-rock group. Hot on their heels, Gram Parsons put together his own country-rock band, the Flying Burrito Brothers, with ex-Byrds Chris Hillman and Chris Ethridge and maverick LA pedal steel guitarist "Sneaky" Pete Kleinow. The cover of their debut album, *The Gilded Palace of Sin,* shows three of them in elaborate suits by North Hollywood country outfitter Nudie's Rodeo Tailors, purveyors of stage wear to some of the more flamboyant Nashville stars (Porter Wagoner, most notably), Parsons's displaying huge marijuana leaves, which hardly endeared the group to Nashville but that went over well with their target audience.

Still, Nashville was, if reluctantly, getting comfortable with some of these new guys. Bob Dylan had recorded the bulk of *Blonde on Blonde* there, and then *John Wesley Harding*, and now he came out with *Nashville Skyline*, which led off with a duet with Johnny Cash, on whose new television program he'd appeared, and continued with a bunch of straightforward love songs backed by some first-call studio musicians, including steel player Pete Drake, fiddler Charlie Daniels, and hot young acoustic guitarist Norman Blake. Cash contributed liner notes in the form of a blank-verse poem. Then Clapton made his move: in May, a new supergroup, Blind Faith, was announced, with Clapton; Steve Winwood; Cream's drummer, Ginger Baker; and bassist Ric Grech, who'd been with Family, a very odd British group that had failed to do much in the United States but was quite hot at home. Despite few memorable songs and a textless cover of a barely pubescent girl, naked, holding an airplane-shaped chrome hood ornament (a shot quickly withdrawn and replaced by a sepia-toned photo of the band), their album rocketed up the charts, and after a short U.S. tour, they went their separate ways. As, acrimoniously, did bluegrass stars Lester Flatt and Earl Scruggs, who'd been together since the early '50s. Earl Scruggs, who'd transformed bluegrass banjo when they'd paired up, was becoming more of a rock star ever since the two had provided the theme song for the TV sitcom *The Beverly Hillbillies* and then revised one of their signature instrumentals, "Foggy Mountain Breakdown," to serve as the theme to the hit film *Bonnie and Clyde*. Their last single, in September 1968, had been "Like a Rolling Stone." It was not a hit.

That was okay; there were brand-new stars in the making and old ones evolving: Doug Sahm was taking to San Francisco very nicely, and had recorded a remarkable album, *Sir Douglas Quintet + 2 = Honkey Blues*, which combined free jazz, country, blues, and psychedelia (and had only Doug from the Quintet). He followed it up with a single, "Mendocino," which did just so-so business in the States but was a smash all over Western Europe, and the resulting album, produced by "Amigos de Musica" (a name that usually meant Doug and his original producer, Huey P. Meaux), was packed with some mature songwriting and featured the original Quintet.

Labels were still trying to figure out how to acquire the right talent. Elektra had wisely chosen Danny Fields, formerly with *16* magazine, as house hippie, a switched-on, in-the-know New York scenester given the power to sign bands; and Fields had made his way to Detroit, where he saw the MC5 do their loud, powerful, political show at the Grande Ballroom. They were the public face of the White Panther Party, a rather confused political group that could have arisen only in a city with an industrial base and a strong working class. Their platform, such as it was, called for "dope, rock & roll and fucking in the streets," and was run out of a commune whose leader, John Sinclair, a poet and rabble-rouser, felt that the White Panthers would be militant white leftist youth in the same way that the Black Panthers were for the black community. He was a force behind the Ann Arbor Blues Festival, forcing it to book avant-gardists like Archie Shepp and Sun Ra, and encouraged the MC5, whom he was managing, to make political statements as well as to program avant-garde instrumentals, such as Ra's "Starship," which appeared on their debut album, and the never-recorded "Black to Comm," which fans swore was one of the all-time greatest rock instrumentals. The band organized their shows like a gospel performance, inciting the audience to frenzy and exhorting them to revolution, and their debut album, *Kick Out the Jams,* recorded live at the Grande, opens with vocalist Rob Tyner saying, "Now it's time to . . . KICK OUT THE JAMS, MOTHERFUCKERS!" This resulted, first, in Tyner having to overdub the offending word with "brothers and sisters," in March, and, in May, after the band had done some touring, in spreading chaos and in Elektra's dropping the band entirely after three months with the label for "unprofessional behavior." On the same trip, however, Fields had signed one of the MC5's fellow Grande acts, the Stooges. They weren't particularly political. In fact, some would say they could hardly even play.

The thing is, the industry still didn't have a great idea of what "the kids" wanted. Groups, okay; everyone knew about groups. But each week, *Billboard*'s list of the new albums showed chaos. Some seemed the result of casting calls: four or five guys in matching clothes and longish hair and a girl and a trade ad emphasizing their producer. The copy would be a nebulous promise of peaceful feelings and sunlit days, not the songwriting or playing. These bands vanished almost immediately. Others were moody, vaguely hostile-looking youth of both genders not quite looking into the camera, promising the sounds of brooding youth, pondering today's problem: who were Pidgeon? Rhinoceros? Kak? The Serpent Power? The Wildflower? Zakary Thaks? The Harbinger Complex? Crow? So many albums were coming out that some interesting, if forgotten, stuff was out there in the wild. Kapp Records was hardly a major cultural force, but they put out an album by Silver Apples, a New York duo who played primitive self-built synthesizers. It would be tempting to say that they influenced '80s bands like Suicide and the many new wave British synth duets, except nobody ever heard them. Columbia put some money into the United States of America, a group headed by an avant-garde composer and grad student named Joseph Byrd and his girlfriend, Dorothy Moskowitz, which played theatrical performances of lefty protest songs with synthesizers and percussion, all of which was rather too lofty for a mass audience. There was also Kaleidoscope, who became legendary later on as the starting place of virtuoso guitarist David Lindley, but also had members proficient on a number of odd instruments, including oud, saz, flamenco-style guitar, and exotic percussion. They offered classical Turkish music, old-timey country, and an avant-garde dissection of classic blues, but didn't have enough focus to have much of a career—an early iteration of the band was supposed to play Monterey but forgot to show up—although they were LA club favorites for several years. Equally diverse, albeit slightly more focused, was Memphis's Insect Trust, named after an organization in a William Burroughs novel, who had members with pasts in country blues (guitarist Bill Barth was a co-rediscoverer of Skip James and involved with the Memphis Blues Festival), avant-garde jazz (wind player Robert Palmer and baritone saxophonist Trevor Koehler), and old-timey folk (Luke Faust). The band had a knack for songwriting that led to some inspired combinations, and also wrote music to "Eyes of a New York Woman," a song Thomas Pynchon put into his novel *V,* and to a song Koehler's six-year-old son wrote (which had Elvin Jones on drums when they recorded it).

But probably the most successful (if one uses the term loosely) of these odd bands was Captain Beefheart and His Magic Band. "Beefheart" was Don Van Vliet, a childhood friend of Frank Zappa, with whom he shared a love of the blues in their early days. He was also a gifted painter whose parents had moved the family into the desert outside LA (where he met Zappa) because they feared that Don's love of art would turn him into a homosexual. He moved back to LA to form a band, and had recorded two off-kilter bluesy albums when Zappa signed him to Straight, one of the labels he and his manager, Herb Cohen, had started. Gathering his band in a remote house in the suburbs, Beefheart rehearsed them relentlessly for eight months, finally emerging with twenty-eight compositions of angular, often dissonant weirdness with titles such as "Neon Meate Dream of an Octafish," "When Big Joan Sets Up," and "Hobo Chang Ba," played by band members whose names had been changed to the likes of Zoot Horn Rollo (for Bill Harkleroad) and Winged Eel Fingerling (for Elliot Ingber). In them, Beefheart's voice, with a range of several octaves, bellowed out incomprehensible lyrics as the band swooped and clanged behind him. Released as a two-record set with the power of Warner Bros. behind it, the album, *Trout Mask Replica,* was indeed one of the most polarizing records of all time, starting Beefheart on the road to stardom of a sort. All the way at the end of the listenability scale was a single on Mercury, "Paralyzed," by the Legendary Stardust Cowboy, a west Texas weirdo named Norman Odam, who played guitar and bugle. Its lyrics and direction are utterly undefinable, and on the record, Odam is backed only by a drummer, J. Henry "T Bone" Burnett. Heartened by the fact that anyone heard it, Odam moved to Las Vegas to become a star, and lives there today.

More palatable to the pop audience were the emerging horn bands. The Electric Flag had had a horn section, which pricked up fans' ears, and the next edition of the Paul Butterfield Blues Band had a horn section, too. Canadian Skip Prokop formed Lighthouse, which had jazz pretensions, and there were mutterings out of England by the likes of Keef Hartley and If, but the big news was Blood, Sweat and Tears, a band Al Kooper had formed to showcase his own songs, to which he'd recruited a number of horn players, studio musicians on the edge of New York's jazz scene, who signed to Columbia. Their first album, *The Child Is Father to the Man*, didn't do particularly well, but the band liked playing together and replaced Kooper with a Canadian singer, David Clayton-Thomas, in 1969. He clicked with the public, which took their next three singles to number two and began a career that would last until the late '70s, with Clayton-Thomas in and out. Columbia, sniffing a trend, signed a band with horns that had been playing rock clubs in the Midwest, and soon, a double album was released by the Chicago Transit Authority (double because they had so much to say, the ads informed us), which did okay, but the group dropped "Transit Authority" thanks to a threatened suit, and their next album, *Chicago II*, kicked off a series of albums that was at *XXXVI* at the time of this writing and fifty charting singles that have sold millions worldwide. Although they were marketed as rock and roll, in the end these bands—and there were a few more—proved to be just an edgier form of middle of the road, although their pretensions were a fit for the times: *Chicago IV*, a boxed four-LP set, featured a vintage cover photo of Carnegie Hall, printed as a poster inside, because some of its content was recorded there.

The big excitement for the summer of 1969 was rock festivals. There were more bands touring than ever, lots of them British, which for some reason often had more cachet than being American, and the model of Monterey was there for aspiring promoters. Every week, *Rolling Stone* would have news from far-flung correspondents of festivals where announced acts didn't show (or weren't genuine, as with some spurious Zombies and Yardbirds), weather shut things down, or, far more common, teenagers smoked dope, the police moved in, and violence ensued. But there was just too much money to be made, whether the event went off or not, so they kept happening. The promoters of the Aquarian Exposition, in White Lake, New York, called themselves the Woodstock Music and Art Fair and announced their event for August 15–18. This wouldn't have attracted much attention initially, but several factors came into play: first, one of the promoters, Michael Lang, had already pulled off a well-publicized, semi-successful festival earlier in the year, in Miami; second, looking at a map, this wasn't actually Woodstock, but it was *near* Woodstock, and everyone knew that's where Dylan lived! Except for the Woody Guthrie memorial concert, nobody'd seen Dylan playing out, but now he'd announced that he'd play the Isle of Wight Festival, in Britain, at the end of August. Well, if he was playing again, why wouldn't he play in his hometown? And secretive as he was, he wouldn't announce it, would he? Dylanology by now had become as complex and rumor-ridden as Kremlinology (our government's "scientific" approach to decoding the Soviet Union's complex domestic political moves), with one notorious figure, A. J. Weberman, dropping out of college to study the "meaning" of Dylan's work and eventually going so far as to rummage through Dylan's garbage for "clues." So, although his management explicitly denied he'd appear, there was a bigger buzz going on. No lineup had been announced as the event got closer, but there were town council meetings aplenty in the surrounding communities as publicity for the festival of festivals filtered upstate. At the last minute, White Lake denied the promoters the land they'd hoped to use, and somehow Max Yasgur, a dairy farmer in nearby Bethel, heard about it and, out of the kindness of his heart (and an undisclosed amount of money from the promoters), let them use one of his large pastures. "If the generation gap is going to be closed," he told a Baltimore paper at the time, "we older people have to do more than we have done." Because August was prime tour time, there was little problem attracting acts from Britain (the Who, the Incredible String Band, Keef Hartley, Ten Years After), both sides of the West Coast divide (Jefferson Airplane, Sly and the Family Stone, Crosby, Stills and Nash, the Grateful Dead, Canned Heat, Janis Joplin, and the new sensation, the Santana Blues Band, who didn't even have an album out yet), New York (Jimi Hendrix, Richie Havens, Mountain), and the neighborhood (the Band, Paul Butterfield, Tim Hardin). How exactly to pay for this was a bit of a problem, one solved when coproducer Artie Kornfeld signed a deal for a film. This would turn out to save the organizers' asses and would form the basis for the Woodstock myth. Despite the posters promising "3 Days of Peace & Music," it wouldn't be an easy ride.

To start with, the site quickly became impossible to get to. It could very well be that despite advance ticket sales (which were approaching three hundred thousand), the promoters didn't think that parking would be necessary. Quite possibly they were unaware that human beings have to eat, because there was very little food on-site, and what there was was expensive. Toilets, too, were hard to find. Oh, and it rained. It rained on the first day and intermittently on the days to come, including a couple of drenching showers. This caused problems not only for the audience, who were, after all, in a cow pasture, but also for the electric instruments and the cables for the sound system, which, by today's standards, was very rudimentary and underpowered. But the bands played on: the first day was dedicated to folk music, sort of: a band called Sweetwater played, filling in for someone who hadn't yet arrived, and Ravi Shankar performed as the rain really started pounding down. Melanie Safka, a twenty-three-year-old who'd been pestering Lang to let her perform, got her lifetime break when the Incredible String Band refused to play in the rain; and Joan Baez, six months pregnant, got up and trilled her way through a set of mostly countryish material, closing with "We Shall Overcome" for her imprisoned draft-resisting husband.

The next day opened with Quill, a band whose album *Rolling Stone*'s reviewer had likened to a shotgun going off in a porcelain toilet. Country Joe McDonald then played a solo set because there was some trouble with the next act, who turned out to be Santana, although Carlos Santana didn't seem to be the source of the confusion; he thought he was going on later, so he'd taken some mescaline to be in a mellow mood by his scheduled midafternoon slot. As he was settling in to the trip, someone ordered him and his band onstage, no discussion possible. Baked as he was, he scored some valuable real estate in the subsequent film, and his career was launched. Other events that day were Canned Heat, playing a boogie jam for almost thirty minutes, a preview of much of the coming decade's live music; the Grateful Dead, whose microphones weren't grounded and delivered a mighty shock if anyone got too close; Janis Joplin, with her new Full

Tilt Boogie Band; Sly and the Family Stone, the festival's only rec-ognition of soul music—Sly had made an effort to reach out to the rock audience from the start of his career; and the Who, who were interrupted by Abbie Hoffman, who seemed to think mid-set was the right time to talk to the audience about John Sinclair's recent impris-onment for the two joints he'd been found with. Pete Townshend dis-agreed, of course; he kicked Hoffman in the butt and then bashed his head with his guitar, yelling, "Fuck off my fucking stage!" The band then finished the set, which Townshend later characterized as "fuckin' awful" and Roger Daltrey remembered as "the worst performance we ever did." That would have been it for the day, but things were so far behind that after the usual futzing around setting things up, the Jef-ferson Airplane took the stage as the sun rose and delivered a perfor-mance that was redolent of the acid they'd consumed, featuring their new, widely banned single, "Volunteers," which preached revolution, used the word *fuck,* and presaged the band's descent into incoherent politics, UFOlogy, and worse. Then came Joe Cocker (as yet unknown, although he had an album out), another act who was made by the film, doing his twitchy ersatz-soul shtick. Two guitar heroes were up next, Alvin Lee of Ten Years After and Johnny Winter, separated by the Band (whom Albert Grossman refused to let be recorded or filmed, and who endured shouts for Dylan the whole time they were onstage). Ten Years After provided another glimpse of the decade to come, with Lee's flashy but content-free playing, but at least Johnny Winter had some years of gigging at roadhouses in Texas's Golden Triangle (Beau-mont, Port Arthur, and Houston) behind him and some experience with black blues. The big buzz was the first public performance by Crosby, Stills and Nash, whose static harmonies were defeated by the sound system. Neil Young, whose first solo album was already out, joined them halfway through to show everyone there were no hard feelings, but they rerecorded the audio for the set for the film. Paul Butterfield showed off his new band and, inexplicably, was followed by Sha Na Na, a camped-up comedy oldies group that had spun off from the Columbia University Glee Club. Sadly, their appearance in the film made their career, too. Finally, as Monday dawned, Jimi Hen-drix, who'd waited patiently to show off the new group he'd formed with air force buddy Billy Cox on bass, Experience holdover Mitch Mitchell on drums, a rhythm guitarist and some percussionists, which he called Gypsy Sun and Rainbows, went on. Much has been made of his performance of "The Star-Spangled Banner," with writers seeing it as rock's ultimate expression of anger at the Vietnam War, but in fact it was an old stalwart in his set. More important was how few people actually heard it: hippies they may have been, but it was Monday by now, and a lot of people had to get back to work, so Hendrix played to only a couple of thousand people out of the estimated four hundred thousand who'd eventually shown up.

Over the years, Woodstock has assumed a disproportionate importance in the myth of "the sixties." Its anthem was written by Joni Mitchell, watching news reports from her Manhattan hotel room: she was booked onto Dick Cavett's late-night talk show, which, the way her albums had been selling (they hadn't been), was much-needed exposure. She hadn't been invited to perform at Woodstock, but she was certainly in a position to pull strings if she'd wanted to. Her manager, Elliot Roberts, counseled her to save her voice for the Cavett show and not risk going to the festival only to find she was unable to get out. (The Jefferson Airplane, on the other hand, took a helicopter to New York City and appeared on Cavett alongside her.)

Another thing worth noting was that the Hog Farm, a commune that had evolved out of Ken Kesey's Merry Pranksters, headed by Wavy Gravy (former stand-up comedian Hugh Romney) showed up, erected a tent, processed bad trips, and fed at least some of the crowd for free. But flashy guitarists aside, the real prophetic moment, one that would echo the dichotomy at the heart of the next thirty years, took root. At some point, a hundred thousand gate-crashers—some of whom rationalized their actions by the idea that the music was made by their peers and, thus, belonged to them and that paying for it was bullshit, man— tore down the site's fences. On the other side was the very real necessity of performers making a living and the business's need to exploit that need for profit. "Woodstock was created for wallets," Wavy Gravy said years later. "It was designed to make bucks. And then the universe took over and did a little dance." This was true enough, but George Clinton, who was also there, noted that "People say Woodstock was the beginning. It wasn't. It was the end. Everything was for sale. No more 'Hey, brother, have a joint, let me lay a tab of this acid on you.' It was 'Wanna *buy* some weed? Wanna *buy* some acid?' And when you went back home, pretty soon that's the way it was on the street." The Woodstock film, which helped pay off the three-million-dollar loss the promoters suffered in the immediate aftermath, was released in March 1970, and eventually grossed fifty million. Despite its three-hour length, you could see it in a movie theater (with clean toilets), where, well-fed and relaxed in a nice seat, you could hear expertly re-mixed sound and sigh with nostalgia over director Michael Wadleigh's wistful shots of young love and grooving youth, and not even get wet. Hell, if you were so inclined, you could smoke a joint in your car be-fore you went in, or time an acid trip so you were peaking when your favorite act came on.

When Abbie Hoffman interrupted the Who's Woodstock set, they were in the middle of playing excerpts from the album they'd put out in the spring, the much-anticipated, much-talked-about (mostly by Townshend, who was beloved of the rock and underground press: ask him a question, and he'd talk and talk, coherently and intelligently at that) "rock opera," *Tommy*. This was a career-defining release: even today, the remains of the band (Townshend and Daltrey, dubbed "The Two" by sarcastic fans) play a suite from it as part of their show. It was also sprawling—it took up two LPs—and fairly incoherent. The plot involves the title character, a "deaf, dumb and blind kid," who becomes a celebrity with his pinball skills. He is exploited by numer-ous folks around him (and molested by his pervy uncle) and finally wins some sort of release and redemption, all announced by crashing guitars and Keith Moon's amped-up military drumming. It had an amazing impact, though; this was "rock as art" writ large at last, and the band announced that it would be performed in full at the Metro-politan Opera (which it was, in 1970, but not before it had been done elsewhere), which led to several songs being dropped from live per-formances. And songs they were, too: unlike a regular opera, where a drama with a plot is presented like a sung play, *Tommy* contained no recitative to help explain the plot, and the players are the band, who obviously couldn't act parts while playing their instruments. It would properly be called a suite, but the idea of a rock opera was already in the air (notably in Keith West's 1967 British hit single "Excerpt from a Teenage Opera," which never saw the light of day as a finished work), so nobody caviled. It would be both the millstone around the band's neck and the pole of pretentiousness against which they continued to write clever, arty pop songs, as they did with the 1971 album *Who's Next*, which came before their next "opera," *Quadrophenia*, in 1973, as well as an ongoing project, *Lifehouse*, that was never wholly realized. All this material was based on Townshend's recent attachment to the guru Meher Baba, an Indian who hadn't spoken since 1925, and who had had a high profile and many followers in the West since the 1930s. *Tommy* inevitably led to more "rock operas" and more thematic pretension among lesser groups in the years to come. Soon enough, "concept albums" became popular.

The other important album, already recorded by the time of Woodstock but not released until the following month, was the Band's follow-up to *Music from Big Pink*, simply titled *The Band*. It would be simplistic to say that this one LP gave birth to the genre of "Americana" that started showing up in the 1990s—for one thing, that would downplay the post-Byrds groups in Los Angeles, who were at least creating the space for this album to exist—but it did have a titanic impact that's still being felt. The brown cover, with its sepia-tinted black-and-white photo of the band and its simple title, was as understated as the music within. The twelve songs were all credited to Robbie Robertson, the Band's guitarist, and their titles all evoked the American past: "Across the Great Divide," "Up On Cripple Creek," "Look Out Cleveland," "King Harvest (Has Surely Come)," and the most covered of them all, "The Night They Drove Old Dixie Down." In his book *Invisible Republic*, Greil Marcus lays out the connections between this album, Dylan's basement tapes with the Band, and Harry Smith's six-LP *Anthology of American Folk Music*, which was an ur-text of the folk revival; Marcus imagines the latter as a map or story concerning "the old, weird America." Laying needle to vinyl for the first time on *The Band* took the listener right there. "With *The Band* album, that's when I really knew who we were," Robbie Robertson said later. "This is when I said 'This is what we sound like, this is what we do.'"

And to a lot of fans, this was what *they* sounded like, if only they could have done it, and this is what *they* wanted to do, somehow. The album was redolent of a better, simpler America at a time when the country was beginning to feel the pain of a changing society. And it came out at about the same time that the other group Danny Fields had found in Detroit, the Stooges, released their first album, which led off with the words "It's 1969, okay / War across the USA." That was true, too.

chapter five

INVENTING "THE SIXTIES"

Memories of a free festival: Cutting the fence at Woodstock
(Photo © Baron Wolman)

As for Britain, if there was a war raging, it was a fairly polite one. Neither the Beatles (who'd retired from live performance, although they never announced it) nor the Stones (who were preparing a new album followed by a U.S. tour) were at Woodstock, but the Beatles, at least, were keeping busy. There was a new "Beatles" single, "The Ballad of John and Yoko," which didn't sound like everyone in the band was on it (and they weren't: it was John and Paul overdubbing) and detailed the travails of the couple, who'd gotten married in Gibraltar on March 20. They stayed on the rock long enough for the papers to be signed—Gibraltar is a British possession, so they were on British soil—and then jetted off to Amsterdam, where the first part of their honeymoon consisted of a "Bed-In," in which they lay in bed in matching white pajamas, invited the press in, and talked endlessly of peace. Room service brought meals, and allegedly the couple never left the bed except to go to the bathroom. Staying there for a week as members of the press filed in and out, the couple rambled on about nonviolence and the scourge of war. Somehow the single rose into the top 10 and was followed by a much better single, credited to something called the Plastic Ono Band, "Give Peace a Chance," recorded during yet another Bed-In, this one at the Queen Elizabeth Hotel in Montreal, after the couple had appeared at a "rock & roll revival" show in Toronto and been denied entrance to the United States because of Lennon's drug conviction (and because the FBI quietly considered him a subversive). Seeing another opportunity for some peace publicity, they invited the press yet again, and recorded the single, helped by the talents of Tommy Smothers, who played acoustic guitar, and the voices of Timothy Leary, Rabbi Abraham Feinberg, and the Canadian chapter of the Radha Krishna Temple. This ramshackle production, however, not only launched a hit but also became an anthem that's still sung at peace marches and other protests today. Just as important to what was to come for the Beatles, though, was Paul McCartney's marriage the week before Woodstock to photographer Linda Eastman, a wealthy New York–based photographer who'd taken some nice portraits of Paul and whose father was an imposing entertainment lawyer whose clients included trombonist Tommy Dorsey and painter Robert Rauschenberg. Paul and Linda had no intention of making their marriage a spectacle, and Paul and his new father-in-law hit it off right away.

All the Beatles, though, jumped into the Apple label immediately, coming up with projects. First out of the gate was a single, "Those Were the Days," by a winsome Welsh teenager, Mary Hopkin, who'd done some TV and whom model Twiggy had suggested to Paul as a natural. The song is an old Russian showbiz number, cloyingly sentimental, and with a bombastic, overbusy arrangement, both of which were to become frequent hallmarks of McCartney's own work. It went to number two, the best Hopkin ever did. Next up was a project from a non-Beatle: Peter Asher was helping run the day-to-day activities of Apple and early in 1968, he heard from a friend of a friend, a New York–based singer and songwriter named James Taylor, who'd been in a band with Asher's friend Danny Kortchmar. Taylor had heard that Apple was looking for acts, Kortchmar had provided the connection, and Taylor just showed up at Apple with a demo he'd recorded a couple of days earlier. Thus began the saga of *James Taylor*, an album that took forever to put together, what with its star's peripatetic ways and penchant for heroin. Paul McCartney and George Harrison (along with Asher) played on the single "Carolina in My Mind," which did absolutely nothing when it finally came out. Also on the Apple label was a brass band single of a theme song Paul had written for a TV show;

another by a Welsh band, the Iveys, "Maybe Tomorrow," which made gentle waves in America, none in Britain, and went top 20 in Holland; a guy who called himself Brute Force, who George thought was a genius songwriter—well, he *had* been in the Tokens—and who made a record called "King of Fuh" (think about it) that EMI refused even to manufacture—a few private copies were run off; and a survivor of the Mersey Beat sound, Jackie Lomax, formerly of the fab Undertakers, who recorded a song George wrote in India, "Sour Milk Sea," backed by George, Paul, Ringo, and keyboardist Nicky Hopkins, with Eric Clapton on lead. Finally, there was Billy Preston (another discovery of George's), who'd been playing gospel keyboards since he was a preteen and who had backed up Little Richard, Sam Cooke, and Ray Charles; Preston's single "That's the Way God Planned It" featured Harrison, Keith Richards on bass, Eric Clapton on lead, and Ginger Baker on drums. Despite all that, it hardly set the charts on fire.

Over on the Stones' pitch, things weren't going all that well. Brian Jones was no longer a Stone by midyear, which was one way of putting it: actually, Jones had been gone for a while, at least mentally. His drug use had gotten to the point of rendering him incapable of playing, and he spent some recording sessions blacked out on the studio floor. The Stones were busy recording an album in advance of their upcoming American tour, and Brian's drug bust still hadn't been sorted out, so between that and his increasingly fragile physical condition, there was no way he was going to tour with them anyway. Keith Richards had stepped in and swiped Jones's German girlfriend, Anita Pallenberg, and finally the band, stymied by a nonplaying guitarist, asked twenty-year-old Mick Taylor, a recent departure from John Mayall's latest crop of Bluesbreakers, if he'd like the job. As a matter of fact, he would. Brian must have been hurt—after all, he'd started the band and was the impetus for their playing blues—but between his worsening asthma and his near-constant disorientation, he'd become a liability. On June 8, a thirty-minute meeting among most of the Stones (Bill Wyman wasn't there) and Brian at Cotchford Farm, Jones's estate (formerly owned by A. A. Milne, author of *Winnie-the-Pooh*) did the trick. Brian issued a statement: "I no longer see eye to eye with the others over the discs we are cutting. We no longer communicate musically. The Stones' music is not to my taste anymore. I have a desire to play my own brand of music rather than that of others, no matter how much I appreciate their musical concepts. The only solution is to go our separate ways, but we shall still remain friends. I love those fellows." This love wouldn't last long: on July 3, 1969, Brian was found dead in the swimming pool at Cotchford Farm by his live-in nurse, Janet Lawson, who called out to the other two people at the house, Brian's girlfriend, Anna; and a forty-four-year-old builder, Frank Thorogood, who was staying in the guesthouse while rebuilding a wall on the estate. He and Anna fished Brian out and started artificial respiration, while Janet called an ambulance. The paramedics worked on him for thirty minutes, but they finally lost him. An inquest found that a combination of alcohol and asthma medication had killed him, and despite an alleged 2009 deathbed confession from Thorogood, who said he'd held Brian's head underwater during a drunken argument, the man to whom he allegedly confessed denied he'd said anything. Occam's razor says the coroner's verdict of misadventure was right. The Stones had already booked London's Hyde Park for a free concert on July 5, so it became both a memorial to Brian and the introduction of the Stones' new guitarist. Mick Jagger opened the Stones' set by reading Shelley's elegy on the death of John Keats, "Adonais," and then tried to release nearly a thousand white butterflies, which, having been sitting cooped up in sacks all day in the sun, were mostly dead.

The Stones then went back to work. They'd tossed out a single, "Honky Tonk Women," whose B-side was a teaser for their next album, "You Can't Always Get What You Want," an elaborate production aided by Jack Nitzsche, featuring French horn and organ by Al Kooper, the London Bach Choir, and a plaintive vocal by Mick, who was already headed to Australia with Marianne Faithfull to shoot *Ned Kelley*, a biopic about the legendary Australian outlaw. On arrival, Marianne collapsed at their hotel in Sydney, eventually going into a coma for several days. Blood tests revealed overdoses of numerous sedatives, and when she awoke, her mother whisked her off to a Swiss clinic. Mick had a film to make (and a TV special, called *The Rolling Stones Rock and Roll Circus*, in which the Stones; the Who;

up-and-coming prog band Jethro Tull; Taj Mahal; Marianne Faith-full; something called the Dirty Mac, featuring Eric Clapton and John and Yoko; and of course the Stones, and which was filmed in 1968 but was still waiting to be edited and finally emerged in 2004 on DVD) and an American tour to start at Fort Collins, Colorado, on November 7. They wisely gave Memphis journalist Stanley Booth exclusive access to cover the tour, and the resultant book (titled *Dance with the Devil* or *The True Adventures of the Rolling Stones,* depending on which edition you find), which took Booth fifteen years to write, documents the first really decadent rock tour: there was nobody else touring yet who was on the level of the Stones, and they took full advantage. After the tour, they repaired to Muscle Shoals to do some recording while working out the details of the free concert in San Francisco they'd announced for December 6. The idea was a West Coast Woodstock in Golden Gate Park, but when the City of San Francisco nixed that, the event was moved to Sears Point Raceway. Then that fell through, and somebody found a man named Dick Carter, who owned another racetrack, the Altamont Speedway, in a rather remote location in the East Bay. Santana; the Grateful Dead; the Flying Burrito Brothers; Crosby, Stills, Nash and Young (Neil Young had joined the group officially by then); and the Jefferson Airplane were the featured acts. "It was a disaster from the start," said Ian Stewart, the "sixth Stone." "It went wrong from the minute we left Muscle Shoals." What happened that day has been tossed about ever since, but at the root of it was the fact that the Dead got their pals the Hells Angels the gig as stage security in exchange for five hundred dollars' worth of beer. That was just one of the substances that came into play that day. Speed had been part of the San Francisco scene since the "Summer of Love," and along with increased alcohol use, especially of cheap wine and potent wine-like beverages, a powerful sedative called methaqualone, sold under the name Quaalude (Mandrax in Britain) was all the rage. It calmed you down without incapacitating you, was reputedly an aid to seduction (or, more accurately, date rape), and reacted viciously with alcohol. This, along with cold, damp weather, overcrowding, and a bunch of Hells Angels whacked out on any substance they could get their hands on (including a bag of acid, courtesy of Owsley Stanley) made

for one of the most horrific concerts so far. Veteran San Francisco journalist Joel Selvin put together a minute-by-minute chronicle in his
Altamont book, aided a lot by footage from the Maysles brothers' documentary film of the concert. The most memorable moment among
the several scenes of violence was the fatal stabbing of Meredith
Hunter, a tall, skinny, eighteen-year-old black kid in a lime-green suit,
by Alan Passaro, a Hells Angel. Hunter, pretty wasted on speed, had
worked his way to the front of the crowd and pulled a gun. Passaro
may or may not have felt a duty to do his job. Hunter may or may not
have intended to shoot Mick Jagger, as someone in the crowd yelled
just before the murder. The Maysles' film, *Gimme Shelter,* has it all,
including a moment of Jagger watching the editing in the studio and
reacting as he sees the altercation between Hunter and the Angel. The
new Stones album, released the day before Altamont, had a title that
was suddenly problematic: *Let It Bleed.* It was a record that deepened
the band's identification with violence and evil, from the title cut to
the remarkable "Gimme Shelter," in which a background vocalist,
Merry Clayton, stepped out in a hair-raising duet with Jagger that sent
talent scouts after her for her own album. (Lou Adler's Ode label won
the race, and she made an album for him. It went nowhere.) Equally
edgy was "Midnight Rambler," a glorification of darkness that would
become a regular part of the Stones' live shows.

Hot on the heels of "The Ballad of John and Yoko," the Beatles released another weak single, "Come Together," on which John poached
some of Chuck Berry's "You Can't Catch Me," and George, on the
B-side, contributed the lovely "Something," which was also something
of a poach of James Taylor's Apple album cut "Something in the Way
She Moves." Just to keep his hand in, John's Plastic Ono Band released
"Cold Turkey," which shocked fans with the realization that with
drugs, too, John was in touch with the times. It may be that Yoko had
introduced him to heroin, or he may have done it to himself, with her
taking it on as part of their partnership in art. Whatever the case, during the summer of 1969, John and Yoko were addicted, just as Yoko
became pregnant and Paul managed to get the band together for a new
album, which he'd titled *Abbey Road,* after the address for EMI's famous studios. Yoko, sick, lay on a bed in the studio reading and knit-

ting as the band worked on the record. John had offered "Cold Turkey" to the Beatles, and they'd turned him down. Whether the couple had actually kicked the drug cold (as Yoko later maintained) or at a private clinic in London, they weren't hooked for the moment. *Abbey Road*, though, was the end of the Beatles—and sounded like it. Many of the songs weren't finished, and George Martin and Paul McCartney did a masterful job of cobbling eight of them together on the second side of the album, which ended with a song called "The End." (It wasn't: the album actually ends with a twenty-three-second snippet called "Her Majesty.") They got *Abbey Road* out for Christmas—Lennon told *Rolling Stone* that it was "a good album but nothing special"—so, now they could turn their attention to another project. On January 30, 1969, the band had gathered on the roof of Apple's Savile Row headquarters building to do an open-air show for a tiny audience, some passersby, and a film crew who was going to make it part of a documentary about the Beatles recording an album. A single, "Get Back," came out a few months later, leading to hopes that the band really was getting back to basics and might tour soon. The simplicity bit was true: the idea was to do an album with no additional personnel and no overdubs. (Touring, considering that the band's interpersonal relations were at an all-time low, with Lennon and McCartney feuding almost constantly, was out of the question.) A couple of tunes were added the next day—the police had ended the outdoor show, but the missing tunes were led by Paul's piano, which was unsuitable for a snowy rooftop—and the album, but not the film, was complete. It was worked on in the early months of 1970, and in March, a single, "Let It Be," came out, and it was announced that that was the title of the film, which would come out in May. John, freed from the Beatles at last, wrote a song, "Instant Karma," at the end of January, and ran into the studio with Phil Spector, who'd been hovering around him, producing. The song shot into the top 10, and in gratitude, Lennon gave Spector the *Let It Be* album tapes to remix. Uh-oh. Paul, encouraged by his own wife, was busy at their Scottish farm readying his own solo album, which he intended to release before *Let It Be*. When he heard Spector's work—among other things, he'd put a huge orchestral backing on "The Long and Winding Road," one of Paul's songs and the single after "Let it Be"—he flipped out, raging at John and Allen Klein, who'd engineered the introduction to Spector. In truth, it was partially his own fault: while making his solo album he'd refused to attend Apple meetings. And there was another thing: Allen Klein, who, for a short while, they'd shared with the Rolling Stones.

In early 1969, John Lennon had granted an interview about Apple to freelancer Ray Coleman that appeared in *Disc and Music Echo,* one of the "inkies," the name given to the weekly pop press whose pages were so cheaply printed the ink came off on your hands. "We don't have half the money people think we have," Lennon told Coleman. "It's got to be business first, we realize that now . . . If it carries on like this, all of us will be broke in the next six months." Klein had been working with the Stones for years, and yet he'd obsessed over running the Beatles' business affairs, so this was just what he'd been waiting to hear since Brian Epstein's death. Eight days after the Coleman interview, he was knocking on the door of John and Yoko's suite at London's Dorchester Hotel. The three of them felt one another out. A short while later, Klein had been retained to handle John and Yoko's finances. John candidly told Klein that Paul had retained his father- and brother-in-law, Lee and John Eastman, on behalf of "the Beatles," whose existence seemed to be ever more in question. Klein then met with John, George, and Ringo, and presented them with some ideas about handling their money. George and Ringo had previously met with John Eastman, and hadn't been impressed, Ringo seeing him as "pleasant but harmless" and George thinking him flat out incapable of the job. Paul, for his part, detested Klein, as, possibly, did the Eastmans, who'd been at entertainment law for a long time and saw the thirty-six-year-old interloper as an opportunist. But Klein needed the Beatles, not only for his own ego but also for additional income: the deal he'd negotiated with Andrew Loog Oldham, the Rolling Stones, and Decca Records would expire in 1970, and with Mick Jagger negotiating with Prince Rupert Loewenstein, a merchant banker whom he knew socially, about perhaps taking over Klein's position, as well as chatting with Ahmet Ertegun while the band was in Muscle Shoals in the days before Altamont, things looked ominous for Klein's continued association with them. But the battles were just beginning, and although it wouldn't be until McCartney's 1970 solo album that the Beatles officially ceased to exist on paper, the end came around the time of McCartney's solo album, which contained a mini self-interview where he said he loved and respected John but that Lennon's work "doesn't give me any pleasure." He answered simply "no" to questions about another Beatles album, further Lennon-McCartney songwriting work, and whether he missed the Beatles and George Martin. Meanwhile, the other guys were busy with solo albums themselves, and nobody could fail to notice the simple ad for *Let It Be* in *Rolling Stone*, which was a picture of the record's cover and the words "Manufactured by Apple, an ABKCO® company," the abbreviation for Allen B. Klein Corporation. The business problems would continue for years, both despite and because of Allen Klein. The Beatles would live forever, in the fans' hearts and in the courts.

As for the Stones, they blew out their contract with Decca/London Records via what would become a time-honored tradition of a live album featuring a solid batch of their hits—a very good live album, it must be said, entitled *'Get Your Ya-Ya's Out!'*, recorded on November 27–28, 1969, at Madison Square Garden. Any further obligations could be taken care of with a greatest hits and miscellaneous album, which duly appeared. Champing at the bit, the band signed with their own record label, Rolling Stones Records, through Atlantic, and on the advice of Prince Rupert, who was part of the new regime, they began spending more time at the Villa Nellcôte, in Villefranche-sur-Mer, just east of Nice, on the French Riviera, for tax purposes. Mick married Bianca Pérez-Mora Macias, a Nicaraguan socialite, after dumping Marianne Faithfull and having a fling with background vocalist Marsha Hunt. On the verge of releasing their first Rolling Stones Records album, *Sticky Fingers*, with its Andy Warhol–designed cover featuring a picture of Joe Dallessandro's denim-clad crotch (with an actual zipper), Decca informed them that they owed the label one more single, so Mick and Keith got together and recorded a blues song, featuring the best blues-singing Mick had done in ages, and delivered it on a take-it-or-leave-it basis. "Schoolboy Blues" was its innocuous title, but when it hit its "Where can I get my cock sucked / Where can I get my ass fucked" chorus—the song is commonly known as "Cocksucker Blues," which was also the title of Robert Frank's documentary on the Stones' 1971 tour, as a result—that was that. Their actual next single, off their new album, was "Brown Sugar," which may not have had dirty words, but whose racial and sexual content was hardly any better.

By this time, the baby boom had taken over, and the world of popular music had definitely installed rock as the default mode. Record companies had learned quite a bit about how to market it. Ads from the period in both the trade and consumer press were emphasizing a commonality among consumers through consumption of rock music. A mid-1968 ad for a Country Joe and the Fish album in *Rolling Stone* read, "Country Joe and the Fish are you. The things that you are: questioning, idealistic, involved, concerned with the love, the confusion, and the excitement of the life you live today." Columbia had a bunch of notorious ads. "If you won't listen to your parents, The Man, or the Establishment," one read, "why should you listen to us?" The answer: because we're you, with albums by Big Brother and the Holding Company and the Chambers Brothers; the *Super Session* album; and the Small Faces' famous swan song, *Odgens' Nut Gone Flake* (which came in a round album cover with nineteenth-century graphics), depicted in the ad. Another Columbia ad showed a mixed-gender, racially diverse set of youth sitting in a circle, one of them with a hand to his mouth, suggesting that he's smoking a joint: "Know who your friends are. And look and see and be together. Then listen." And then there was the most notorious one: "The Man can't bust our music," which features a bunch of kids in a holding cell along with their oddly worded protest signs ("Take Hold"). In that one, the records being advertised were all classical: Charles Ives, Edgard Varèse, Karlheinz Stockhausen, Terry Riley's revolutionary composition *In C,* and the Moog triumph *Switched-On Bach.* Warners's ads were even more subversive, positing an audience that knew better and that rose above the top 40 to appreciate artists who made a difference and who were signed to a record company that happily lost money to further the artists' careers. This project was overseen by Stan Cornyn, who'd been with the company since 1958, mostly writing liner notes, but whose approach when he became director of creative services at the label definitely made the Warners name stand out. As he explained it to *Billboard,* "From the start, I knew I didn't want to write the kind of ads that everyone else was writing in the record business . . . My way was to do something different: some white space, a catchy headline, a couple of paragraphs, a small photograph, some wit, all the while embracing the artist . . . The attitude of these ads was such that many people believed that Warner/Reprise was more interested in great music than great profits. Actually, we wanted both. But the ads accentuated the former[,] and over time, the company's reputation with the hip music-buying crowd was very positive." Among his memorable ads were a couple of "Pigpen Look-alike" contests to promote the first couple of Grateful Dead albums; the "How We Lost $35,509.50 on the 'Album of the Year' (Dammit)" ad for Van Dyke Parks's *Song Cycle;* and an offbeat promotion for Randy Newman's *Twelve Songs* album, headlined "Once you get used to it, his voice is really something," which noted that "These things don't happen overnight." Warners also offered two-dollar loss-leader double-album samplers with nonalbum tracks, singles, and oddities (Parks's music for the Ice Capades) and other mail-in promotions (a bag of Topanga Canyon dirt, for instance) to sell the label, which worked so well that within a couple of months, several other labels were copying it. It was a brilliant strategy, and it paid off. In the trades, Warners offered a book of "our most insulting ads, mostly from America's spicy underground press."

In mid-1969, another phenomenon hit the record business: a blank album cover with the words "Great White Wonder" stamped on it appeared in some record stores, and it proved to have a bunch of Dylan's "basement tapes" tunes on it, hardly studio quality, but unheard Dylan material nonetheless. Nobody knew who'd put it out (although, since all the tracks on the album came from a copy of a tape Dylan's publishing company had circulated to bands in the hope of having them cover the material, it wasn't as if a robbery had occurred), but it was scary enough that it existed. Soon, there was a live recording of the Stones entitled, *Live'r Than You'll Ever Be,* which some fans preferred to their official release; and a record of the Beatles at the Hollywood

Bowl (which *was* an outright theft from the Capitol vaults, given that the label had considered and then dropped the idea of issuing it; it finally relented in 1977) and some of the unissued tracks from the *Abbey Road* and *Let It Be* sessions. The bootleggers were brazen enough that they had their own labels: GWW, Trade Mark of Quality (its logo a pig), and even more brazen, The Rubber Dubber, a collective under the leadership of a guy with film studio experience and a high-end portable stereo recorder with two professional microphones, who issued stereo recordings of live concerts in Los Angeles and who argued that by paying for a seat, he'd been given permission to record the show. He also claimed to put a percentage of the label's earnings into an escrow account to pay the artists directly if they asked. Probably the apogee of his career came in 1971, when Atlantic, unhappy with the amount of studio vocal work it was faced with before it could release the live Crosby, Stills, Nash and Young album *4 Way Street*, offered to buy the Dubber's CSNY tapes, which were better than it had been able to get, with the advantage of being totally undoctored. The Dubber declined, but rock bootlegs were enough of a presence that when the Who released *Live at Leeds* in 1970, its cover was brown cardboard with the title rendered as a faux rubber stamp. It's only a slight exaggeration to say that it got so record companies worried when an act *wasn't* bootlegged: didn't the kids like him?

Boutique labels, as they came to be known, were booming. Capitol had given the Beatles Apple, and the Beach Boys had (briefly) had Brother. Now offering a label could be part of negotiations with whomever a label was signing. Warners gave Frank Zappa and his manager/partner Herb Cohen two labels: Straight and Bizarre, one for signings like Tim Buckley and Captain Beefheart and the other for Zappa's own musical projects. When Warners acquired the directionless Beach Boys, reviving the Brother label was part of the deal. And late in 1969, Denny Cordell took on management of Leon Russell, a longtime studio musician for Phil Spector and the Beach Boys who was now putting a band together for new star Joe Cocker, resulting in another label, Shelter, which started out being distributed by Capitol but later switched to ABC. All these labels were kept fairly autonomous from the companies that distributed them, as long as they kept shifting units. Meanwhile, transatlantic labels looked for ways to get their product released in the States. Island, founded by confectionery heir Chris Blackwell, a white Jamaican in London who had made a small fortune releasing Jamaican music to the city's immigrant population, started surveying the capital's rock scene and began to handle some fairly large players. Initially, A&M had first refusal on Island product, which is how Fairport Convention and Spooky Tooth wound up there, at which point Island switched the deal to Atlantic, which was aggressively acquiring British talent in the wake of Led Zeppelin's success.

Probably the oddest trend of 1970 was the so-called "rock-and-roll revival." The "love crowd" discovered that it had a past, and suddenly there were "revival" groups like Sha Na Na and Flash Cadillac, and older performers hooking up with youngsters, as Carl Perkins did with NRBQ, an unclassifiable bar band who'd signed to Columbia. Cat Mother and the All Night Newsboys, a New York band produced by Jimi Hendrix, put out a single, "Good Old Rock 'n' Roll," an inane medley of five classic tunes, including "Sweet Little Sixteen" and "Blue Suede Shoes," that got to number 21; and rockabilly star Gene Vincent (of "Be-Bop-a-Lula" fame) appeared from out of nowhere with an album of new songs on Dandelion, a boutique label at Elektra run by the innovative British radio personality John Peel. Frank Zappa had been ahead of the trend in 1968, with his tribute to his youth, *Cruising with Reuben & the Jets,* which included a new recording of a song he'd written for the Penguins, "Memories of El Monte," after the El Monte Legion Stadium, an East LA venue where many a vocal group show had taken place. For those who needed an education in the classics, SSS International, a label headed by Nashville wild man Shelby S. Singleton, who'd made a fortune in 1968 with Jeannie C. Riley's recording of Tom T. Hall's "Harper Valley P.T.A." when it unexpectedly topped the pop charts for weeks, bought Sun Records and was putting out cheapo collections of its classic artists. Although, for practically nothing, anybody with the patience to riffle through the two-dollar bargain bins at drugstores, department stores, and even some record stores, where cut out albums and discount labels from the majors were sold, could amass Chuck Berry's entire Chess catalogue (and a lot of Muddy Waters's and Howlin' Wolf's, among others on Chess), much of Buddy Holly's, Sun albums by Johnny Cash and Roy Orbison, and plenty of other classic material. And a label called In-crease started issuing the year-by-year *Cruisin'* series of albums, which not only showcased the hits of each year, but also formatted them as radio shows with classic disc jockeys talking and playing vintage com-mercials in between. There was much talk (and little action) about "getting back to basics," which hardly fazed the "progressive rock" crowd.

Brian Jones had also started a trend: toward the end of the sum-mer of 1970, Canned Heat's Al "Blind Owl" Wilson, twenty-seven, had succumbed to downers and alcohol; and, shockingly, Jimi Hen-drix was found dead on September 18 in his London apartment, from aspirating his own vomit after accidentally mixing alcohol and sleep-ing pills. He, too, was only twenty-seven, he hadn't made out a will, and his business affairs were such a mess that it took years to settle his estate. This resulted in a lot of unauthorized records appearing, and legendary tapes (supposedly one of him jamming with Miles Da-vis in Woodstock, for instance) being sought after, as well as "Hen-drix was murdered" conspiracy theories, fueled in part by the death of one of his managers, Michael Jeffrey, in a mysterious plane crash a few years later. Then, on October 4, 1970, while laying down tracks for her next album, *Pearl*, Janis Joplin died of a heroin overdose in a Hollywood motel. She was also twenty-seven. There was one more to go: The Doors had been living a paradox, putting out albums that were increasingly dubious in quality but that went gold nonetheless and having to put up with an increasingly erratic Jim Morrison, who was often so drunk onstage that he was an embarrassment at best and a riot-causing provocateur at worst, which caused him to be arrested sev-eral times, twice for whipping his penis out during a performance (or so it was alleged; certainly he simulated doing so). *Morrison Hotel*, their fifth gold record in a row, had been a slight step up from the *Soft Pa-rade* album, which was practically MOR, and they seemed to be get-ting back to form on *L.A. Woman*, scheduled for early 1971 release, when Morrison quit the band at the end of 1970. On July 3, 1971, his lifeless body was found in the bathtub of the Paris flat on rue Beautreillis that he and his wife, Pamela, were renting. Earlier in the day Morrison had been drinking at a bar named Rock and Roll Circus, on the rue de Seine, where he was a regular. He was waiting for a shipment of heroin to take back to his wife, who was a regular user, while he used only it casually. By the time the dealer's courier showed up, Morrison was pretty drunk, and curious: he took some of the heroin into the club's bathroom to check it out. Unaccustomed as he was to powerful, uncut Marseille Golden Triangle heroin, he snorted some, and it killed him. Eventually the club's manager realized that Morrison hadn't come out, and he went into the bathroom to find the singer unconscious. The club had been under surveillance for a while, so the owner knew he had to get Morrison out of there. One of his friends escorted the "drunk" Morrison to his apartment, where his friend Alain Rosnay and film director Agnès Varda filled the bathtub with ice water and put him in, hoping to revive him. He was already dead, however, and the coroner, finding no needle marks on his body, ascribed the death to "heart failure." The death wasn't announced to the general public until July 9, by which time Morrison had already been buried in the legendary Père Lachaise Cemetery, where his grave quickly became a blight thanks to people leaving drugs and alcohol at the site. The Doors announced they'd continue as a trio. Finally, almost nobody noticed when it was announced that, on October 12, rockabilly singer Gene Vincent, his latest relationship over, had gone on a drinking binge and, while visiting his mother, vomited blood and fell face-first onto the floor, dead. He was thirty-six.

The Jimi/Janis/Jim deaths, along with Altamont and the Beatles' disbanding, have been widely regarded as the end of the Sixties, which is hardly true. Certainly the aesthetic that had powered the youth movement was still alive: the Allman Brothers (former names: the Allman Joys and the Hourglass), a band based around session guitarist Duane Allman and his brother, Gregg, were just getting started with their Southern take on the Grateful Dead's improvising (the Allmans being tighter and more blues-oriented, unsurprisingly); and Led Zeppelin was making albums of stylized blues that would inspire an entire genre of slowed-down, solo-oriented bands whose sound would become known as heavy metal. Still, things were changing: at the end of 1970, Led Zeppelin displaced the Beatles in *Melody Maker*'s year-end poll (the Fabs were number two, and the Stones in fifth place); the Dead repaid Warners' faith in them with a back-to-back duo of song-rather-than-jam-oriented albums, *Workingman's Dead* and *American Beauty*, which sold very well indeed and contained material that also went over well in concert.

The Jefferson Airplane, after two bombastic studio albums, a live album, and a greatest hits album, reorganized under Paul Kantner and Grace Slick, who fired the rest of the band and added a keyboardist; a new guitarist; a new drummer; bassist David Freiberg, from the increasingly confused Quicksilver; and weirdest of all, Papa John Creach, a fifty-three-year-old black violinist who had befriended the band's new drummer, Joey Covington. (Creach had played electric violin since the 1940s, with everyone from Nat King Cole to Greek dance bands.) The Airplane's former guitarist and bassist, Jorma Kaukonen and Jack Casady, formed a popular duo, Hot Tuna, who mostly jammed (acoustic or deafening electric) blues. The revamped Airplane renamed themselves the Jefferson Starship, and RCA gave them a gift of their own boutique label, which they called Grunt, where everyone concerned was able to indulge themselves with all manner of projects—and did.

Keeping track of all this was *Rolling Stone*, whose year-end circulation filing indicated an readership of 270,811, and whose pages pushed a rock-centric, determinedly San Franciscan agenda. The Sixties weren't dead, they were just filing incorporation papers.

New groups continued to pop up, sometimes with disastrous results. At the end of 1969, a couple of young music biz vets in London, Eddie Molton and Dave Robinson, started up a management firm called Famepushers, and put a classified ad in *Melody Maker*: "Young progressive management company require young songwriting group with own equipment." As usual, this resulted in an avalanche of tapes, mostly horrible, but one caught their ear: Kippington Lodge, from Tunbridge Wells. Robinson called them into his office, which he shared with a woman named Dot Burn-Forti, and went on about his experience and expertise, based on his having been a roadie for Jimi Hendrix and, later, an Irish group Hendrix had produced, Eire Apparent. The band hadn't quite solidified its sound, but they went over well live, and Robinson was impressed by a bunch of songwriting demos the band's bassist, a rangy fellow named Nick Lowe, had written for the meeting. Eventually, Famepushers took the band, who'd renamed themselves after their guitarist, Brinsley Schwarz; got them a deal with United Artists in England and Capitol in the States; and, for their world debut, managed to set up a showcase at Bill Graham's Fillmore East. They'd have two days in the country: April 4–5, 1970, but would play only on the fifth, doing an early and a late show. That day, an airplane chartered by Famepushers would deliver the cream of the British and Irish music press (accompanied by a few contest winners from a *Melody Maker* competition) to report on this Next Big Thing wowing the Yanks. It didn't turn out that way: the charter, an Aer Lingus plane, developed mechanical problems, delaying the trip and seriously injuring the split-second timing Famepushers had relied on. A replacement plane was ordered, but there were more delays. Famepushers provided drinks for the journalists, who happily accepted them. Finally, a plane was brought out and, hours late, the passengers boarded. With an 8:00 show to attend, they landed at Kennedy Airport, where they cleared customs and got into a fleet of twenty-two stretch limos. By the time the first cars got to the Fillmore, it was 8:15, and everyone had been traveling for seventeen hours. Meanwhile, Dave Robinson was trying to hold the curtain so that the press contingent would at least be in the building when the band went onstage, and complicating matters even more, the venue was refusing to let the film crew he'd hired to document the triumph set up their gear. At 8:25 the band, terrified at the size of the venue and underrehearsed, took the stage for their thirty-five-minute set. The Americans weren't expecting the band to sound quite so American, and were unimpressed, and the press, either tripping or drunk, sharpened their claws. (Brinsley Schwarz had opened that night for Van Morrison and Quicksilver, both of whom far outplayed them, although years later,

Nick Lowe remembered the midnight show as having gone very well.) The resulting coverage should have buried Dave Robinson, Famepushers, and Brinsley Schwarz. In fact, only Famepushers went down as a result of the boondoggle. Robinson and the band would be back.

"Rock" now ruled utterly and completely. Few were wondering where the "roll" had gone.

chapter six

I AM THE SONG THAT
MY ENEMY SINGS

Downbeat "sound," with Clement "Coxsone" Dodd at the microphone
(© Jean Bernard Sohiez/Urbanimage)

In 1964, Ahmet Ertegun went to a party. In fact, Ertegun being who he was, it's likely he went to many parties in 1964, but this one had been organized by Edward Seaga, the head of social welfare and economic development for Jamaica, to showcase the island nation's music. It was held in Kingston, at Ken Khouri's Federal Records studio, the nation's most high-tech operation, capable of recording and pressing records under one roof (although they had to send out for mastering) and also providing printing for labels and album covers. The island's music, along with tourism, would be the focus of Jamaica's national pavilion at the upcoming 1964–65 World's Fair in Flushing Meadows, Queens. Music at the event was provided by a band that earned most of its money playing calypso and American pop tunes at upscale tourist resorts, Byron Lee and the Dragonaires. In New York they'd be backing up such hot Jamaican artists as teenage Jimmy Cliff (who'd had a smash hit the year before with "Miss Jamaica," celebrating Carole Crawford, who'd won the 1963 Miss World contest), Millie Small (whose song "My Boy Lollipop" had originally been recorded by Chris Blackwell on his Blue Beat label and was rocketing to the top of the U.S. charts, thanks to its being a huge hit in Cleveland and Detroit), and Prince Buster, a charismatic performer who owned a record store, jukebox repair shop, and studio on Orange Street, "the street of the beat," in Kingston. Ertegun flipped over the

music, which, he was told, was called "ska," a term of obscure prove-
nance that referred to a rhythm heavily accented on the second and
fourth beats of a 4/4 measure. Not only did he flip, but he went into
Federal's studio with his top engineer, Tom Dowd, and cut forty tracks
by the Blues Busters, Stranger and Patsy, the Charmers, and the Maytals, none of which has ever surfaced but was referenced in a May 23
Billboard story headlined "Atlantic Hot on Ska." What did surface,
though, was an album, *Do the Ska*, by Byron Lee and the Dragonaires,
complete with a diagram on the front with numbered feet showing
you how to dance to it. It went nowhere, not even among the sizeable
West Indian communities in New York, Miami, and Baltimore, likely
because they'd already been exposed to less watered-down versions on
records sent from home and because, of course, they already knew how
to dance to it. Blackwell, for his part, saw a business opportunity, and
left Jamaica to set up a label in London, Island, which had licensing
agreements with numerous Jamaican producers, including first refusal
on all productions by Chinese Jamaican reggae producer Leslie Kong,
which turned out to be a very wise move.

   Jamaica had long had a music industry, first with productions for
regional offices of British labels and then, after independence in 1962,
for the flurry of independent labels that grew out of the country's
"sounds" (short for sound systems), which were owned and operated
by fiercely competing entrepreneurs. These entrepreneurs would set up
their sounds on "lawns," large grassy areas behind clubs, sometimes
dueling with exclusive records that were treated with great secrecy.
Some were American (Fats Domino and Memphis bluesman Roscoe
Gordon, whose eccentric piano style influenced ska tremendously) and
some were local, and the practice of keeping the titles secret involved
all manner of stratagems: scratching any visible information off a record's label, using test pressings on metal for local releases (many of
which had been recorded by the sound's operator), and blatantly rerecording a hit with one's own musicians. Sounds were large, loud, quite
heavy on the bass, and were operated by the owner, a "selecter," who
generally, in those days before cross faders, would have only one turntable, which necessitated manual dexterity to keep the flow going,
and a deejay, who had a microphone and would announce records, ex-

hort the crowd, and sometimes talk over the record. Those in attendance varied in age but not economic status: they tended to be poor folks, "sufferahs," as they called themselves, and lots of them aspired to hearing themselves over the sound's speakers. Or *someone's* sound's speakers: a couple of record producers held open auditions once a week: one by one, young hopefuls would show up to sing a song they'd written or stolen from somewhere, in the hope of scoring a record deal.

None of this was on display at the World's Fair in Queens, which had been carefully sanitized to keep that element at arm's length. Byron Lee was a chubby Chinese Jamaican—Chinese immigrants owned a lot of businesses in Jamaica at the time, including "Chineyman shops," as black Jamaicans called them, ghetto grocers and liquor stores that doubled as bars—Jimmy Cliff and Millie Small were cute teenagers, and among the dancers who'd show you how to "do the ska" at the fair was the aforementioned Miss World, Carole Crawford. As for the band, they referred to the stuff they played as ska-lypso. Back in Jamaica, though, the real players were all sorts of people. Arthur "Duke" Reid, an ex-policeman, owned a liquor store and a sound and knew just enough people on both sides of the law to keep the peace; Clement "Sir Coxsone" Dodd, a jazz fanatic from way back, would bring records to listen to at work in his mother's liquor store; Cecil Bustamente Campbell, known by all as "Prince Buster," was primarily a sound operator, repairing amplifiers and jukeboxes in his shop on Orange Street. His parents had made him get a certification in carpentry before they'd assent to his being in the music business, and it came in handy for constructing and repairing speaker boxes. Sir Coxsone (so called because of his resemblance to a cricketer of that name) operated Studio One, one of the first Jamaican labels and studios, and Buster helped him with that and Sir Coxsone's Downbeat Sound System. The first three ska records appeared in the last months of 1959, when a couple of tricks from a form of folk music called mento were applied to the latest attempt to copy New Orleans music, and veered into something new: Joe Higgs and Roy Wilson's "Manny Oh," Theopholus Beckford's "Easy Snappin'," and the Folkes Brothers' "Oh Carolina." Despite the lack of airplay for such "ghetto trash"—the JBC, the only station on the island, was still aping the BBC—and the lack of record players in individual homes, each of these sold around twenty-five thousand copies apiece. Thus ska was born.

The fact that it was a people's music, created by both instrumentalists and singers from Kingston's sprawling slums, fired up nationalist feelings: Jamaica had a pop music nobody else had. Buster began calling himself and his new sound—he split from Coxsone around the start of 1960—the Voice of the People. And among the teenagers who showed up to hear it were Robert Nesta Marley, Winston Hubert McIntosh, Neville Livingston, Franklin "Junior" Braithwaite, and sometimes Cherry Smith and Beverley Kelso, collectively known as the Wailing Wailers, who'd been taking singing lessons at Joe Higgs's house, and went on to win the Wednesday night talent shows at the Vere Johns Opportunity Hour at the Carib Theatre. Johns not only hosted the show, but also had a column in the *Gleaner*, the island's daily paper, and a radio show on the JBC, so winning the contest could mean a lot more than the few pounds you got as a prize. One thing it got the Wailing Wailers was a steady association with Studio One at the height of the ska days, not only recording their own songs, but also singing backup on other people's records. They were ghetto, all right: Marley was the son of a white British soldier who'd abandoned his mother, a country girl he'd met while stationed in the hills; Livingston was a kid from the country who had been sleeping on the Marleys' floor, and McIntosh was a tall skinny kid who, abandoned by his parents in the country, gravitated to Kingston, where he, too, took singing lessons from Higgs and taught himself guitar. They were also, like a lot of Jamaican musicians and instrumentalists, followers of a religion called Rastafarianism. Rastas endorsed Marcus Garvey's back-to-Africa movement, regarding the black man's current circumstances as equivalent to the Jews' captivity in Egypt and Babylon. Following a prophecy of Garvey's, they worshipped Ethiopian emperor Haile Selassie as God's representative on earth. They also considered marijuana, a plant that grew all over the island thanks to Indians brought to work in the fields by the British, a sacrament. Rastafarians were, of course, scorned by decent Jamaicans, despite their musical ability, which was great—the Alpha Boys School, a reform school in Kingston, had a cracking school band and produced a disproportionate number of Jamaica's instrumentalists over the years—and the big producers, namely Coxsone and Duke Reid, kept the Rastas' easily identifiable drumming off most of their productions and wouldn't tolerate smoking ganja (as marijuana was known) in the studio. (Outside in the yard was often another matter.)

Ska took hold in Jamaica and Great Britain, and as studios and, especially, performers increased in number, the Jamaican music business, free of such silly things as publishing contracts, managers, recording contracts—many musicians would walk into whatever studio was convenient if they felt they had a hit; sometimes two, if the first try didn't take—and live performances (the backing band on those hits was too busy to take time off to go play a show) became a study in anarchy. It was a durable form, with hundreds of records recorded and hundreds of heroes (the Skatalites, Alpha alumni who served as the backup band on numerous records, still exist today), martyrs (Don Drummond, the Skatalites' trombonist and an unapologetic Rasta, was considered the most innovative instrumentalist on the island, but ended his days in a mental hospital after being convicted under murky circumstances of murdering his wife), and fads (the Judge Dread–versus–Rude Boys records of 1966). This last was a nice piece of local sociology: with youth gangs running amok with guns and razors, Buster invented his "Judge" character to upbraid them, as Judge Dread, played by Buster, showed no mercy to three hapless, sobbing youths who, collectively, he sentences on "Judge Dread," to 1,700 years in jail and 500 lashes. Although ska sold very well in England, the United States would have no part of it, although once again, it was the Voice of the People, Buster, who scored a mild U.S. hit on RCA in 1967, with his silly, sexist "Ten Commandments," in which he lays down the law to women. His album also has a reply, by one "Princess Buster," that is just as silly.

The rhythm, however, was changing, and the new music had definitely taken the side of the ghetto sufferahs. Under a new generation of producers such as Sonia Pottinger, Leslie Kong, and Joe Gibbs, the rhythm on the lawns slowed a bit, a reaction to a brutally hot summer. The new thing was "rocksteady," which started off as sloweddown ska and rapidly acquired its own rhythmic subtleties. By the time Alton Ellis and the Flames' "Rocksteady" hit the lawns, it was an established fact, heard on such hits as Joe Higgs's enigmatic "I Am The Song That My Enemy Sings," the Jamaicans' 1967 song festival winner "Ba Ba Boom," the Paragons' "The Tide Is High," and in the work of Desmond Dekker and the Aces. Dekker, a welder by trade, had played both sides of the rude boy fad with "Honor Your Father and Mother" and "Rudy Got Soul," but in 1967, as the rude boy thing was fading, he had a number-one hit in England with "007 (Shanty Town)," as a white youth tribe known as skinheads decided that Jamaican sounds such as ska and rocksteady were *their* music. (Oddly, skinheads were known not only for drinking and brawling, but also for "Paki-bashing," attacks on Pakistani immigrants. Apparently they thought Jamaicans were okay.) Dekker went for it again with "Israelites," which flopped initially, but after Dekker and the Aces toured England, the song became massive, a true sufferah's anthem that explicitly made the Rastafarian connection between Kingston's striving ghetto dwellers and the captive Israelites in Egypt. A Leslie Kong production like all Dekker's early records, it not only conquered the British charts, but somehow got licensed in America to Uni, Decca's "hip" label, which propelled it into the top 10 in 1969. Sadly, the follow-up, "It Mek," was rumored to mean "fuck you" in Turkish—it doesn't; it means "it makes" in Jamaican dialect; where was Ahmet when they needed him?—and died. The album, however, was listened to by a few daring souls, who took note of a song called "You Can Get It If You Really Want." With runaway violence and the Jamaican economy floundering, the sounds started feeling like the daily paper, especially when a harmony trio called the Ethiopians made records like "Everything Crash," "Hong Kong Flu" (which was reputed to have saved many lives by making people aware of the epidemic), and "Poison Flour" (ditto). A spell in jail was becoming routine for some ghetto youth, as the Maytals emphasized in "54-46 Was My Number," about the nine months that lead singer Frederick "Toots" Hibbert spent in jail for possession of ganja (and it really was his number, too). But it was another Maytals song that put the next rhythm in focus: "Do the Reggay."

Nobody seems to know where the word came from. Some say it's a corruption of *ragamuffin*, used to describe the ghetto youth who were recording and dancing to the new beat, but Jamaica being what it is, histories of reggae tend to skip the issue. What's most important is that a new generation of producers appeared and started making hits. Leslie Kong had had his crossover hit, but Joe Gibbs's Amalgamated label had the Pioneers ("Long Shot Kick de Bucket"), who had a string of hits; Harry J, who was famous for his instrumental hits (most notably the Harry J All Stars' "The Liquidator," one of the bestselling reggae singles ever, still used in advertisements in the United Kingdom); and the man who started his career by storming out of Joe Gibbs's studio and starting his own sound and studio, Lee "Scratch" Perry, also accurately known as "the Upsetter." Perry had eccentric ideas about production, and a charisma that drew musicians to him. He started his career with "People Funny Boy," which unloaded all his rancor on Gibbs (who fired back with "People Grudgeful") but was soon approaching outer space with his experiments in his Black Ark Studios. "Until reggae it was all Kingston, Kingston, Kingston," he told an interviewer. "Then the country people come to town and they bring the earth, the trees, the mountains. That's when reggae music come back to the earth. They used to think of country men as madmen, but so what? Sometimes it takes a madman because these madmen can't do the same thing the same way because it don't mean nothing to them." He was dead right: a lot of the new records' vocals were loaded with so much countryman patois that they were practically unintelligible to foreigners, and to Jamaicans of the middle class and up. "High-class" records were still being made, a light reggae beat behind a soul delivery, resulting in covers of songs by the Impressions or, in the case of Joe Gibbs, Nina Simone, whose "Young, Gifted, and Black" was an immense hit by vocal duo Bob (Andy) and Marcia (Griffiths). Scratch homed in on the weirder, rootsy stuff, producing the Ethiopians, the Mellotones, and, in 1969, the Wailers, now down to a trio of Bob Marley, Bunny Wailer (the former Neville Livingstone), and Peter Tosh (formerly McIntosh). They knew that Perry wouldn't shy away from songs about ganja ("African Herbsman"), country superstition ("Duppy Conqueror") or revolution ("Small Axe," "Soul Rebel," "Four Hundred Years"), and most reggae fans consider the hundred or so tracks the Wailers cut with Scratch to be their best work. (Even after Marley had gone on to rock stardom, he returned to Perry in 1975, when Haile Selassie died, to record "Jah Live," which he put out on his own Tuff Gong label.)

By 1969, Jamaica was awash with talent, reggae was on the pop charts in England, and it was natural that some of the talent would spill over to the United States. It was Jimmy Cliff, whom Chris Blackwell had brought to London, who did the trick. With Blackwell's label offering first refusal to A&M Records, Cliff managed to record an album in Jamaica with Leslie Kong and have a hit off its title tune, "Wonderful World, Beautiful People," which reached 25 on the American pop charts. People who bought the album, though, got an earful: "Many Rivers to Cross" was a gorgeous straight-out ballad; Cliff's take on "You Can Get It If You Really Want" outshone Dekker's; and the magnificent "Viet Nam" was acclaimed by none other than Bob Dylan as the best protest song ever written—and it might just be. Meanwhile, filmmaker Perry Henzell was running around shooting Kingston scenes, such as the Maytals and Leslie Kong in the act of recording their landmark hit "Pressure Drop" for a film he was putting together starring Cliff as a character based on a legendary Robin Hood–style outlaw named Rhyging (real name Vincent "Ivanhoe" Martin; Cliff's character was named Ivan) who ran Jamaican authorities on a merry chase in the late 1940s, becoming a sufferahs' legend. (Kong was riding high: just before his premature death in 1971, he hosted a recording session for Paul Simon, lately separated from Art Garfunkel, and Kong's killer studio band can be heard on the song "Mother and Child Reunion.")

In 1970, Denny Cordell, who was now managing Leon Russell and Joe Cocker, vacationed in Jamaica, and wound up licensing a few tracks, including "Pressure Drop," U-Roy (on the record label as "Hugh Roy') with "Flashing My Whip," and Scotty's "Draw Your Brakes"; issued them on some singles on his Shelter label, with different artists on each side; and tried to stir up some interest. That interest (and a number of the songs from that bunch of singles) was given a boost in 1972, when Henzell's film, titled *The Harder They Come*, was released to mostly uncomprehending reviews, although its soundtrack sold well and the film rapidly became a cult hit for its inside look into not only reggae but also the Rastafarian movement and its massive consumption of ganja. Its soundtrack album sold steadily for years and years, and the film became a campus and midnight movie staple.

Two of its tracks pointed to a rising phenomenon in reggae: "toasting," or "talkover." Jamaican singles routinely featured the instrumental backing track on the reverse side, sometimes with bits of the vocal dropped in, or the reverb amped up here and there, and a good selecter with two turntables learned to segue into it to keep dancers dancing. Also, the title would use the word *version* in some fashion. A good sound wouldn't let that go to waste. As we've seen, sounds employed deejays to comment on records, hype the sound itself, and get the crowd up. Then, in the late ska era, the deejay would make percussive counterpoint (". . . chicka . . . chicka" or the like), which propelled the Skatalites' "Al Capone" and "Clint Eastwood," from Lee Perry's house band, the Upsetters, up the charts. Then along came Count Machuki. Although he never recorded, he went from being a dancer in the crowd to a selecter with the Tom the Great Sebastian sound, where he not only demonstrated dance moves, but also inserted rhyming couplets into his talkover. When Tom got a gig uptown, he cut Machuki free, and the chatty dancer wound up with Prince Buster. But the first deejay to cut a record was U-Roy, real name Ewart Beckford, who started with a sound called Dickies Dynamic and worked his way up to Coxsone's B-team, which was run by Osbourne Ruddock, aka King Tubby. Tubby's day job was as a mastering engineer, so he had access to a lot of raw tape of new songs, which he'd remix into backing tracks especially for U-Roy's work, pressing them into one-off records. One of his first experiments with a talkover sold like crazy: "Wear You to the Ball" was introduced at a dance in 1970, an hour after Duke Reid had cut it onto a demo record, and those who were there never forgot the way the audience reacted. Soon, other toasters began to appear: Dennis Alcapone, I-Roy, Scotty (who appeared on *The Harder They Come*'s soundtrack with a version of Keith and Tex's "Stop That Train," titled "Draw Your Brakes"), and a new generation a couple of years later that included, most notably, Big Youth (Manley Augustus Buchanan), whose "C90 Skank" immortalized the Honda motorcycle that most ghetto youths lusted after. Big Youth's almost demented single, "Screaming Target," was a revelation to fans as he started out screaming repeatedly into the mike, and the album that came after it had a good underground following in Britain and the United States. One deejay record was even a mild hit in the States, leaking over from England, where it was massive: Dave and Ansell Collins's "Double Barrel" got to 22 on the pop charts in 1971.

At the same time as, and parallel to, the rise of deejays was the rise of dub, initially in the hands of Lee "Scratch" Perry. Again, versions played a role, as the Upsetter experimented with various effects machines, loops, and the like, playing with versions late into the night at his Black Ark Studios. The haunting sounds he was producing eventually became known as "dub." Once again, King Tubby's access to recordings became important as he, too, started experimenting. Tubby had one thing Scratch didn't, though: a busted Fender reverb, which he would kick on occasion, making the spring inside go *boiiiiing*. Then it got to the point where the two were remixing each other's work, which resulted in albums—dub was the first Jamaican form to demand an album because it wasn't primarily for dancing—with titles like *King Tubby Meets the Upsetter at the Grass Roots of Dub*. As the 1970s moved on, credible reggae bands based in London introduced live performance into the mix, with bands such as Aswad and Matumbi enjoying national reputations. Britain also had a Jamaican label, Trojan, which began when Chris Blackwell's infant Island label moved into its first London offices and the landlord, Lee Gopthal, noticed a lot of traffic in and out of the building. As Blackwell turned away from licensing Jamaican records to concentrate on his own productions, Gopthal started Trojan to pick up the slack, issuing singles and garish albums in the *Tighten Up* series, with scantily clad black women on the covers as much an attraction to British teens as the carefully assembled tunes on the platter. Chris Blackwell, however, was watching carefully, and in 1972, he released his first Wailers album, *Catch a Fire*, aimed squarely at the American market, where he'd done so well with rock music. He was going to make Bob Marley a rock star, and a black culture hero.

He failed, at least at first. The reason can be put down to two factors. First, there was a long-standing loathing of West Indians among U.S.-raised black people, who saw them as obsessed with making money—"Black Jews" they called them—and secretive, not to mention speaking funny (a mockery that goes all the way back to Louis Armstrong's day). That problem never really went away, but there was another reason: black American music was producing more great stuff than its target audience could really consume, and the rise of increasingly segregated rock radio in the early '70s meant that more and more of it wasn't crossing over. Led by Curtis Mayfield and, to some extent, Motown, with some of Norman Whitfield's productions and Stevie Wonder's songwriting, soul was becoming socially conscious. Starting with "Keep On Pushing" in 1964, Mayfield led the Impressions through a number of increasingly forceful statements: "People Get Ready" in 1965, "We're a Winner" in 1967, "This Is My Country" in 1968, "Choice of Colors" in 1969, and then, as a solo artist, nearly everything he recorded for a while after "(Don't Worry) If There's a Hell Below, We're All Going to Go," including the immortal "Move On Up." The Staple Singers, although not worrying the soul establishment much, were also working for social change, albeit, for the moment, exclusively in the church: the civil rights movement, after all, had taken no anthems from pop music in the South. Pops Staples was a fervent supporter of Martin Luther King Jr., unlike some in the black church, a stance that distinguished him from just about every other gospel performer. All these records did much better on the soul charts than on the pop charts, but it's worth noting that both Mayfield and the Staples were based in Chicago. It's likely that in the home of "deep soul" (i.e., the South) their records didn't do as well.

The South was still in a golden age for black popular music. Otis Redding's death had initiated a rush to replace him, and when it became apparent that nobody at Stax was going to fill his huge shoes, people looked elsewhere. The most deserving candidate was James

Carr, a tall, gospel-bred, Mississippi-born Memphian who'd had hits as far back as 1966, with "You Got My Mind Messed Up" and "Pouring Water on a Drowning Man," followed by the definitive version of the Chips Moman–Dan Penn classic "Dark End of the Street." These were all recorded for Quinton Claunch's Goldwax label, home to many obscure classic Memphis recordings. Carr had all of Redding's virtues but was totally irresponsible in terms of showing up for gigs and sessions, owing to psychological issues; his records, though, are amazing. Another candidate was James Govan, a popular club attraction on Beale Street who made a number of records for Fame and who showed a real talent for interpreting Bob Dylan. He was even more obscure than Carr but wound up becoming a star in Italy, of all places.

Then there were the artists who were popping up on Joe Cuoghi's Hi label, which had scored a couple of instrumental hits with trumpeter Willie Mitchell and his band, and agreed to take him on as a producer. He'd been working with a young singer, Ann Peebles, and while her early records were blues—a fine version of Little Johnny Taylor's "Part Time Love" was a hit in late 1970, which she followed up with a take on Bobby Bland's "I Pity the Fool"—she was headed to soul territory. What turned Mitchell and Hi around was when Al Green, whom Mitchell had written off as a mistake, knocked on his door. Thinking he was a carpenter he was expecting, Mitchell waved him in and was instead confronted with a guy introducing himself as Albert Greene. "You're the son of a bitch with my money, ain't you?" Mitchell said, recalling that time in Detroit when he loaned Green $1,500 to get out of a contract. To get it back, they started working long hours at an apartment Mitchell rented for Green. "The biggest thing I had to do with Al was soften him up," Mitchell remembered later. "He wanted to sound like Otis Redding, he wanted to sound like Stax's Sam and Dave. I said, 'We don't need that. You can't compare with those guys. You need to be smooth and sweet, you don't need to scream.' And finally I got him to settle down." The breakthrough came in late 1970, with Green's version of the Temptations' "I Can't Get Next to You," in which he drops the tempo to near funereal and in which the minimal, muted backup—using absolutely no echo was a trademark of Mitchell's—emphasizes the surrealism of Norman

Whitfield and Barrett Strong's lyrics. It wasn't a huge hit, but it established Green, and after back-to-back smashes in 1971 with "Tired of Being Alone" and the crossover number one "Let's Stay Together," Green and Mitchell (and the house band Hi Rhythm Section comprising brothers Leroy "Flick" Hodges, Charles Hodges, and Mabon "Teenie" Hodges; Howard Grimes; and Archie Turner, which would take over from Booker T. and the M.G.'s as Memphis's hot studio band) were on their way, minting gold and platinum through 1977 and opening the door for other Mitchell-produced Hi artists such as Ann Peebles, Otis Clay, Syl Johnson, and O. V. Wright to hit the charts.

As for Stax itself, it wasn't doing too poorly, either. The Al Bell regime at the label found an unlikely new star in songwriter/pianist Isaac Hayes, not a strong singer but an excellent songwriter and producer, even of his own material. Hayes started out with the gimmick of reciting a long introduction that commented on a song's lyrics before singing it with the double-sided hit "Walk On By"/"By the Time I Get to Phoenix" in 1969, for the new Enterprise label, which Stax had added for rock groups. He most firmly found his ground in 1971, though, recording the theme to a blaxploitation film, *Shaft*, which went to the top of the pop charts and which nicely shows up his strengths and weaknesses as a performer. Bell also managed to talk the Staples into recording for Stax, at first with "Long Walk to D.C.," and then with the family group recording politically tinged material while lead singer Mavis also did secular songs. They began to break through in late 1971, with a song that took a line from a popular preacher who had marched with MLK, Dr. King's associate Jesse Jackson, who was attracted to Stax's tentative commitment to soul and activism. "Respect Yourself" had an undeniable groove, even if some of the lyrics are a bit silly—putting your hand over your mouth when you cough isn't going to do a thing about pollution, but someone was apparently stuck for a rhyme. Their big breakthrough, though, was "I'll Take You There," recorded in Muscle Shoals in 1972, which has an unmistakable reggae rhythm: the backup band, the Muscle Shoals Rhythm Section (aka the Swampers), had just toured Britain with Steve Winwood's newly reinvented Traffic, and their opening act was the Wailers. Bassist David Hood had been astounded by the music, and helped build the arrangement on the Staples' session; on the record, you can hear Mavis Staples urging him on.

Elsewhere at Stax, they were still mixing blues and contemporary soul: Albert King sang blues, accompanied by his giant Gibson Flying V guitar, and scored on the soul charts; Stax did a record with John Lee Hooker, who was still recording prolifically; and the label tried like hell to break a harmonica player named Little Sonny, to no avail. Pervis Staples brought a Chicago gospel trio, the Hutchinson Sunbeams, to the label, hearing they wanted to do secular music, and after a little image tweaking, the Emotions were born, starting a run of hits that continued into the next decade. Ollie and the Nightingales was another gospel group being reshaped in the Stax studios, while a local vocal group, the Soul Children, was doing what could be called progressive vocal group music, along with the slightly more conservative Mad Lads; and a reconstituted Bar-Kays started having hits again, even if they did kick off their revival with "Son of Shaft." Stax's revamped organization announced itself to the world at its 1969 sales convention, May 16–18, at which a whopping twenty-eight albums—albums, not singles—were announced for release (although the Rufus Thomas one never actually came out). Jim Stewart was still head of the company, but Al Bell was definitely positioning it as the social force that Motown was not: the convention featured keynote speaker civil rights activist Julian Bond, and it introduced a new organization, called SAFEE, the Stax Association for Everybody's Education, which would run day care centers and trade schools for underprivileged youth. At the end of the weekend, Stax had spent a quarter-million dollars on the bash and was looking at two million dollars in orders from its wholesalers. What could go wrong? And there were even more ambitious plans afoot: in 1972, the annual Watts Festival in Los Angeles culminated in a gigantic Stax-only concert (which was being filmed and recorded) that would be known as Wattstax. Admission was a dollar, and it was held at the Los Angeles Coliseum, where 112,000 people saw as many of the Stax stable of stars as had time to play. The schedule was disrupted when Sammy Davis Jr. canceled his evening engagement in Las Vegas so he could go off and get hugged by Richard Nixon, so the Staple Singers, who were opening for him, had time to make it in for a set. The organizers had just plain overbooked the thing, but the day ended without incident, the crowds had seen lots of acts that local radio wasn't playing, and Stax not only had a double album but also a film that, with some touching up, hit the theaters with a bang.

Things at Motown up in Detroit were unsettled. There was some social commentary sneaking into Norman Whitfield's writing for the Temptations, what with "Psychedelic Shack," "Ball of Confusion (That's What the World Is Today)," and "Ungena Za Ulimwengu (Unite the World)"; and Edwin Starr had surprised everyone with a couple of big hits in 1970, "War" and "Stop the War Now"; while Martha and the Vandellas had released "I Should Be Proud" that year, the lament of a woman whose man has died in the war, which included some really embarrassingly bad lyrics that went unheard. Berry Gordy was eyeing Hollywood and his new mistress, Diana Ross, as his passports into world showbiz, but the trouble was that some of the folks who'd gotten him as far as he'd gone were chafing at their restraints. For one, little Steveland Morris was well aware that the contract his guardians had signed would become null and void on his twenty-first birthday, in 1971, and he'd been mulling over offers from other labels, paying heed to the kind of freedoms rock groups were getting, including concessions on royalties, publishing, and freedom of expression. There wouldn't be anything new out of Stevie Wonder until that got settled, although he did have stuff in the can, which Motown released. Then there was an even bigger problem in the person of Berry Gordy's brother-in-law, Marvin Gaye. Although he was the label's bestselling male artist and Motown's sex symbol, he hadn't had it easy while consolidating that role. The label had paired him with former James Brown backup vocalist Tammi Terrell, for a run of smash duets that paralleled his own hits from 1967–69, and her segment was one of the highlights of his live show. But Tammi had her own problems: she'd been having violent headaches, possibly due to beatings she'd gotten from Brown, and one night during a concert, she blacked out in Gaye's arms. She kept working with him, and on her own Motown records, but she was diagnosed with a brain tumor and was clearly not well, having multiple surgeries and long hospitalizations.

(A couple of the records released under her name had Valerie Simpson doing most of the vocal work.) Finally, on March 16, 1970, she died in a hospital in Philadelphia. Although the two weren't involved other than professionally, Terrell's decline hit Gaye hard. He retreated to his house, spent hours lost in thought, doing some praying.

Shortly after Tammi's funeral, Obie Benson, one of the Four Tops, showed up with a song that he and songwriter Al Cleveland had written, "What's Going On," a protest against a crumbling American society, poverty, the Vietnam War, police violence—a lot, but handled with the kind of deft touch that a delicately forceful voice like Gaye's might be able to deliver without it sounding too hectoring. Marvin, who'd been learning production by sitting behind the board (with a company-approved producer, of course) on some very successful sessions for the Originals, didn't like it at first, but eventually he called a session that, in defiance of company rules, he intended to produce himself, on June 1, 1970. He worked out some basic arrangements with Motown's David Van De Pitte, had a bunch of percussion instruments on hand, invited a couple of members of the Detroit Lions football team to do background vocals, and placed Motown's legendary studio band the Funk Brothers, itching to play the arrangement, in front of them. It was unlike anything Motown had done before: loose, oddly structured, relaxed. Tape was rolling while Eli Fontaine was warming up his alto sax, and he blew a couple of swooping lines that clicked in Marvin's head: here was the intro. Fontaine was told to pack up and go home. Then, as the session evolved, Marvin asked the engineer to save two vocal tracks, so they could select the best take; he mistakenly played both back at once, which made it sound like the singer was duetting with himself. That idea, too, was a keeper. Instead of standing behind a stationary microphone, Gaye was singing into a handheld mike, wandering around the studio as if he were onstage. Bassist James Jamerson came home from work that day and told his wife he'd just cut a classic record—something he'd done enough times before to be sure of. And Berry Gordy? He hated it. Fine, his brother-in-law told him; he wouldn't record another note for the company. So, they released it in January 1971, and it rocketed to the top of the soul and pop charts. Okay, now for an album: Marvin had been writing songs in this new style with his wife, Anna, with Benson and Cleveland, and others. God, he said, had been using him as an instrument to deliver a message of love, a message that was repeated in the rambling liner notes he penned for the album, which came out on May 21, 1971. Its cover showed Gaye's uplifted head, evidence of a recent rain shower in his hair, worn short and natural, and on the vinyl raincoat he's wearing. *What's Going On* was its title. No question mark. And for the first time in Motown history, the musicians' names were printed on the gatefold sleeve. Now people knew them. And in short order, it became Motown's bestselling album ever.

While it was a breath of fresh air for Motown creatively, *What's Going On* was also a blow to the Motown factory system, and an indication that that system might well be outdated. The next bomb was Stevie Wonder. After exploding onto the scene with "Fingertips" in 1963, he was basically buried by the Motown machine, although he continued to tour with the Motortown Revue and to record harmonica instrumentals and insubstantial material while hanging around Hitsville absorbing everything he heard. Finally, at the beginning of 1966, he grabbed on to a hit, "Uptight (Everything's Alright)," which had the classic Motown sound and which he'd cowritten with Sylvia Moy—she'd just sat through a meeting at which Gordy muttered that if Wonder's next single wasn't a hit, he'd be gone from the label. Wonder's voice had changed, his sound had changed, and he was writing material, but nobody knew what to do with him. A punchy horn chart, an urgent delivery, and everything was, indeed, uptight and all right. Next, he did one of his own projects, a version of Bob Dylan's "Blowin' in the Wind," which puzzled everyone at the company but Wonder's mentor, Clarence Paul, who was encouraging this sort of thing; Wonder again went to the top of the charts. By the time he turned twenty-one, he'd shown his value to the company, but he was biding his time, and when the big day came, he was a married man (to former Motown secretary Syreeta Wright) and had come into a fortune. Berry Gordy presented him with a check for a million dollars, a fraction of what Wonder had made for Motown and, he came to feel, not a particularly generous fraction. To celebrate his emancipation, he packed up and moved to New York, away from the Motor City, where he'd grown up, and from the growing Motown operation in California. The next thing he did was form his own publishing company, Black Bull, riffing on his astrological sign, Taurus—1970s black and hippie culture kept a wary distance from each other, but one bit, astrology, sure struck a chord in black life—separating himself from Motown's Jobete publishing. He got a lawyer, too, introduced to him by Richie Havens, a guy named Jonathan Vigoda, a kind of hippie himself, but sharp enough to sit down with the offers Stevie was getting from Atlantic, Elektra, and Columbia—oh, and Motown—and read them carefully. And as the final proof that there was a new Stevie Wonder, he found a new instrument: the synthesizer. Synthesizers were in a pretty primitive state in 1971, usually able to deliver only one line and requiring a lot of setting up before they could be played, but Stevie had heard an album, *Zero Time,* by TONTO's Expanding Head Band—in reality, Malcolm Cecil and Robert Margouleff, two guys in Ontario who'd figured a way to link together a bunch of synthesizers in the studio; TONTO stood for "The Original New Timbral Orchestra." Stevie went to meet them, and they showed him their gizmo. He played with it awhile and then told Cecil and Margouleff to pack it up and reinstall it at Electric Lady Studios, which Jimi Hendrix had built for himself and where Stevie was planning to record. The three, with occasional input from other musicians, managed to spend $250,000 in studio fees during the subsequent year, creating all the tracks for Stevie's next four albums (*Music of My Mind, Talking Book, Innervisions,* and *Fulfillingness' First Finale,* which came out between 1972 and 1974) and, according to Cecil, forty other songs recorded and mixed and 240 others in one stage of completion or another. Those albums basically make up the classic Stevie Wonder canon, and contained "Superstition," "You Are the Sunshine of My Life," "Higher Ground," "Living for the City," and more, all crossover pop and soul hits. His new contract with Motown left the company with hardly anything but the right to manufacture and distribute his records, making him one of the label's richest entertainers, but not one who was enriching the label.

He'd eventually be joined by Michael Jackson, who came to public attention with his family group, the Jackson 5, in 1969, when their single "I Want You Back" stormed the charts. The Motown story was that the group had come to Diana Ross's attention and she'd brought them to Berry Gordy—which was nice, but not true. In fact, the Jacksons' father, Joe, had been drilling his sons relentlessly for several years to develop an act, both to realize his own stymied career and to lift the family out of the poverty of their hometown, Gary, Indiana. They'd had a couple of singles out on a local label and had been performing awhile when they wound up on the bill with Gladys Knight and the Pips a couple of times; Gladys had her management contact Motown about them. Their next connected fan was Bobby Taylor, who'd had a hit with his interracial band the Vancouvers ("Does Your Mama Know About Me"), on Motown's V.I.P. subsidiary, and actually managed to get the 5 an audition, which of course they passed. At eleven years old, Michael was an insanely talented front for his brothers Marlon, Jermaine, Tito, and Jackie, and the poise and precision of their stage act only improved once they got to the West Coast and met the mentor whom Gordy and Ross had picked for them, a woman named Suzanne De Passe, who'd recently joined the company. The Jackson 5 were the future of Motown, building on its factory past but based in Los Angeles. De Passe and her cousin Tony Jones groomed their image, and the company turned their songwriting and production over to three men, Deke Richards, Fonce Mizell, and Freddie Perren, who were kept anonymous under the collective title "the Corporation." The 5 were adorable, particularly Michael; they appealed (unsurprisingly) to that cash-flush demographic, young kids, to the point where a Saturday morning animated series was built around them for a couple of years; and their first four singles hit number one on the pop charts and the next two made it to number two. Michael also made solo albums starting in 1971, heavy on ballads, and hit the top pop slot in 1972 with the only known love song to a rat, "Ben." There would be no *What's Going On*, no *Innervisions*, from this crew.

There was a time at Motown when the discovery of a phenomenon like the Jacksons would have set in motion some furious activity in the writing suite of Holland–Dozier–Holland, but they were long gone; after a period of forced inactivity while settling their suits against Motown, HDH had started a couple of labels, Invictus and Hot Wax, through Capitol and Buddah, respectively, and there they released some of the best Motown records Motown never made. Invictus had Freda Payne, who hit in 1970 with "Band of Gold," a strong pop cross-over, but who really showed what she could do the following year with "Bring the Boys Home." The latter was the kind of protest song Motown could have been doing, an anthem that resonated in the black community, even if top 40 radio's response, doubtless out of fear for their FCC licenses deep in the Nixon era, wasn't as strong. Freda's sister, Scherrie, was in the Glass House, a boy-girl group on Invictus who also made social commentary with their biggest hit, "Crumbs off the Table." The label's other big act was the Chairmen of the Board, a trio whose leader, General Johnson, was a triple-threat songwriter, singer, and producer, and who had led the Showmen on "It Will Stand," a pop semi-hit in both 1961 and 1963 whose chorus declared that "rock and roll will stand." "Give Me Just a Little More Time" was their 1970 hit, but other records, such as "Pay to the Piper," were equally strong, and they even managed a strong political and musical statement with their later album *Skin I'm In*. Over at Hot Wax, the action started with a white rock band, the Flaming Ember, whose one-shot hit "Westbound #9" established the label, but the ladies had the day for the rest of the label's existence. Honey Cone was a trio that included Darlene Love's sister, Edna Wright, and recorded a clutch of hits in the early '70s, including "Want Ads" and the insanely catchy "One Monkey Don't Stop No Show." Proudly pop-feminist, they shared the stage with Laura Lee, adopted daughter of one of the gospel Meditation Singers, who were even more pop-militant, with "Wedlock Is a Padlock," "Women's Love Rights," and "Rip Off." And over on Invictus was the group Parliament. Nobody was quite sure what to do with them, but it was that never-say-die crew from Revilot Records who'd lost the rights to the name "the Parliaments" in the label's death throes. Dropping a letter saved them from that, and HDH was smart enough not to meddle with their songwriting. It gave them to Ruth Copeland, a British singer who'd married Jeffrey Bowen, a former Motown songwriter who'd helped HDH set up their labels, and she produced an album, *Osmium*, for the band; they contributed to her albums, but nobody knew how to market them. No matter: if one change of name could give them freedom, two were even better. Retaining the idea of Parliament as basically a vocal group, George Clinton, their leader, took pretty much the exact same musicians and peddled them as a hard rock band, Funkadelic, and went to Armen Boladian, a Detroit record guy who'd been recording gospel, and pitched them to his Westbound label. At pretty much the same time as *Osmium* appeared, so did an album called *Funkadelic*. The fun was just beginning.

The fact is, the hippies and the subsequent warping of the pop narrative that came from their music affected the black audience, too. The most visible exponent of this was Sly Stone, who had a huge influence on reshaping a lot of givens in the black music world, and would have had a bigger career over a longer period of time had drugs and paranoia not derailed him. His welding of white pop and the rhythmic innovations that James Brown and Dyke and the Blazers had birthed, plus his proud interracialism—only Sly could have gotten away with a song called "Don't Call Me Nigger, Whitey"—pointed to a direction for soul that white kids were enthusiastically accepting.

Jimi Hendrix, too, provided a path that some black musicians were investigating, particularly in jazz circles. Miles Davis heard Hendrix's potential early on, and looked for an opportunity for both of them to play together that was probably never realized (nobody's sure if they ever played together). Davis was an early advocate of racially integrated bands, starting in the 1950s, when Bill Evans played piano for his famous quintet, but really taking off with 1969's *In a Silent Way*. He'd told his pianist, Herbie Hancock, "We're not going to play the blues anymore. Let the white folks have the blues. They got 'em, so they can keep 'em. Play something else." Hancock had already heard the message, and was about to leave Davis, who augmented him with two other keyboard players, Chick Corea and Joe Zawinul, both white; a white bassist, Dave Holland; and a white British guitarist, John McLaughlin, for the album. Davis famously told *Rolling Stone*, "You've got to have a mixed group—one has one thing, and the other has another. For me, a group has to be mixed. To get swing, you have to have some black guys in there." He referenced the Jimi Hendrix Experience along with the group Lifetime, led by Davis's drummer, Tony

Williams, in which McLaughlin also played, as did organist Larry Young. With his producer, Teo Macero, Davis sculpted *In a Silent Way* out of long sessions whose modules they spliced together, itself a technological advance for jazz.

Davis's next album, 1970's *Bitches Brew,* was even more unconventional, with two drummers on some tracks, and Harvey Brooks, who'd been with Michael Bloomfield's Electric Flag, on bass. Also, with a shock only a bit more muted in the jazz world than the folk world had felt with Bob Dylan, Miles "went electric," with a group of sessions in 1970 that drew together some new young players with some of his veterans for material that would be released on a number of albums in the years to come, seemingly formless jams (actually carefully constructed after the fact, as with *In a Silent Way*) sizzling with funk, wah-wah pedals, electric keyboards, and stop-start rhythms. The earliest release of these sessions was on an album called *A Tribute to Jack Johnson,* one track to each side. In contrast to *Bitches Brew,* which earned a gold record, *Jack Johnson* barely sold at all, but Miles forged on.

So did his alumni. Tony Williams had several versions of his Lifetime band, including a short-lived one with ex-Cream bassist Jack Bruce in it; and Joe Zawinul put together Weather Report, an explicitly rock-oriented band with Davis veteran saxophonist Wayne Shorter and bassist Miroslav Vitous (later replaced by Jaco Pastorius), which went on playing rock venues throughout the '70s, eventually becoming very commercially successful. Herbie Hancock formed the Mwandishi Sextet, whose first album, *Mwandishi,* on Warners in 1971, thoroughly confused jazz fans who'd been watching Hancock since his 1965 *Maiden Voyage.* The music they purveyed eventually became known as jazz-rock fusion. Others in the fusion camp, such as Lenny White, Alphonse Mouzon, Chick Corea's group Return to Forever, Billy Cobham, John McLaughlin's Mahavishnu Orchestra, Airto Moreira, and Michael Henderson—all of whom were on the *Jack Johnson* sessions—would go on to make records that outsold Miles's. While derided by the critics most of the time, fusion was taken up by some segments of the rock audience, and lives on today.

Much harder to come by was black hard rock, which may have

stumbled because no black artists had the skills or experience to take on Jimi Hendrix's legacy. Only Funkadelic's Eddie Hazel (and then, later, Michael "Kidd Funkadelic" Hampton, whose profile grew after Hazel was imprisoned for biting a flight attendant) took up the challenge, although Funkadelic was way, way underground. This seems odd when one listens again to such early masterpieces as "Maggot Brain," a long showcase for Hazel, a slow scream over gentle arpeggios, legendarily the result of Clinton asking him to play as if his mother had just died. But the fact was, the band's personnel was unstable, Westbound wasn't yet much of a label, and most of all, FM radio was becoming more and more segregated. Hey, with all the rock albums coming out, who could keep track? And Funkadelic—and Parliament, which, after Invictus let them go, Clinton had signed to Casablanca, a label started by former Buddah bubblegum magnate Neil Bogart—just sounded, well, too black. There was one segment of the population, however, for whom this wasn't a problem, and Clinton and his motley crew (which soon contained castoffs from James Brown's J.B.'s, including the very young William "Bootsy" Collins, who'd revolutionized Brown's thinking about bass playing) toured the campuses of black colleges to growing numbers of enthusiastic fans. They were also huge around Washington, DC, which they called "Chocolate City," and Parliament would eventually pay tribute to it in the song of the same name.

The musical revolution the J.B.'s had introduced had been evolving for some time. A lot of it was in Brown's head, and it was just a matter of finding the right people to make it happen. There was the weird music that Dyke and the Blazers had made. There were the odd rhythmic experiments Sly Stone had begun to make with "Thank You (Falettinme Be Mice Elf Agin)," aided by his bassist Larry Graham. There were regional weirdos such as Virginia's Maskman and the Agents, and a bunch of people in Phoenix hoping to pick up where Dyke had left off. Eventually, this music of sprung, melodic bass lines; powerfully minimalist drumming; and wide-open spaces in the arrangements, all circling around to land on the first beat of the next line (which was called "the one"), acquired a name, one that had been around for a long time, but now, in the early '70s, became known as funk. It drew from a lot of sources: At one point, Brown took the J.B.'s (and his new wife) on a short tour of West Africa, and with a couple of days off in Lagos, Nigeria, they were honored guests at a compound known as the Shrine, a sort of commune based around a saxophone player who'd spent time in England and the United States (where he'd fallen under the spell of the Black Panthers) and who was a big James Brown fan. Fela Ransome-Kuti was the son of a well-known Nigerian evangelist, and at the Shrine, he'd put together a band, Africa 70, that was capable of fusing the funk innovations he'd heard overseas with some traditional Nigerian drumming. He'd dubbed the result Afrobeat. Bootsy Collins, who was riveted by it, called it "another dimension," and said, "When I heard them, that was the deepest level you could get." But unlike his American fans (but much like Bob Marley in Jamaica, to whom he was later compared), Fela was committed to exposing the deeply corrupt Nigerian regime in songs like "Zombie" and "Coffin for Head of State," and it was only his international connections, and his popularity as a recording artist for international labels that followed, that had kept the government forces from killing him.

Black protest music did exist in the United States, although the furor over *What's Going On*, a fairly nonmilitant, nonstrident record, shows the extent of the conservatism of American radio, always, during the Nixon years, afraid of losing a broadcast license for playing controversial content. But until Stevie Wonder's quartet of TONTO-produced albums came to market with songs such as "Higher Ground" and "Living for the City," black protest was limited to occasional flukes like "Bring the Boys Home"; the Chi-Lites' 1971 Sly-esque "(For God's Sake) Give More Power to the People"; its less successful follow-up, "We Are Neighbors"; and the Dells' Vietnam non-hit "Does Anybody Know I'm Here." There were also deep underground oddballs such as Jerry Williams Jr. A performer from the same part of the country as the Chairmen of the Board, Williams reinvented himself in 1970 as Swamp Dogg, with an album called *Total Destruction to Your Mind*, which got raves in *Rolling Stone*, had a few of its songs covered by the likes of Jimmy Cliff, and launched a career that, thanks to Williams's superb songwriting, continues to this day. (His next album, *Rat On!*, was with Elektra, and showed him seated atop a huge white rat.) For the moment, though, serious young black musicians were investigating jazz-funk, or watching the ascent of post-Motown soul. They were beginning to get the message: FM radio was no longer "underground"; it was the new Establishment, and it was white.

chapter seven

LONG LIVE ROCK!

Led Zeppelin with the private aircraft they toured in
(© Bob Gruen/www.bobgruen.com)

B eatles or Stones? This famous metric determining someone's basic taste in popular music has endured throughout the decades, and has even been asked of American presidential candidates. But it's an excellent filter for looking at the state of things as the 1970s began. The question, of course, is not as simple as which band one preferred over the other, but on which side of a growing fault line one stood. The Beatles, for all their ability to be noisy, were firmly in a camp called pop. In the end, pop is more about craft than virtuosity, about finely shaping a musical experience to fit within the three-minute length of a single, and as such, it is quite amenable to being created in a factory-type situation, although that's not essential. Pop has a long history in the United States and Britain, each country creating its own flavor, which is why the Beatles were recognized and understood immediately: the past they looked back to was a pop one, as were the American records they emulated—along with the English music hall tradition that Paul McCartney in particular mined, there was early Motown, girl groups, and early country-soul, all American pop genres. The records the Stones put out in the first part of their career were also pop, but pop made from less-contrived raw materials: blues, early soul, and even a bit of country. Not as genteel as their supposed competitors, the Stones were the equivalent of folkie authenticists. And, ironically, despite the class differences between the two bands—the Beatles very working class from provincial Liverpool; the Stones, mostly middle-class and from sophisticated London and its suburbs—their audiences were the opposite: there was much to-doing among musicologists and the art crowd about the Beatles' compositional (and, in the case of John Lennon, artistic) sophistication, with pooh-bahs like Leonard Bernstein publicly admiring them; while the Stones' confrontation, their supposed grittiness, endeared them to political radicals and the great unwashed, as well as to some of the nascent rock press. As the Beatles' records became increasingly sophisticated and dependent on studios for their creation, the band's ability and desire to perform to live audiences waned. The Stones, post-Altamont, saw their tours attracting more and more people, and their new material was easily adaptable to live performance.

This was also the divide opening up between the singles market and the album market. *Billboard,* in its February 28, 1970, issue, printed its annual roundup of the previous year's charts. Top singles, in order: the Archies' "Sugar, Sugar"; the 5th Dimension's "Aquarius/Let the Sunshine In," from *Hair;* "I Can't Get Next to You," by the Temptations; the Stones' "Honky Tonk Women"; Sly's "Everyday People"; "Dizzy," by Tommy Roe; "Hot Fun in the Summertime," by Sly; Tom Jones's "I'll Never Fall in Love Again"; the Foundations' "Build Me Up Buttercup"; and Tommy James and the Shondells' "Crimson and Clover." By contrast, the albums were *In-A-Gadda-Da-Vida,* by Iron Butterfly; *Hair,* the original cast recording; *Blood, Sweat and Tears;* Creedence's *Bayou Country; Led Zeppelin; Johnny Cash at Folsom Prison;* Barbra Streisand's *Funny Girl* original cast LP; *The Beatles* (aka the "White Album"); *Donovan's Greatest Hits;* and *The Association's Greatest Hits.* Not quite a pop/rock divide, what with two Broadway shows on the list, but *In-A-Gadda-Da-Vida*'s title song was seventeen minutes long and took up an entire side of the record. The Iron Butterfly album was also slowed down and rhythmically ponderous, as most of Led Zeppelin's first album was. The singles on the *Billboard* list were topped by an actual manufactured American pop product, followed by another confected group singing Broadway rock, but the list also included two Sly and the Family Stone tracks, the beginning of Norman Whitfield's rejuvenation of Motown, and a memorable Stones track. (The reason the Stones weren't on the album list was both because they'd spent much of the year touring and because they weren't releasing new product until they could get out of their deal with London Records.) It wasn't quite as stark a divide as it would become. It's also notable that the only two San Francisco–area bands in either list were Creedence, a band that had never played the Fillmore or the Avalon and that was derided by many on that scene for being too pop, and Sly and the Family Stone, outliers because they were interracial and had a black leader.

Nineteen seventy would continue to heighten this divide. In its first months, Warners released *Sweet Baby James,* by James Taylor, and *Black Sabbath* (on Friday the thirteenth of February), kick-starting the '70s. One was the continuation of a singer-songwriter's confessional journey, the other a morphed British blues band from grimy industrial Birmingham. One was mostly acoustic, and hardly dancing material. You couldn't dance to Black Sabbath, either, but they made both Iron Butterfly and Led Zeppelin sound like the Orchestra of St. Martin in the Fields. And with the success of each, the floodgates opened. *Mellow* became a new catchword, and a lot of FM stations leapt on the quieter music, because its subject was almost invariably personal and nobody was asking anyone to kick out the jams or go street-fighting, although a new Stones album was always welcome. Taylor's album rocketed to the heights of the LP charts, and Atlantic announced they'd signed his brothers Livingston and Alex and his sister, Kate, to deals. Joining him was Van Morrison, whose critically acclaimed *Astral Weeks* hadn't performed so well, but whose subsequent albums, using a band he'd put together in Marin County, California, where he and his wife, Janet Planet (née Gauder), had moved, used horns and a jazzy sensibility to put across songs like "Moondance," "Domino," "Wild Night," and "Tupelo Honey," all singles that charted well and became FM mainstays along with his album tracks. From England came Cat Stevens, who'd had a couple of pop hits over there but switched labels to Island in 1970 and began purveying mellowness with enigmatically titled albums like *Mona Bone Jakon, Tea for the Tillerman,* and *Catch Bull at Four,* which gave him a very successful career until his 1979 conversion to a particularly severe kind of

Islam (and a change of name to Yusuf Islam) caused him to disappear from the public eye for many years.

Carole King became the queen of mellow with *Tapestry*, recording with James Taylor on occasion after her earlier albums, one with her band, the City, and a solo effort called *Writer: Carole King*, had failed to catch on. *Tapestry*, released in 1971, became one of the best-selling albums of all time, with the single "It's Too Late," backed with "I Feel the Earth Move," clinging to the top slot on the charts for weeks, while the duet with Taylor, "You've Got a Friend," was ubiquitous on FM. (In an ill-advised move that was probably an accident, Don McLean, who'd had a smash with the cringe-inducing nostalgia-fest "American Pie" in 1971, chose to title his second album, released shortly after King's, *Tapestry*, which all but killed it.) Record companies loved the mellow crowd, whose albums and singles could easily be (and were) marketed to the MOR crowd, which included post-college consumers, for whom a bit of rock was okay, and who were buying new, rockier performers like the Association, the Carpenters (a clean-cut brother-sister duo in which the lead vocalist, Karen Carpenter, was the drummer, while brother Richard played keyboards), Neil Diamond, and soft soul artists like Dionne Warwick, Roberta Flack, and Donny Hathaway.

On the other pole was "heavy," an appellation that included loud bands that improvised to a greater or lesser degree. The Allman Brothers Band released their self-titled debut at the start of 1970, and a follow-up, *Idlewild South*, in October. Guitarist Duane Allman had been a house virtuoso at Fame Studios, where he fit in well with the soul records being produced. (Listen to, for instance, his solo on Wilson Pickett's "Hey Jude.") Combined with a second guitarist, Dickey Betts, and his keyboard-playing brother Gregg, who wrote and sang some of their best material, they proved to be at their most potent live, so Atlantic cut a double LP of them live at the Fillmore East in March 1971, giving them their first platinum album (one million *copies* sold, as opposed to gold, which meant a million *dollars' worth* sold.)

Truly one of the most exciting live albums of its period, it gave inspiration to dozens of less-talented bands and showed a new way for improvised electric guitar music. But Duane, four days after the record went gold in late October 1971, was riding his motorcycle in the band's new home of Macon, Georgia, when he swerved to miss a truck and lost control of his bike, and was killed almost immediately. The band kept on under Gregg's and Dickey Betts's leadership, and continues in much-changed form to this day. Johnny Winter, after two albums of heavy blues, hooked up with, of all people, the former McCoys, of "Hang On Sloopy" fame, whose guitarist, Rick Derringer, was a perfect foil for him. As Johnny Winter And, they were welcomed by FM stations, where their single "Rock and Roll, Hoochie Koo" caught on right away, as did a 1971 live album. Winter's keyboard-playing brother, Edgar, followed suit, first with a kind of East Texas show band called White Trash and then with the Edgar Winter Group, and topped the charts with an instrumental, "Frankenstein," in 1973. Detroit came up with Grand Funk Railroad (a pun on the local Grand Trunk Railroad System), a power trio of very limited virtuosity who started out as Terry Knight and the Pack and had some minor local hits in the late '60s. Knight quit to manage his backup as a power trio, and under his Svengali-like guidance, they ground out platinum album after platinum album from late 1969 to 1973, with almost no radio play. Knight taunted radio and the press and toured the band relentlessly, but despite selling out Shea Stadium, thus outselling the Beatles, they left behind almost no legacy. Once John Eastman (Paul McCartney's brother-in-law) got them a divorce from the increasingly unhinged Knight, they were able to hire Todd Rundgren to produce *We're an American Band,* whose title track gave them their first number-one single.

Cleveland birthed the James Gang, with lead guitarist Joe Walsh; ex–Mitch Ryder guitarist Jim McCarty joined ex–Vanilla Fudge members Tim Bogert and Carmine Appice to form Cactus; Fleetwood Mac went from emulating Chicago blues to emphasizing their guitarists Peter Green and Jeremy Spencer on songs like "Oh Well" and "The Green Manalishi (With the Two Prong Crown)" only to lose both guitarists to mental illness and to the cult Children of God, respectively, necessitating a complete do-over, with American singer-guitarist Bob Welch.

Many other heavy British bands, such as Uriah Heep and Deep Purple, appeared on the circuit, while some ex–Small Faces tried their luck with Humble Pie, and Free had the good luck to be both heavy *and* pop with their classic top 10 single "All Right Now," a feat that they never repeated. The kings of heavy, of course, were Led Zeppelin, whose early career decision to focus on the United States, to tour relentlessly, and to forget singles paid off magnificently: their first four albums went multiple platinum, and by the time of 1971's *IV,* which actually had no title but four "runes" Jimmy Page had come up with (hence causing some fans to call it *ZOSO,* a crude typographical rendering of the runes), they'd found a mixture of heavy and British mysticism that lifted the album to eventual sales of thirty-seven million copies, despite the fact that the most-played song on the album, "Stairway to Heaven," was never released as a single.

During all this, former guitar gods Michael Bloomfield and Eric Clapton tried to disappear, each in his own way, while ex-Yardbird Jeff Beck saw his former Yardbirds colleague Jimmy Page raking in the dough and rearranged his own career for higher visibility. Bloomfield basically retreated to his home in Marin County, playing in local clubs and going into the studio mostly to produce other artists, like Otis Rush.

Clapton's track was different. Delaney Bramlett was a young white guitarist from Mississippi who, in the mid-'60s, had washed up in LA at just the right time, and became a Shindog, playing guitar in the house band for the popular TV show *Shindig!,* which also featured Leon Russell and Elvis sidemen James Burton and Glen D. Hardin. While he and his wife, Bonnie, a seasoned soul backup singer, were performing around town in 1969, they caught the ear of Don Nix, a white Stax producer who'd been hanging in LA looking for acts to send Al Bell. Nix signed them to do an album, which the label sat on. Undaunted, they signed with Elektra, who released an album on them that didn't sell so well but got a lot of radio airplay. Switching to Atco, an Atlantic label, they went on tour, where they were joined by labelmate Clapton, who stayed out of the limelight, seemingly enjoying just being in a band. Clapton then took three of their backup players, Bobby Whitlock, Carl Radle, and Jim Gordon, holed up in

Miami, and announced that they were his new band, Derek and the Dominos. The double album that resulted, *Layla,* was noted not only for mad drug excess during the sessions, but also for the presence of Duane Allman, who dropped in briefly to execute some twin-guitar work with Clapton, ensuring that the album became a classic, particularly its long title cut, which was a coded love song to George Harrison's wife. It also meant the end of Clapton for a while: he went into seclusion after the band (minus Allman) finished its tour and Leon Russell jumped on the remaining band members.

As for Beck, once out of the Yardbirds, he formed the Jeff Beck Group, featuring vocals by Rod Stewart, a former British folkie with blues tendencies who had a rough voice capable of lyricism. They never had any hits (except backing up Donovan for a single), and lost pianist Nicky Hopkins to Quicksilver, while Stewart quit to try a solo career with a band he assembled himself. Over the course of three years, Stewart became a star, beginning with 1971's *Every Picture Tells a Story,* by which time (just to confuse matters more), he'd also joined up with several ex-Small Faces (including ex–Jeff Beck Group bassist Ronnie Wood), who'd dropped the Small from their name. Stewart was inescapable in the early '70s, as a Face or solo, while Beck soldiered on with new groups.

Confusion was the name of the game, actually: singers performed as bands, bands featured singers. Detroit was a loud, energetic band fronted by Mitch Ryder in a bid for the new market, and another Detroiter, Bob Seger, played guitar in front of organ/drum duo Teegarden and Van Winkle, until he quit to go back to college, dropping out to form yet another band, the Bob Seger System, which wasn't successful, either. The safest career path for now seemed to be fluidity: Neil Young, for instance, had done well in 1969 with his second solo album, *Everybody Knows This Is Nowhere,* on which he was backed by a band called Crazy Horse (formerly the Rockets, with an album on White Whale), who played loud and crude. Young was also a sometime member of Crosby, Stills, Nash and Young, and also made country-flavored solo albums with studio musicians, one of which, *Harvest,* in 1972, was his only number-one album due to the presence on the record of his only number-one single, "Heart of Gold." Singing backup on it were James Taylor and Linda Ronstadt. During this time, Crosby, Stills and Nash also each produced solo albums, and Stills and Nash a duo album. Linda Ronstadt fronted a countryish band made up of Don Henley, Glenn Frey, Randy Meisner, and Bernie Leadon, all Troubadour bar veterans. Not everybody had such a dynamic backup, but songwriters were definitely the current thing in LA. Gathering at the Troub, or for inexpensive meals and margaritas at Lucy's El Adobe, across the street from the Paramount lot on Melrose, were not only Ronstadt but also songwriters such as John David "JD" Souther, Jackson Browne, Ned Doheny, Dan Fogelberg, and Judee Sill, most of whom wound up with at least a cameo on each other's albums. It was a kind of community.

Hovering over it were two men, David Geffen and Elliot Roberts, who would, together and separately, mold the LA scene for years to come. For one thing, Geffen, Roberts Management handled most of these acts, with the hands-on work done by Roberts, a pot-smoking, laid-back guy to his clients, but a total hardnose to those who wanted the firm's services. Geffen, who did the business side, had famously risen out of the mail room at the William Morris Agency, where he'd met Roberts. Roberts was the guy who'd fight for an artist's right of expression, and Geffen was the guy who saw that the artist got paid, and paid well; both seemed like people you could talk to. Eventually, it made sense for Geffen to start a label, which he called Asylum, because it was a retreat where artists could produce art or find refuge from the general insanity of the scene. The core act would be the four guys in Ronstadt's band, who'd been talking a lot among themselves about what it took to make it. The first generation of LA country-rock was passing: ex-Byrd Gene Clark had talent but also substance abuse problems, but he was rivaled in both departments by Gram Parsons, his fellow ex-Byrd and, by now, ex–Flying Burrito Brother. Parsons had gone solo and attracted a singer from the Washington, DC, folk scene, Emmylou Harris, who was a great interpreter of his songs, while he, having not only a number of bad habits but also the trust fund to pay for them, managed to career around Hollywood and get chucked out of the Stones' entourage in France before dying of an overdose in September 1973, aged twenty-six, just before the release of his debut solo album. This, Henley, Frey, Meisner, and Leadon decided, was not the way to do it. They walked into Geffen's office and auditioned some songs they'd worked up, and he was sold. Two of them had an outstanding record contract to fulfill, so Geffen bought it out, also paying for them to get their teeth fixed. In a way, this band—they'd been calling themselves the Eagles—was the Monkees, only much, much hipper, a bit more of an organic group, and with an appeal to an older, wealthier, less fickle demographic. In another way, they were the culmination of the efforts of a lot of people's work in the LA country-rock singer-songwriter world: they didn't write all their own material, and indeed, of their first three singles in 1972, the first, "Take It Easy," was a cowrite between Frey and Jackson Browne, and "Peaceful Easy Feeling" was by Jack Tempchin, a Troubadour bar regular.

While the Eagles were off in London recording their debut album with producer Glyn Johns, Asylum put out its first albums, by Judee Sill (an odd, neurotic woman with a seedy past and a miraculous touch with melody and lyrics) and David Blue (aka David Cohen, a longtime New York folk scene figure), with Jackson Browne, JD Souther, Ned Doheny, Joni Mitchell (who'd ditched Warners for Asylum), and Essra Mohawk (a Frank Zappa protégée formerly known as Sandy Hurvitz) soon to come. Was there gold in those California hills? Record companies thought there could be, and the stampede was on: country-rock bands, such as Pure Prairie League, the New Riders of the Purple Sage (who had Grateful Dead connections), Dr. Hook and the Medicine Show (who performed only songs by Sausalito-based songwriter/children's book author/*Playboy* cartoonist Shel Silverstein), and the Nitty Gritty Dirt Band (who seemed genuinely interested in forming a rapport with Nashville veterans, recording with a number of them on their album *Will the Circle Be Unbroken* in 1972), ran the gamut from opportunism to, well, a kind of folkie authenticity.

The thing was, you didn't have to be a performing songwriter to make a go of things, and a number of writers were emerging to prove this. Laura Nyro, an early client of Geffen's, was one of them. A reluctant performer who had more or less retired from the stage after being booed at Monterey, Nyro had become a millionaire in her mid-twenties, thanks to writing hits for the 5th Dimension, Barbra

Streisand, and Blood, Sweat and Tears, and had a cult following for her Columbia albums. She was one of Geffen's earliest management clients, and when he created Asylum, she was among the first he asked to sign, but she changed her mind at the last minute and stayed with Columbia (reportedly devastating Geffen), making albums until the mid-'80s.

Another example was Harry Nilsson, who started his career as a contract songwriter in Teen Pan Alley West, penning songs for the Monkees and Three Dog Night and recording an album, but who had the spotlight turned on him in 1968 when John Lennon was asked what his favorite American group was and answered "Nilsson." Signed to RCA, he refused to perform, instead lurking in the studio making more albums, which did very well. Ironically, his two big hits were written by others (Fred Neil's "Everybody's Talkin'," featured on the soundtrack of the hit film *Midnight Cowboy*, and the number-one record "Without You," by Tom Evans and Pete Ham of Badfinger, a Welsh band signed to Apple formerly known as the Iveys), but he also used his prominence to lift a friend from his contract songwriting days, Randy Newman, into the spotlight with the *Nilsson Sings Newman* album. Newman himself wasn't too big on live shows, either, although a promotional album of him playing an industry showcase promoting *Twelve Songs*, his debut, got enough FM airplay that Reprise released it commercially.

And then there was Jimmy Webb, from Oklahoma, who started his songwriting career in Los Angeles in 1966, when Johnny Rivers recorded his "By the Time I Get to Phoenix." This led to his being in demand for other artists, including the 5th Dimension, who were Rivers protégés, and Glen Campbell, who took many a Webb composition onto the charts, including "Wichita Lineman," "Galveston," and "By the Time I Get to Phoenix," which sold outrageously well. In 1968, Webb was responsible for one of the weirdest (and most derided) hit singles of the era, "MacArthur Park," by British actor Richard Harris, with its passionately delivered line about leaving a cake out in the rain. Silly as it was, it was a hit again the next year, for Waylon Jennings, who even managed to cop a Grammy for it. From there, Webb became a recording artist for Reprise, where his albums sold modestly. He almost never performed, but his income from his ever-expanding catalogue, including Isaac Hayes's left-field smash "Phoenix," made it unnecessary. Webb, like Nyro and Nilsson, was a pop composer with uncool clients, so he was largely ignored by the hipoisie.

But pop could also be hip, under the right circumstances. Uni Records put on a huge push for a performer it had picked up from Dick James, the London publisher who'd owned some of the Beatles' catalogue for a while. Elton John (real name Reginald Dwight) had toiled in James's employ, writing an album, *Empty Sky,* scoring a film called *Friends,* and writing with lyricist Bernie Taupin, but he was determined to strike out as a performer. The self-titled debut album that Uni released in 1970 was paired with a high-profile tour and laudatory coverage in some of the rock press, although his first single, "Border Song," barely scraped the Hot 100. Thereafter, he routinely hit the top 10, assembling a rather subdued rock band to tour with and honing his stagecraft—it had been a while since a major star spent most of a show seated at a piano—while Taupin, whose lyrics were often opaque, investigated American themes; indeed, John's next album was titled *Tumbleweed Connection,* although the cover photo and the title were the only countryish things about it. He nonetheless had immense crossover success, beloved by AM and FM alike.

The next hip-pop hype was a big deal: gay men had been an increasingly visible presence in popular culture, but marketing a gay male pop star *as* a gay male pop star—there were plenty in the closet, including Elton John—was considered too hot for the culture and the industry to handle. But gay liberation had been on the rise since the 1969 Stonewall riots in New York City, where gay pride established a beachhead, and indeed invitation-only gay dance parties at deejay David Mancuso's loft at 647 Broadway, which began in 1970, were a hot ticket. Gay bathhouses, where men could meet one another and hook up, were much easier to get into. One of the best was the Continental Baths, in the basement of the Ansonia hotel, at 2109 Broadway, which featured not only deejays who'd learned their trade at Mancuso's, but, eventually, a live act in the person of Bette Midler, whose gently Jewish mother persona, sharp tongue, and passion for old show tunes caused the curious, gay and straight, to flock to the Continental when she was performing. Ahmet Ertegun (himself bisexual and, of course, a connoisseur of New York nightlife) took the leap and signed Midler to Atlantic, where her pianist, Barry Manilow, produced her first two albums and then went on to a solo career of his own. Midler's debut, *The Divine Miss M,* was heavily promoted in *Rolling Stone* and the underground press, where at least some of the readers could decipher the code embedded in the title. Midler, like Manilow, became a '70s superstar, although while Manilow cowrote a lot of his own material (his biggest hit, "I Write the Songs," however, was written by sometime Beach Boy Bruce Johnston), Midler was dependent on outside writers, including a lot of former Teen Pan Alley stars like Ellie Greenwich and Barry Mann.

A lot of the East and West Coast songwriter material was marked by introspection and, all too often, unbearable solipsism, as well as a lack of substance. Another style of songwriting, which owed more than a little to frequent visitor Bob Dylan, was gaining strength in Nashville. There, two camps existed side by side. The more traditional-sounding was based largely around Mercury staff producer Jerry Kennedy. A first-call dobro and electric sitar studio player, Kennedy got his break by producing Jerry Lee Lewis's hard-core country hits and two albums by him in 1969, each entitled *The Country Music Hall of Fame Hits,* which served the dual purpose of showing how deep Lewis's commitment to country was and to promote the as-yet-tiny hall of fame/museum that was anchoring Nashville's Music Row. Kennedy's production style was very bare-bones, with no strings except a fiddle and with a dobro sometimes standing in for the pedal steel guitar, and Jerry Lee's masterful reading of the classics. Kennedy's own taste in lyricists ran to the likes of Tom T. Hall, and it turned out that Hall, too, was a quietly appealing singer, and his storytelling songs, such as "Ballad of Forty Dollars," "That's How I Got to Memphis," and the smash hit "The Year That Clayton Delaney Died," sustained his long career as both performer and writer. This encouraged folkier songwriters to push their material, including Kris Kristofferson, who started the 1970s with two huge country hits, "Help Me Make It

Through the Night" (recorded by Sammi Smith) and "For the Good Times" (a hit for Ray Price); Mickey Newbury, whose songs were as close to James Taylor's as they were to the Nashville crowd's and who rebelled by signing as an artist to Elektra; and Billy Joe Shaver, an irascible Texan (also championed by Cash) whose bare-bones approach recalled Hall's but had a characteristic darkness Hall's lacked and who broke when Waylon Jennings did a whole album of his songs, *Honky Tonk Heroes*, in 1973. Also lurking in this crowd was Shel Silverstein, who was writing songs that he was pitching to Nashville, starting with Johnny Cash's "A Boy Named Sue," in 1969, and Bobby Bare's hit "Sylvia's Mother," in 1972. (Silverstein was also hedging his bets by mentoring Dr. Hook and the Medicine Show; their "Sylvia" went pop at the same time as Bare's went country.) These new Nashville artists sometimes hit the pop charts, and Kristofferson went a bit further, with his song "Me and Bobby McGee" turning into a posthumous number one for Janis Joplin and his rugged good looks giving him an movie-star career that included, early on, a silly remake of the Hollywood classic *A Star Is Born*, with costar Barbra Streisand.

Elsewhere in Nashville, a very different ethos obtained. For all its omnipresence in the South, at radio outposts in places like New York (New Jersey, actually) and Boston, and at the occasional Big Event, such as Buck Owens and the Buckaroos playing Carnegie Hall (where they cut a fine live album), the actual sales necessary to propel a country single were tiny. Forget albums—nobody considered country an albums market. Sometimes, as few as twenty-five thousand units could get you well into *Billboard*'s country chart, which in 1972 had seventy-five slots on it. Both the occasional crossover hit and the new, rock-influenced MOR, typified by the Carpenters and the 5th Dimension, emboldened some Nashville producers to think they were under-achieving with their records, that pop success could be had by beefing up arrangements, mixing down or omitting the fiddles and steel guitars, and hiring less-traditional songwriters for material. Probably the most important figure in this was Billy Sherrill, who'd worked at Sun Records' short-lived Nashville studio and had subsequently been one of the founders of Fame Studios. In 1966, having returned to Nashville and achieved the status of house producer for Epic Records, he met a young hairdresser named Wynette Pugh who had a voice that appealed to him—but not a name: he changed it to Tammy Wynette—and he began writing songs for her and producing them in the new, pop-oriented style that was just beginning to appear in country music. When her "Stand By Your Man" broke the pop top 20 in 1968, he knew he was onto something, and started looking for other performers. A natural was George Jones, who'd married Wynette; another was Johnny Paycheck, an Ohio-born singer who sounded a lot like Jones and who'd recorded some of the hardest honky-tonk music in the late '60s, on the Little Darlin' label. Epic signed Paycheck in 1971, and Sherrill grabbed him and gave him a recent soul hit by Freddy North, "She's All I Got," to record as his debut. It took him to the top of the charts and won that year's Song of the Year award from the Country Music Association. At the award ceremonies, when the song's writer, Jerry Williams Jr. (aka Swamp Dogg), stepped up to accept the plaque, he recalled with relish later, "Man, it went *silent* in there." Charley Pride notwithstanding, Nashville was still a very white town.

The next artist to feel Sherrill's magic touch was Charlie Rich, an Arkansas chicken farmer who'd recorded a bit for Sun in its later days and had then gone on to Hi, RCA, and, finally, Smash, where he was one of the few artists Jerry Kennedy couldn't sell to the public. All along he made fantastic records, due to his deep love of jazz (and facility at performing it), but he didn't have real commercial success until Sherrill started grooming him in the late '60s, putting him in front of an orchestra with his piano, and finding him songs. (Although, Rich found plenty himself: his wife, Margaret, was a fine songwriter.) Starting with 1972's "I Take It on Home," he started hitting big, and in 1973, his two number-one country hits, "Behind Closed Doors" and "The Most Beautiful Girl" (the latter a pop number one as well), made him into a crossover superstar big enough that his former labels were able to chart older records nearly as high as Epic was doing with the new ones. He really hadn't changed.

The "countrypolitan" sound had been born; Nashville was more sophisticated than ever, and to prove it, the Grand Ole Opry announced that it was moving out of its home, the Ryman Auditorium downtown, a repurposed church from which it had been broadcasting since 1943, and broke ground (using a mule, no less) on Opryland, a country-themed amusement park with a much larger auditorium featuring built-in television production facilities. It opened in 1974, as country-politan came to dominate country and exert a strong presence on AM pop radio as well in the hands of Kenny Rogers, Crystal Gayle (Loretta Lynn's youngest sister), and Ray Price.

And then there was the uncategorizable Johnny Cash, who was revered by pretty much everybody, old and young. Cash championed Kristofferson by recording "Sunday Morning Coming Down" in 1970 and hitting the top slot on the country charts with it, and had his own TV show from 1969 to 1971, on which he picked the musical guests, who included Bob Dylan (in 1969, his first sighting in public since his accident), Stevie Wonder, Louis Armstrong, Pete Seeger, Neil Young, Creedence Clearwater Revival, Derek and the Dominos, Neil Diamond, and Ray Charles, along with a strong list of country singers. Cash also had plenty of hits, balancing his classic sound with protest material like "What Is Truth" and "Man in Black." His tolerance stood in perceived opposition to the right-wing sounds coming from the West Coast, most notably Merle Haggard's 1969 smash "Okie from Muskogee," a huge hit that began with the line "We don't smoke marijuana in Muskogee" and then continued to say nasty things about hippies and protestors; Haggard followed it up with "The Fightin' Side of Me," which was similarly abrasive. (It's quite likely someone in Muskogee was smoking pot by then, and it's absolutely true that a bunch of them were on Merle's bus, because the inspiration for the song, as Haggard revealed years later, was a crack by one of his band, the Strangers, "I bet they don't smoke marijuana in Muskogee," as they entered the city limits.)

And then there was Jesus. Of all the trends of the early '70s, the spate of religious rock operas and "Jesus rock" was one of the silliest. It started in late 1970, with the release of a double album called *Jesus Christ Superstar*, a rock opera by Andrew Lloyd Webber and Tim Rice, a couple of British songwriters, Lloyd Webber having written some musicals in school and Rice just looking for a way into showbiz as a songwriter. It began as a record, which sold well enough that Robert

Stigwood snapped it up for exploitation on the stage. The two young writers were quite talented, and a couple of the songs from the show were recorded right away, especially Mary Magdalene's "I Don't Know How to Love Him," which hit the U.S. charts in two competing versions by Helen Reddy and Yvonne Elliman. The problem was that Stigwood was readying a big stage production, and in America and Britain, church groups and amateurs were mounting versions and even getting ready to tour them, as they thought that, legally, it was like performing a rock album in its entirety, which bands more or less did all the time. Stigwood had his hands full serving injunctions against churches, which didn't look good.

Meanwhile, Lloyd Webber and Rice cooked up another, much campier concoction, "the first rock cantata," *Joseph and the Amazing Technicolor Dreamcoat*, which parodied a number of rock styles and was announced early in 1971, adding to Stigwood's problems as more performance requests came in. *Superstar* hit Broadway in May, with road companies going out in August and Stigwood confidently predicting twenty million dollars from it. The race was on: an Off-Broadway show called *Godspell* opened and spawned touring companies; Paramount announced a double-album rock opera based on the life of Joan of Arc by the unfortunately named band Smoke Rise (which sort of gives away the end); and an even more preposterous project, *Truth of Truths*, purported to cram the entire Bible into two LPs of rock opera, with seven listed composers who allegedly labored four years on the product. Actor Jim Backus, renowned for his voicing of cartoon character Mr. Magoo, was the voice of God. Motown released a "rock gospel" album with some of its artists, including a rock signing on its new Rare Earth label, Stoney and Meatloaf, and religious labels in Waco, Texas, and Nashville belatedly started chasing hippies while a very bewildered looking Tommy James, sans the Shondells, stood carrying a big stick, clad in white robes, on the cover of his latest album, perplexingly titled *Christian of the World*.

By the end of 1971, *Superstar* had been banned in South Africa for blasphemy, a welcome jolt of publicity Stigwood must have loved. It's possible that nobody could have predicted this, but in the post-hippie world, a lot of young drug takers were looking for unequivocal answers, and "Christian" groups, such as the cultish Children of God (who had a lot of money and whose big trophy was former Fleetwood Mac guitarist Jeremy Spencer) and Jews for Jesus, were all over the streets seeking converts. So were the Hindus, with the Hare Krishnas (the popular name for the adherents of Swami Bhaktivedanta's International Society for Krishna Consciousness) pulling kids into a cultlike atmosphere—and being funded heavily by George Harrison, who recorded London's Radha Krishna Temple doing the "Hare Krishna Mantra" (as well as an entire album of their chants), a mild hit in Britain. Jesus rockers started appearing: Mylon LeFevre quit his family gospel group to do a much-hyped solo record for Atlantic, later joining forces with Ten Years After's Alvin Lee for an album. Then there was Marjoe, a former child evangelist (named for Mary and Joseph), who renounced his ministry in a huge article in *Rolling Stone* after a documentary about his last preaching tour, showing his gimmicks, hit the screens—and yes, he made a record, which sank without a trace. And while they may not have been Jesus rockers per se, an awful lot of the LA singer-songwriters hedged their bets by recording songs of more or less fervent faith, or at least imploring Jesus for help with their current problem.

Ex-Beatles, too, were everywhere in the early '70s, competing to see who could outsell the others with solo records. John had the advantage of being first: it had been his bonding with Yoko Ono and heading in another direction that had widened the fissure in the band. He'd had the first hit as a solo Beatle, and also the first solo album, the infamous *Two Virgins*. That album, and the subsequent *Life with the Lions*, was not so much a John Lennon album as a John and Yoko art project, as was *Wedding Album*, a box with an LP and reproductions of various documents. The real solo debut was *John Lennon/Plastic Ono Band* (which was released simultaneously with *Yoko Ono/Plastic Ono Band*, whose cover was nearly identical), composed under the influence of radical psychotherapist Arthur Janov, whose "primal therapy" sessions the couple was attending as part of their attempt to wean themselves from their nasty heroin habit. Lennon's was mostly raw confessional material such as "Mother" and the infamous "Working Class Hero," an obvious broadside aimed at Paul.

But the other Beatles weren't sitting still. The moment Apple had formed, George Harrison came out with the soundtrack he'd written for a 1968 film called *Wonderwall*, which had come out and then vanished almost instantly; six months later, he was back (on the new subsidiary, Zapple) with *Electronic Sound*, which was exactly that: the tape of his instruction session on the Moog synthesizer with Paul Beaver and Bernie Kraus. But with Phil Spector now working with Apple, Harrison did a whopping three-LP project: four sides of his songs and an extra disc called "Apple Jam," of the core band (on their way to becoming Derek and the Dominos) jamming with various musicians. The album, *All Things Must Pass*, also contained a number-one single, "My Sweet Lord," which incorporated the Hare Krishna chant—and the seeds of an interesting lawsuit, which claimed Harrison had lifted most of the song from the Chiffons' 1963 chart topper "He's So Fine," which George, as a Beatle, would inevitably have heard. The judge ruled that George had unconsciously copied the song, and ordered him to pay more than $1.5 million in damages (which was all he'd made from the song at the time of the trial) plus a lot of the album's royalties. Next up was a gala benefit concert to aid victims of the civil war in Bangla Desh, as the Bengali provinces of East Pakistan called themselves while attempting to break away from the country ruling them from the other side of India. The concert was held at Madison Square Garden on August 1, 1971, and featured appearances by Ravi Shankar, Ali Akbar Khan, Bob Dylan, Eric Clapton, Ringo Starr, Badfinger, Billy Preston, and Leon Russell. *The Concert for Bangladesh* was rush-released for Christmas 1971 (another triple album) in order to maximize royalties, which, like the proceeds from the concert itself, were being donated to UNICEF. (Although *New York* magazine claimed that music publisher Allen Klein was skimming royalties, which led to a war in the press.)

Ringo was busy making movies, but he managed an album of old standards, *Sentimental Journey*, with a photo of the house he'd grown up in, and, a few months later, *Beaucoups of Blues*, a country album recorded with Nashville's A-team of studio musicians, a lifelong dream come true.

But it was Paul, implacable opponent of Allen Klein and Phil Spector, blissfully wed to Linda Eastman and recording on his Scottish farm, whom a lot of Beatle fans were waiting to hear from (the Beatles' own Beatles-or-Stones dichotomy being Paul-or-John), and his first album, blandly titled *McCartney,* came out in April 1970, with the obligatory hit, "Another Day," backed with "Oh Woman, Oh Why," followed by another portrait of domestic life on the farm a year later, titled *Ram,* whose cover showed Paul grabbing the title animal by the horns—causing John to retaliate with a postcard included in his *Plastic Ono Band* album showing *him* grabbing a pig by the ears. Finally, Paul assembled a band, which he dubbed Wings, featuring an ex–Moody Blues guy and Linda on keyboards and vocals, thereby giving fans who objected to Yoko's caterwauling something additional to complain about. Certainly, Wings' debut album at the end of 1971, *Wild Life,* didn't sell nearly as well as hoped, and their subsequent political statement, "Give Ireland Back to the Irish," was so ill-conceived that their next single was the anodyne "Mary Had a Little Lamb." In fact, for a minute, it looked like Paul and Linda and John and Yoko were in a contest to make the most embarrassing ex-Beatle record. John and Yoko found a crazed busker in New York, David Peel, got him a band, and then released *The Pope Smokes Dope,* on Apple, and followed it up with a Plastic Ono Band album, using their new backup band, Elephant's Memory, and affirming their commitment to their new home, the United States, in particular New York City. The album, *Some Time in New York City,* was preceded by a single, "Woman Is the Nigger of the World," which, astonishingly, made it to 57 on the pop charts despite its title. The rest of the album was just as "political" and as well crafted, with songs about the Attica prison uprising, Angela Davis, the Irish Troubles, and White Panther John Sinclair's incarceration, all on the live side; the B-side, predictably, was a jam, this time with Frank Zappa and some of his people. This political activity drew the attention of Richard Nixon's famously paranoid State Department, which began investigating Lennon, who'd applied for a green card and still had a pot bust on his record. (This wasn't an issue for Yoko, who had been married to an American, with whom she'd had a child.) The government vowed to prevent him from getting it.

There was still interest in the Beatles, as *Rolling Stone*'s editor, Jann Wenner, proved at the start of 1971 with a two-part, far-ranging interview with John that ran in subsequent issues of the magazine (along with, in a third issue, one with Yoko); Wenner later put both parts together into a book, *Lennon Remembers,* and issued it on his new Straight Arrow Press imprint, horrifying Lennon, who'd thought he was doing a routine magazine interview and rightly pointed out that he'd never agreed to its becoming a book. Wenner, however, had every right to feel cocky. *Rolling Stone* had just won a National Magazine Award for Specialized Journalism, and had been praised for its June 11, 1970, issue on youth turmoil throughout the United States. It had introduced a book division—besides *Lennon Remembers,* there was a biography of Swami Satchinanda, a health food cookbook, and a guide to making your own clothes, with more titles to come—and a poster division featuring shots of stars by the new in-house photographer, straight out of the San Francisco Art Institute, Annie Leibovitz. The staff had been almost completely replaced, and new hires such as David Felton, Jon Landau, Paul Scanlan, and "sports editor" Hunter S. Thompson took on politics and were about to take the music coverage in a different direction (deemphasizing dope a bit), toward the new royalty of rock, the Taylors, Elton John, and of course Mick Jagger. (When Jagger married Bianca Pérez-Mora Macias, *Rolling Stone* had gotten the scoop.)

As for the Stones, they were largely resident in France at that point, tax exiles driven out of England for making too much money. Their new record company, distributed by Atlantic, had debuted with *Sticky Fingers,* with its Warhol-designed unzippable-crotch cover. (Unlike Warhol's notorious *Velvet Underground and Nico* peelable-banana cover, though, there was nothing to see if one unzipped this cover.) As part of the band's agreement when parting with Allen Klein, they'd had to give him the two singles from that album, "Brown Sugar" and "Wild Horses," but now that they were free, they were recording their next album, to be called *Exile on Main Street,* at their rented French château, Nellcôte. The scene there, with sidemen such as saxophonist Bobby Keys (another Delaney and Bonnie alumnus who would be a de facto Stone for a while) was memorably debauched, with plenty of heroin around. So, it was something of a shock when Richards kicked Gram Parsons out for inviting the wrong people to visit and drawing the attention of the gendarmes. But the album—a double, of course; everyone was doing them—came out in mid-1972, the band mounted another tour, and the soon-to-become-familiar Stones cycle of album-tour-album-tour began again.

Beatles and Stones, Beatles and Stones, mellow and heavy, pop and rock—it seemed like there should be change in the air, but everyone was making too much money, not to mention moving their performances from clubs to Fillmore-type rock halls to a circuit that toured the more successful acts through stadiums and sports arenas, with plenty of room on the bill for warm-up acts, making each show a bit of a rock festival before the headliner. But one man saw another possibility, and was doing something about it. David Bowie's sheer ambition was monumental. He had been lusting after fame since he'd been just plain David Jones in the mid-'60s, finally breaking through in Britain with "Space Oddity," in 1969, but getting nowhere in America, where the single got to only 124 on the charts and where subsequent songs, like "Memories of a Free Festival" and "The Man Who Sold the World," did worse. (His doing a radio promo tour in America wearing a long dress couldn't have helped.) Bowie signed with RCA in 1971, and late in the year put out an album, *Hunky Dory*, that finally got him some attention in America, thanks to "Changes," a clever song that was a minor hit. He knew he should be the next big thing, but the love the British were showing him wasn't translating where it mattered, where the money was: in the United States. It was his time but he'd been unable to grasp fame totally. The germ of his idea for doing so was clearly apparent in a song he'd written and given to Mott the Hoople, a favorite band of his. (They had been about to give up, so he gave them a hit, produced their album, and saved the day.) "All the Young Dudes" was a meditation on the change of generations: "Brother's all alone with his Beatles and his Stones," Bowie had written. The coming generation spoke rock like natives because

it was all they'd known, in part because of such television entertainment as post-Monkee shows *The Brady Bunch* and *The Partridge Family*,
whose creators had learned from the Monkees' weaknesses and exercised far more control over content and image. Now these kids were
getting older and were far less interested in the stars of just a few years
earlier. They'd grown up with not only the same threat of nuclear an-
nihilation that their elders had had, but also the seemingly endless
(and pointless) war in Vietnam. With the British economy falling
apart, with the corruption of the Nixon administration and its war
on drug users and, particularly, black citizens—blacks were now demanding to be armed for self-defense and to patrol their own communities (an idea that was anathema to the administration's policy
makers)—and with gay liberation and women's liberation everywhere
raising issues the hippies had for the most part ignored or, at best,
never considered, this cohort needed a hero to believe in. Bowie became that hero, by turning himself into a fictional character: Ziggy
Stardust. The resulting album: *The Rise and Fall of Ziggy Stardust and
the Spiders from Mars*, as dystopian a vision as the hippies' had been
utopian. Its story was simple: the earth has five years left, according
to scientists, which, to Ziggy (or whoever was to become Ziggy) meant
he had to sum up everything in the songs he was writing quickly and
then transform himself into the voice of a doomed generation. Simultaneously engaging the watching audience and the performing ego,
and with the help of what's probably an extraterrestrial spirit, Ziggy's
persona empowers the crowd, and the album ends with Ziggy assur-
ing the crowd that "You're wonderful" and "You're not alone," and asking them to "give me your hand." What with its gender fluidity and
space ships, the message certainly wasn't for everybody, but margin-
alized kids (boys, for the most part) heard what was being said and,
gradually, bought into it. The album was a transformative moment live.
Of course, it didn't hurt that Bowie had found a genius musical partner in Mick Ronson, an ordinary working-class guy with a major talent for guitar and band arrangements.

It also didn't hurt that Britain was a small enough country that pop
stars could become major phenomena overnight, a sort of greenhouse
whose controlled environment—it was an island and could be traversed

north to south by train in two days, with the population concentrated in a string of major cities, and the media, including the all-important "inkies" like *Melody Maker, New Musical Express* (aka *NME*), and *Sounds,* centered in London—made it easy to test a pop phenomenon. America was geographically sprawling, requiring massive amounts of touring just to expose an act, and its media, radio and television weren't centralized the way Britain's were; nor was there a national must-watch weekly program like *Top of the Pops,* or its late-night, more "underground" BBC Two program *The Old Grey Whistle Test.* As with the Beatles, you could start off being huge locally, then regionally, and then take off in London and, eventually, export your act to the rest of the world. This was how Bowie's new manager, Tony deFries, was working his growing act. In 1972, he signed Bowie worldwide to RCA Records, a stumbling company whose biggest act was still Elvis Presley, who was making enough money for RCA to take chances on acts it didn't actually understand. This resulted in the label's having few notable acts in 1972, when Bowie came on the horizon. They promoted him, sure, rereleased his earlier albums, and he toured, even recording at Santa Monica Civic Auditorium for a potential live album, and the press was polite, but he wasn't shifting units. He was, however, helping out: deFries had also signed Lou Reed, whose first solo album for RCA had stiffed, and six months later had a second album, *Transformer,* produced by David Bowie, and in it, a top 20 hit, "Walk on the Wild Side" (his only pop hit, although he'd be an FM fixture for years to come).

Rolling Stone finally caught up to Bowie in November, with a cover story sneering at his career's calculation and audience manipulation, anathema to the groovy, organic California rock ethos. The writer was sent to Cleveland for the story, and other press was interviewing Bowie at the same time, including a magazine the reporter said was named *Cream.* It wasn't: it was *Creem. Creem* had started in 1969 when a couple of guys who owned a Detroit head shop realized that the local rock scene needed coverage it wasn't getting anywhere else, a view that was eagerly embraced by John Sinclair, whose White Panthers had the MC5 as a house band but who also enjoyed the loud "high-energy" bands playing the Grande Ballroom, Detroit's local Fillmore equivalent. He proposed an ambitious young teen named Dave Marsh, steeped in White Panther politics and living at their commune, as editor. The first few issues aped *Rolling Stone* in format, and the whole thing rapidly ran out of money, but after a retrenchment, a change to a magazine format (a glossy cover and some glossy pages inside suitable for color ads), *Creem* relaunched in 1971 with a cover showing the cartoon images of the Jackson 5, who'd become the latest band to be marketed to the preteen set with a Saturday morning cartoon, as the Beatles briefly had been. Just as *Rolling Stone* had caught the perfect moment to start promoting San Francisco, *Creem* appeared just as the bands *Rolling Stone* disparaged or ignored were coming to the fore in the Midwest. The biggest one was Alice Cooper, who'd been signed to one of Frank Zappa's labels, but who'd moved to Detroit from Phoenix to get serious. Their rebellious image, boosted by songs like "I'm Eighteen" and "School's Out," was aided by the fact that they recorded in Canada with a Canadian producer, thereby giving themselves access to the "Canadian Content" (CanCon) rule, whereby Canadian radio stations were mandated to play a certain percentage of music created in Canada or by Canadians. (Neil Young and Joni Mitchell eventually qualified, too, along with 100 percent Canadian groups like the Guess Who and Edward Bear, and the career-renewing *Procol Harum Live in Concert with the Edmonton Symphony Orchestra*). CKLW-FM, located in Windsor, Ontario, just across the river from Detroit (and, oddly, somewhat south of it), was a highly popular station in Detroit, and launched Cooper's career. (Among CK's deejays was Martha Jean "the Queen" Steinberg, sister of Lewis Steinberg, Booker T. and the M.G.'s' original bassist). *Creem* eagerly endorsed Cooper, while also going for Led Zeppelin, the J. Geils Band, Lou Reed, and locals like the Stooges, the MC5, Brownsville Station, Bob Seger, and Mitch Ryder (whose rock band Detroit *Creem*'s publisher, Barry Kramer, managed for a short while). It must have been galling, though, to realize that Detroit's rival, Cleveland, had picked up on Bowie first, but it had: the city where Alan Freed had started a revolution was aiding another. No matter: *Creem*'s Bowie story didn't condescend or make fun of his audience.

Bowie was well aware that he had competition, and once again, it's in "All the Young Dudes," where he sighed that he wanted TV but he got T. Rex. This was an odd little band driven by an odd little man, Marc Bolan, who was no less ambitious than Bowie but not as well focused or as talented a songwriter. Bolan first emerged as Marc Feld (his birth name) in a London mod band called John's Children in 1967, but perceiving the changing winds, he next showed up in a twee folkie duo called Tyrannosaurus Rex with bongoist Steve Porter, who styled himself Steve Peregrin Took. They made an album called *My People Were Fair and Had Sky in Their Hair . . . But Now They're Content to Wear Stars on Their Brows,* featuring songs that were, well, what one would expect from the title. Bolan's weird, quavering voice was put into service for anodyne hippy-isms, the percussion barely audible, and by 1970, Bolan had changed again, assembling an electric band that was now called T. Rex and working with producer Tony Visconti. Invisible in the States, it had two top U.K. singles, "Ride a White Swan" and "Hot Love." In 1972 came the album *Electric Warrior,* with a full band, a top 10 single, "Bang a Gong (Get It On)," and a hope for T. Rex mania. It also signaled a new British movement called "glam rock," which, the inkies said, was all about (male) androgyny and outlandish stage clothes. Next on the glam assembly line was a quartet of working-class yobbos called Slade, who'd initially made the mistake of touting themselves to American audiences as "skinheads," which, initially, they were. Unfortunately, skinheads were already known in the States as racist thugs who mouthed bigotry and went "Paki-bashing" in mobs. The band reemerged in 1972 wearing bizarre haircuts, cartoonish costumes, and giant platform shoes, with near-bubblegum songs like "Mama Weer All Crazee Now," "Gudbuy T' Jane" (which barely dented the American charts but ruled the British ones), and 1973's "Merry Xmas Everybody," which has had a way of showing up on British radio at the end of each year and has placed in the *NME* charts several times since its initial release.

America's attempts at glam were somewhat less successful. In 1973, Jerry Brandt, former head of the music department at William Morris—he'd mentored David Geffen there—and the founder of the Electric Circus, a contemporary rival of the Fillmore East in New

York, announced he'd signed someone named Jobriath, America's first explicitly gay rock star ("a true fairy," the hype read), to a mammoth deal with Elektra Records. A large billboard of the album cover hovered above Times Square for a bit, and Brandt hit the press with ill-advised quotes about his client's being on the same level as Elvis and the Beatles. The album hit neither of those marks, and after a second record for Elektra sank without a trace, Jobriath and Brandt went their separate ways, with the star later succumbing to AIDS in 1983. If America did produce a glam rocker, it would have been Lou Reed, who'd signed with Tony deFries's Mainman agency for *Transformer*, put out a depressing (and, at the time, much-reviled) rock opera called *Berlin* (which had little to do with the German city, which Reed hadn't yet visited), and put him on the road with a killer band fronted by guitarists Dick Wagner (from Detroit cult band Frost) and Steve Hunter, another Detroiter who'd worked with Mitch Ryder's short-lived band Detroit. This was the band that played on Reed's first gold record, *Rock 'n' Roll Animal*, a live set that became an FM staple.

None of this weirdo behavior, no matter how it might claim a part of the rock-and-roll ethos, was much in the mainstream yet. Led Zeppelin continued to record and tour, leaving behind them tales of epic debauchery. As did the Grateful Dead, who, after two very successful records of CSNY-sounding short songs, *Workingman's Dead* and *American Beauty* (which made tons of money for all concerned, thereby lessening Warner's doubts about signing them), realized that they weren't a pop group, even if they sold pop quantities of records, and decided to stick to the road and doing the same thing they'd always done. Along the way, a few personnel changes happened, with classically trained Keith Godchaux and his wife, Donna, joining on piano and vocals and, in early 1973, the Dead's original keyboardist/vocalist, Ron "Pigpen" McKernan, dying after a long spell of alcoholism. His death occurred after the band had pulled off a 1972 tour of Europe (where they were virtually unknown) that resulted in the *Europe '72* double live album, the last record of theirs to be enthusiastically embraced by a mass audience for many years. Still, the Dead were doing better than their first-generation San Francisco contemporaries.

RCA's granting the Jefferson Airplane their own label, Grunt, gave the band members freedom to do whatever they wanted, which they sure did. Vocalist Marty Balin quit the band, and one record in the deluge of records they produced was credited to Paul Kantner and the Jefferson Starship. Kantner and Slick had a daughter, whom they named China (much preferable to their original choice, which was god, with a small *g*), and the general direction of the craziness was evident in the title of their 1973 album, *Baron von Tollbooth and the Chrome Nun*. Quicksilver Messenger Service was still putting out albums, although by now they were largely a vehicle for Chet "Dino Valenti" Powers's songwriting, which seemed to be in decline. The major force from the Haight-Ashbury days was Bill Graham, who'd vacated the Fillmore Auditorium for his slightly larger Fillmore West, to contrast with his New York venue, a former theater from the days when Second Avenue was the hot center of Yiddish theater. The Fillmore East was always a risky venture, especially as the nearby "East Village," as part of the Lower East Side became known, got politicized, and in June 1971, after some serious confrontations with radicalized locals (who, as always, argued that the music was theirs and should be free), he closed it. The Fillmore West wasn't far behind: increasing real estate pressures and Graham's own changing idea of his relationship to the music business caused him to close it with a show on July 4, 1971, which was recorded and filmed. The participants give a good snapshot of where the scene (and Graham's growing management firm) was at the time: the Grateful Dead, Quicksilver, Tower of Power, Boz Scaggs, New Riders of the Purple Sage, the Elvin Bishop Group, It's a Beautiful Day, Hot Tuna, and Lamb. Graham had been booking Winterland, a huge indoor ice arena, for his larger shows and now settled on it as his default San Francisco venue. He also went into the record business, assembling a stable of next-generation Bay Area acts and putting out their albums on two labels, San Francisco (distributed by Atlantic) and Fillmore (distributed by Warners), overseen by former Columbia staff producer David Rubinson, who'd been the producer for Santana's highly successful records. Nothing much came of these labels (and, indeed, they were folded into Warners before long), but they did introduce one of the Bay Area's longest-lived bands, Tower of Power, who maintained a string of hits throughout the decade, including "You're Still a Young Man," "So Very Hard to Go," and "What Is Hip?" whose hook contained the cautionary but accurate couplet that "What's hip today / May soon become passé." Tower of Power, like Sly and the Family Stone, were multiracial, and their horn section was always the star, so much so that long after the band as such broke up, the Tower of Power Horn Section has continued.

As for the East Bay's other phenomenon, Creedence, they blew up in the early '70s, releasing the hitless *Mardi Gras* in 1972, at which point Tom Fogerty came out with a solo album that disappeared immediately. His brother John, a year later, made a record as the Blue Ridge Rangers, a stiff bluegrass attempt on which he played all the instruments. He then disappeared, suing Saul Zaentz, Fantasy Records' president, to get out of his publishing contract. Although he made an album for Asylum in 1975, it would be ten years before John reappeared, still bitter. But despite such attempts to recapture the past, such as Stoneground (a Warners band featuring ex–Beau Brummel Sal Valentino and original Family Dogger Lynne Hughes) and the disastrous cross-country, Tom Donahue–led bus-and-music extravaganza the Medicine Ball Caravan (also funded by Warners), which was supposed to bring the hippie lifestyle to Middle America (which had been working on its own version of it all along and didn't need help, but thanks anyway), such action as there was happened in Marin County. There the laid-back life (funded by the record companies) and faux-rustic surroundings nurtured everyone from Van Morrison to the Youngbloods to Lee Michaels to Dan Hicks and His Hot Licks (an acoustic swing band featuring former Charlatan Hicks, virtuoso fiddler Sid Page, and two peppy female singers, all in support of Hicks's mordant lyrics) to, of course, the Grateful Dead.

The East Coast equivalent was, essentially, "Woodstock." The festival and its aftermath had drawn unwanted attention to the cluster of towns around Woodstock (Saugerties, Bearsville, Wittenberg, Glenford), but it wasn't so much because of Bob Dylan, who was rarely there, as of Albert Grossman, now Dylan's ex-manager, and his expanding interests, which included a French restaurant, the Bear, and a studio complex, Bearsville Studios, which quickly spawned a label, Bearsville Records (which, after a brief stint at the doomed Ampex

Records, wound up as another Warners imprint). The region was also home to one of the era's odder figures. Todd Rundgren had appeared out of Philadelphia with his teenage band, the Nazz, who scored locally with a couple of pop hits. He then signed to Ampex as Runt, playing all the instruments himself, in 1970. Grossman took an interest in this tech-obsessed young popster and became his manager, particularly for production gigs, which Rundgren had been doing all along, engineering the Band's *Stage Fright* album in 1970 and plowing the profits from such gigs as his highly successful production of Grand Funk Railroad's *We're An American Band* into his own eccentric solo records, which were producing the occasional hit, like 1973's "Hello It's Me," a rerecorded song from the Nazz days. (Indispensable as a producer, Rundgren was also constantly pushing the envelope, and managed to open a video studio in Bearsville well before anyone actually needed one.) One wag called him "a producer with an expensive hobby," but over time, he acquired a fan base, toured, and actually sold records.

Other notable area residents included Paul Butterfield, Geoff and Maria Muldaur (who'd been with the now disbanded Jim Kweskin Jug Band and now made two wonderful Joe Boyd–produced albums for Warners), Happy and Artie Traum (veterans of the Greenwich Village folk scene who'd moved upstate well before the rush), Ed Sanders (poet and scholar whose hippie band the Fugs celebrated the Lower East Side and actually managed to get signed by Warners), Bobby Charles of "See You Later, Alligator" fame, and Van Morrison (who became disillusioned with California and his wife, Janet Planet, at about the same time). It rocked a bit harder than Laurel Canyon, but it, too, was pretty mellow. And the thing was, mellow was selling. *Billboard* even had a new term for it: *progressive MOR*. This covered a number of things that might be said to be to the left of the Carpenters: duos like Seals & Crofts, the Mark-Almond Band, and Batdorf & Rodney; quiet singing groups like America, who debuted with a Neil Young soundalike, "A Horse with No Name," which fooled people until they realized Young would never have written such ludicrous lyrics; Bread, an aggregation of studio musicians and pro songwriters; and the Doobie Brothers, from Santa Cruz, who looked like bikers but sounded like, well, progressive MOR. The market for re-corded music was so huge that the opportunity existed to sell just about anything if you could get it onto the radio and into the stores.

Supporting all this was increasingly sophisticated technology, both in the studio and for consumers. The transistor was taking over, and tubes were on their way out, which, from the audiophile's viewpoint, was unfortunate, since the warm sound tubes gave to a home unit was remarkable. They would live on, but only in high-end components. Transistors allowed the stereo to be on as soon as you threw the switch—no waiting for it to warm up—and they never overheated. They were also cheap and never needed replacing, so all you had to watch out for was the needle. Or you could do without a needle en-tirely, although the world of tape was a mess. Few consumers liked reel-to-reel tapes, and indeed, very few nonclassical titles were avail-able; tapes were more for audio buffs. The problem was, the tape in-dustry had a real investment in eight-tracks, which, except in cars, consumers hated: they broke (an industry term for them was *eggshells*) and, worse, interrupted the musical program with a *KA-THUNK* to switch tracks. Also, their tracks were often presented out of order from the original record and played hob with the increasing number of long tracks on rock albums. The eight-track's patent was American, unlike the far simpler, Dutch-patented cassette, which, like a record, had two sides. Into all this came an entirely new thing: they called it quadro-phonic (or quadrosonic), or four-channel sound, with the speakers set up two in front and two in back of the listener. This, of course, re-quired an entirely new playback device, matched with four identical speakers, a hefty investment once the industry figured out whether the music would be on a tape cartridge or a disc, and, if a disc, which of the two competing quad disc systems would rule the market. What nobody even considered was that consumers were deeply indifferent to this, even the minority who could afford it: money for replacing your stereo and buying new speakers could buy a lot of albums, and there sure were a lot of albums to buy. (Plus, record companies were hiking the price by a dollar in response to higher vinyl costs due to the oil crisis.) Stereo could mimic being at a concert, with the per-former in front of the listener. Quad mimicked nothing except perhaps playing in the band or orchestra oneself, and although it took a long time to die, die it did, in the mid-'70s. In the studio, however, things were zipping right along. Four-track recording had given us *Sgt. Pepper*, but increasingly, technology found ways to improve on that. Eight-track, even sixteen-track studios were emerging, giving producers and engineers new vistas for experimentation, which bands eagerly exploited. Some of the new recording technology, however, was patently absurd. *Billboard* announced on the front page of its May 22, 1971, issue that "A new process for recording sound which involves encoding sound signals into digital pulses has been created by Samuels Engineering." Sure, it was theoretically possible, but at that time a computer big enough to handle the resulting files would take up a building! Nice try, Samuels; this'll never fly.

One place where mellow started showing up like crazy was on the soul charts. Not everyone was following Sly, James Brown, and Funkadelic into outer space, and there was still a lot of traditional soul music. Aretha, of course, continued her million-selling ways, but there were other currents emerging. Bill Withers was a quiet acoustic guitar-playing songwriter whose first record, "Ain't No Sunshine," captured America's ears in 1971 and began a career that, with its ups and downs, has continued to the present day. A slightly similar figure was Terry Callier, who emerged from the Chicago folkie scene in the mid-'60s but was so uncategorizable—he was a running buddy of Curtis Mayfield's in his teens and wrote songs for both the Chicago psychedelic band H. P. Lovecraft and the Dells—that his jazz/folk hybrid recordings for Chess in the early '70s sold mostly in England, where in later years he became a star. But, inevitably, it was vocal groups that were popping up again, mostly on smaller labels. The Stylistics, from Philadelphia, appeared in 1971 on Avco-Embassy Records, after a few tries elsewhere, and went into the soul top 10 with their first single, "You're a Big Girl Now"; conquered the pop charts with their third, "You Are Everything"; and kept going like that through 1975, with Russell Thompkins Jr.'s silky tenor in the lead. The Chi-Lites were on Brunswick, a label best known up to then for Jackie Wilson, and between

Eugene Record's vocal arrangements and masterful songwriting (sometimes in tandem with Barbara Acklin, another Brunswick star) and Robert "Squirrel" Lester's falsetto, they broke through with an across-the-board smash, "Have You Seen Her," in 1971; topped all the charts the next year with "Oh Girl," and just kept going. Their two concept albums, *A Lonely Man* and *A Letter to Myself,* were landmarks of lush soul harmony, with help from Brunswick's master arranger, Tom "Tom Tom" Washington. Next door in Detroit, Motown's exit had created a hole in the soul ecosystem, not to mention leaving a lot of very talented instrumentalists with no work. Record producer Armen Boladian took advantage of this by putting out mainstream vocal group sounds with, among others, the Detroit Emeralds, a trio who'd be a footnote (albeit one with the delightful "You Want It, You Got It" to their credit) had it not been for their 1972 non-hit "Feel the Need."

But the most remarkable eruption onto the soul scene in the early '70s was in Philadelphia. Songwriters Kenny Gamble and Leon Huff had been around the block a few times, starting with Gamble's early performing and songwriting efforts on Philly's Arctic label; they were noticed by Columbia, which signed him to a deal. At this point, he'd hooked up with Huff, a keyboard player who was playing with a group called Candy and the Kisses, and along with Gamble's friend Thom Bell, a gifted songwriter, arranger, and producer who'd later work with the Stylistics, they began looking for talent. They found it in the Intruders, four guys from the 'hood; a song they wrote for them, "(We'll Be) United," in 1965, released on the Gamble label, became a hit the next year. In 1970, Gamble and Huff made a proposition to Columbia, citing the nice catalogue of hits they'd written and produced by then, and suggested creating their own label, Philadelphia International, which would issue singles and albums—mainstream soul companies like Motown still hadn't grasped albums, Marvin Gaye notwithstanding—with Columbia's distribution and promotion power behind it. Columbia wasn't doing much in the way of cracking the soul charts, so it bit. Armed with a new recording studio, Sigma Sound, and a genius engineer, Joe Tarsia—he was able to take the sharp edges off the big backing bands the duo favored and make the tracks sound effortlessly musical—they got to work. From their years in the business, they knew a lot of underused talent: the O'Jays, who'd been on the road forever, recording unsuccessfully for a bunch of labels, large and small; Harold Melvin and the Blue Notes, another road-weary act that seemed to lack one ingredient to put them over the top; Billy Paul, a lounge singer working the local clubs; Walter "Bunny" Sigler, a rotund gentleman who'd had a hit in 1967 with a medley of "Let the Good Times Roll/Feel So Good"; and, of course, their old friends the Intruders. Everything blew up in 1972: The O'Jays released "Back Stabbers," a social message forcefully delivered by lead singer Eddie Levert, over a dynamic Thom Bell arrangement. Next up was a dreamy ballad, "If You Don't Know Me by Now," credited to Harold Melvin and the Blue Notes but driven by the voice of their drummer, Teddy Pendergrass, their missing spark, who was to front many more hits for them before going solo. Simultaneously with that came Billy Paul's "Me and Mrs. Jones," another ballad, which put him on the charts for the next eight years. And finally, the O'Jays opened 1973 with "Love Train," an across-the-board number-one record preaching the message that Gamble and Huff were now establishing as company policy: universal love. (The song was written by Bunny Sigler, whose own version, seven minutes long, was released as a single and album track in 1974, and is as close to a church service as Philadelphia International ever released.) And in 1973, Gamble and Huff served notice that they were in command by recording the theme song for a new after-school television dance program, *Soul Train*, "TSOP (The Sound of Philadelphia)," performed by what was essentially their house band, MFSB (Mothers, Fathers, Sisters, and Brothers, although alternate names were commonly suggested), with vocals by the Three Degrees, another discovery. The new Motown was in Philadelphia, and like the old one, it would lead an interracial musical revolution on the charts.

The old Motown was in sad shape. Not financially: the Temptations were entering another golden period under Norman Whitfield; the Jackson Five were printing money; the Supremes and Smokey Robinson and the Miracles were doing okay; and Diana Ross was doing television specials and was soon to star in a Billie Holiday biopic produced by Berry Gordy, called *Lady Sings the Blues*. The Jackson kids, in fact, were doing well enough that both Jermaine and Michael were also recording solo without the group. Jermaine even married Berry's daughter Hazel, while turning out a few hits. But other acts who'd made the label what it was were edging toward the door: in September 1972, *Billboard* announced that the Four Tops had signed with Dunhill, which seemed a curious place for them to land but, as it turned out, not a bad idea at all, given that they started having hits again. And in mid-1973, Gladys Knight and the Pips showed up on Buddah. In August 1972, Motown officially moved to Los Angeles, although its attention had been concentrated there for some time, and that same month, William "Smokey" Robinson, its vice president, announced that he was leaving his childhood friends, the Miracles, and in 1974, he and his wife, Claudette, who'd sung with the group since the beginning, separated, although they'd later reconcile briefly.

On March 1, 1973, Harvest, a division of Capitol that featured progressive British rock, released the latest album by Pink Floyd, *Dark Side of the Moon*. The band had been a disappointment, compared to how they'd done in Britain, where they'd emerged in 1967 as, in Joe Boyd's words, "the soundtrack of the Underground," famously playing hours-long improvisations during UFO club nights at the Roundhouse, a mammoth former railroad building in Camden that served as ground zero for psychedelic London. Led by Syd Barrett, the quartet had come down to London from Cambridge, and were soon signed to a record deal. Pink Floyd produced a couple of hit singles in Britain, including the Barrett-penned "See Emily Play," which scraped the bottom of the American charts. Their albums, though, hadn't done so well, even after the band determined that Barrett had become their Brian Jones and parted ways with him after their first album. (He managed a couple of albums for Harvest before becoming a recluse, and died in 2006.) Harvest in the United States was a graveyard for the outré acts EMI released in the United Kingdom: Roy Harper, Quatermass, Babe Ruth. The best Pink Floyd had done was *Obscured by Clouds,* a film soundtrack. Then came *Dark Side of the Moon.*

The album wasn't much different from the post-Barrett albums that preceded it: some drones, sound effects, sludgy tempos, and extensive use of an early synthesizer, the VCS 3, a small, easily portable machine that not only generated sounds, but also could modify sounds fed into it. Only six of *Dark Side*'s nine tracks had lyrics, although "The Great Gig in the Sky" had an improvised vocalise by studio singer Clare Torry, which was for the best, because bassist Roger Waters's lyrics tended toward the crushingly obvious: life is to be lived, not wasted; money will change you, and not for the better; mentally ill people can be a problem (firsthand experience there). This time, though, the record sold. And sold. And sold. FM radio discovered it and played it to death, particularly the track "Money." There were bits of spoken dialogue mixed way down, and the album became a favorite for playing through stereo headphones (which had come down in price and were now a standard accessory for a hi-fi) while smoking a joint. It sold and kept selling: It remained on *Billboard*'s album chart continuously for 741 weeks between its release in 1973 and 1988, when it dropped off. (Rereleased in 1992 on CD, it reappeared; in all formats, it spent well over a thousand weeks on the chart.) It sold tens of millions of copies worldwide and made the members of the band very, very wealthy. Not that this would stop Roger Waters from developing a dour worldview and using his band to complain.

This was the commercial breakthrough of a gathering tendency in British rock, progressive, or "prog" rock. It had been going on since psychedelia, of course, but Pink Floyd's triumph made it official. It came in all flavors: Jethro Tull, with their odd front man, Ian Anderson, standing on one leg as he blew flute solos in songs with pretentious, incomprehensible lyrics. Tull's music became increasingly herky-jerky as the personnel started to change, but they managed a number of high-charting concept albums like *Aqualung, Thick as a Brick,* and *A Passion Play,* the latter two of which went to the top of the U.S. album charts. *Rolling Stone* noted that Anderson favored Homeric epics, while being no Homer himself, which was on the money. Shortly after *A Passion Play* (which featured his new girlfriend as cover model; she was also the star of a short film projected at Tull's concerts), Anderson whined about being misunderstood and said he was going to quit to make films. He didn't.

Emerson, Lake & Palmer—Keith Emerson, from the Nice; Greg Lake from King Crimson; and Carl Palmer from Atomic Rooster and the Crazy World of Arthur Brown—debuted in 1971 with speeded-up, loud versions of classical compositions, including an album-length desecration of Modest Mussorgsky's *Pictures at an Exhibition*, which had already been hammered by lots of amateur orchestras. Atlantic rewarded them with their own label, Manticore, which then signed an Italian band, Premiata Forneria Marconi. King Crimson started out with *In the Court of the Crimson King*, a bombastic 1969 album that was in many ways the template for all this, with very serious (albeit obscure) songs and the guitar playing of Robert Fripp—he would become something of a godfather to this scene, with many versions of the band continuing to the present day. Genesis, a bunch of friends from a private school, Charterhouse, in Surrey, was led by vocalist Peter Gabriel and keyboardist Tony Banks. They didn't really come together until 1970, when Tony Stratton-Smith signed them to his new, prog-oriented Charisma label, whereupon they, too, began releasing concept albums, but their career moved slowly at first because they had drummer problems and were still in school when they started. They solved the drummer question by recruiting a non-Charterhouse lad, Phil Collins, who, readers might remember, was an extra in *A Hard Day's Night* when he was a child actor. A band from Canterbury, Soft Machine (a name taken from William Burroughs's novel of the same name), released an album in 1968 that went nowhere, then decamped for Cannes, where they spent the summer providing a soundtrack for *Desire Caught by the Tail*, a play by local resident Pablo Picasso. Upon their return to England, they set up as an instrumental outfit, with the three core members, guitarist Kevin Ayers, organist Mike Ratledge, and drummer Robert Wyatt, keeping the band together while working on other projects with the many prog-oriented local musicians. Among these was Matching Mole, a band Wyatt had put together, who recorded two instrumental albums. In 1973, at a party before going into the studio for the third, Wyatt fell out of a fourth-floor window and was paralyzed from the waist down. Pink Floyd organized benefits for him, and he taught himself keyboards, which resulted in a series of song-oriented albums that have a dedicated cult following. The rest of Soft Machine has soldiered on, sometimes with horns, sometimes not, playing music that can be considered prog rock or jazz fusion for their dedicated fan base.

Probably the number-two commercial success in prog after Jethro Tull was Yes, whose first and second albums show a hard-rock band with a few pretensions. With a change of keyboard players, starting with 1972's *Fragile*—its cover was by artist Roger Dean, who would be associated with them from then on—the band took off for parts unknown, writing long compositions with ponderous lyrics but set to melodies with a pop sensibility, which vocalist Jon Anderson sang in a clear, high voice. What on earth did an album title like *Tales from Topographic Oceans* mean? Who knew? It sold anyway, squatting in the top 10 album charts for weeks. Their keyboard player, Rick Wakeman, departed after that and became a critical punching bag for specializing in all-keyboard historical concept albums depicting, for instance, the six wives of Henry VIII, a rock opera based on Jules Verne's novel *Journey to the Center of the Earth,* and, most ludicrously, *The Myths and Legends of King Arthur and the Knights of the Round Table,* for which he recruited an orchestra and choir for live performances and, just for fun, mounted the production on ice skates. Eventually, tax problems forced Wakeman back to Yes, who have continued cosmically, going through a bewildering series of personnel changes. Many of these groups used an unusual keyboard instrument, the Mellotron, which featured what would today be called "samples" of strings, voices, flutes, and brass, all recorded on a complex tape setup. Players could use it to mimic an orchestra or choir or play single-note lines. The Mellotron was heavy, broke easily, and wasn't too versatile, which relegated it to the studio. It can be heard to good effect on the introduction to the Beatles' "Penny Lane," but was a defining sound of the prog '70s.

Probably the most significant prog recording, but not primarily for musical reasons, came in 1973, when a former folk singer, Mike Oldfield, who'd had a duet with his sister before joining the band of Soft

Machine member Kevin Ayres. At that point, he met Richard Branson, who owned a record shop called Virgin Records, which he'd built up from a mail-order business he'd run out of his bedroom as a teenager; Branson was considering starting a record label himself. He was captivated by Oldfield's explanation of how modern recording technology could build tracks up, with instrumental lines layered into complex compositions, and so, although nearly broke himself, he sent Oldfield to Abbey Road Studios. Impressed by what he heard, Branson then bought a manor house in Oxfordshire with money borrowed from his parents and turned it into Manor Studios, where a band could live for weeks or months at a time, as long as its label agreed to pay (which, at this point, labels were happy to do). Oldfield was the test run for Manor, and he emerged with a fifty-minute instrumental epic called *Tubular Bells*, which became the first release on the Virgin Records label. It was already a smash hit as an album in both Britain and the United States when William Friedkin used an edit from it as the main theme in his huge hit film *The Exorcist*, thereby cementing the album to the charts for many more months. This unexpected windfall gave Branson a lot of confidence, and a lot of money, enabling him to start a galaxy of business enterprises, including not only a chain of "megastores" branded with the Virgin name but also, eventually, an airline, hotels, a couple of British railroads, and a space exploration company. Richard Branson became a billionaire off one album, although discovering his talent for business probably had something to do with it, too. As for Mike Oldfield, he didn't do too badly, either, although the much-awaited follow-up, *Hergest Ridge*, didn't do nearly as well, and subsequent albums even worse than that.

It would be inaccurate to say there was no American prog around this time, but it was a genre dominated by Brits, with, on the one hand, their "public" school culture (like Genesis) and their national mythologies (King Arthur or even the made-up one of J. R. R. Tolkien). America was, indeed, the New World, and in the first half of the 1970s, it had a different quest: to find a New Dylan. The first one had gotten domesticated, and wasn't writing protest or abstract stuff as much, and the record business, at least, seemed to think American youth were pining for the thrill Bob Dylan had given them in 1965 and '66. Nor were the troubadours of Laurel Canyon going to produce him: their songs were far too solipsistic to be visionary or to protest anything more than lost love or dope-fueled anomie induced by touring. But lots of kids had lots of guitars, and just from the monkeys-with-typewriters theorem alone, there had to be someone out there. And it's true, they *were* popping up from time to time. Arlo Guthrie was a natural, being the son of Woody and a friend of Pete Seeger, although he'd sort of shot himself in the foot with his first release, a side-long album track that was more talk than song: "Alice's Restaurant" became a favorite FM go-out-back-to-smoke-a-joint or hit-the-bathroom number for late-night deejays, who largely ignored the LP's other side. His next album led off with a song about dope smuggling ("Coming in to Los Angeles") that was catchy but maybe not what the mass audience was looking for. But there were others. Loudon Wainwright III was, as his name implied, a child of privilege—his father had had a column in *Life* for years, and he became the magazine's editor toward the end of its existence—but he came up through the New York folk clubs like everyone else. Some of his songs were brilliant (self-lacerating, wryly observant, with some good melodies), but in performance, he screwed his face up and stuck his tongue out, mannerisms that made him hard to watch. Still, Atlantic took a chance on him, but let him go after two albums. What really killed his career, though, was a hit single: Columbia had snapped him up after Atlantic released him, and he made a record, *Album III*, that included a song called "Dead Skunk": funny, catchy, and . . . about a dead skunk in the middle of the road. It went to number 16 in early 1973, and from then on, Loudon Wainwright was the "dead skunk" guy, although he has managed a good career despite that.

John Prine was a former mailman who was hanging out in the Chicago folk clubs at night, writing a good mixture of protest and personal songs that impressed a broad spectrum of fans. Nashville's new country writers loved him, and even Swamp Dogg recorded his "Sam Stone," about a returned Vietnam vet with a heroin problem. But his more adult themes—he was married and didn't mince words in his

songs, all virtues in what has turned out to be a long career—didn't
excite the younger crowd, so, good as he was, he wasn't the new Dylan.
His friend Steve Goodman wasn't the new Dylan, either, but it didn't
seem to faze him. He got a decent living from writing "City of New
Orleans" (which became Arlo Guthrie's only top 20 hit and was recorded by lots of other people), before dying young of leukemia. What
was needed was someone less adult, a bit more of a rocker, less on the
mellow side of the equation, but with that Dylanesque verbal sensibility and mass appeal.

And then, early in 1973, although almost nobody knew it yet, he
appeared, and through the same channel as Dylan had: Columbia
Records' John Hammond. Bruce Springsteen had a past in the Jersey
Shore rock clubs, a working-class family life, and, as the songs on his
debut, *Greetings from Asbury Park, N.J.*, showed, an active imagination.
The songs weren't quite ripe yet, in retrospect, but there was something there, which became even more evident in September, when his
second album, *The Wild, the Innocent & the E Street Shuffle*, appeared.
Springsteen toured with the band that played on that record, which
became known as the E Street Band, and featured a huge black saxophonist named Clarence Clemons, whom Springsteen used as an onstage foil, causing the band to become known as an astounding live
act. Not only that, the rock critics loved him: Jon Landau, reviewing
a Springsteen show in the Boston *Real Paper*'s May 22, 1974, issue,
stated, "I saw rock and roll future and its name is Bruce Springsteen."
For a change, an outpouring of critical raves wasn't the kiss of death.
As Springsteen's star began to rise, though, management problems
prevented the release of any more music, and it would be two long
years before he reappeared.

America's nonconforming bands had a tenuous connection to British prog, if only because they didn't fit in with the mainstream, which
was still filled with guitar-solo bands and mellow rockers. Blue Öys-
ter Cult had started as a folk-rock band called the Stalk-Forrest Group
at SUNY Stony Brook, on Long Island, and had even signed a development deal with Elektra in the late '60s. They were managed by their
friend Sandy Pearlman; another friend, rock critic Richard Meltzer
(whose master's thesis from Yale was published in 1967 as *The Esthet-*

ics of Rock) helped out with lyrics. By the time they caught the ear of Columbia president Clive Davis, they'd changed their name and had a solid book of quirky songs, and a three-guitar lineup that was capable of intense soloing. Most of their songs were a bit brainy for the mass audience—critics, of course, loved them—but the first album had an anthem, "Cities on Flame with Rock and Roll," that became a live favorite and an FM perennial. Another brainy band from a New York State college was Steely Dan (named after a steam-powered dildo in William Burroughs's *Naked Lunch*), the product of two determined songwriters, Donald Fagen and Walter Becker, who'd met at Bard College. They sold their first song to Barbra Streisand, accumulated other players in the New York rock/jazz underground, and were offered a deal by Dunhill, whose New York office was headed by up-and-coming producer Richard Perry. Their debut album, *Can't Buy a Thrill,* was seized upon by FM, and produced two hit singles, "Do It Again" and "Reelin' in the Years." Still, touring proved disastrous, even though the band put on an excellent show, and soon the original members fell away, leaving Fagen and Becker to work with the cream of America's studio musicians on records and cease touring entirely. Steely Dan's run on AM faded after 1974's "Rikki Don't Lose That Number," but they remained kings of FM until announcing their split in 1981, with occasional reunion gigs happening right up to Becker's death in 2017.

Much more typical of what America was producing in those days was a trio from Houston, ZZ Top. Centered on guitarist Billy Gibbons, who'd played Hendrix-esque guitar in a popular Houston band called the Moving Sidewalks, the band included bassist Dusty Hill and drummer Frank Beard, who had been two-thirds of a popular Dallas outfit, the American Blues. They signed with Houston music biz gadfly (and, as Huey Meaux liked to remind people, former meat cutter) Bill Ham for management, got a deal with London Records, and began to tour in 1971, mostly in Texas and the Deep South. America was still in thrall to Grand Funk Railroad, and ZZ Top was a little more steeped in blues, but after Grand Funk dissolved, ZZ's third album, *Tres Hombres,* rocketed into the top 10. The band didn't stop touring for seven years, recording during infrequent times off, until their contract with London and Ham expired in 1977. Ham was an old-school manager, having near-complete control over the band and their publishing—for one thing, Gibbons was forbidden from guest starring on other acts' albums or from jamming in public at all, which limited his exposure to some audiences—but they managed a quartet of popular singles (including "La Grange," about the fabled Chicken Ranch brothel, later the subject of the musical *Best Little Whorehouse in Texas*), and the years of toil paid off as they became one of the top acts in the country after signing to Warner Bros. in 1979.

Americans kept searching for a great guitar hero after Michael Bloomfield semi-retired into local gigs and a long relationship with heroin. Polydor thought it had found the answer with Roy Buchanan, a longtime fixture in Washington, DC, bars. He was a cousin of Ronnie Hawkins, brought to the label's attention by country-rocker and Youngbloods producer Charlie Daniels; Daniels had produced some sessions on Buchanan in Nashville in 1970 (which remained unreleased until 2004). Polydor believed in him, though, and released a self-titled album that showcased Buchanan's reserved, almost conversational style in his showstopper, "The Messiah Will Come Again." A second record went gold, but Buchanan was never comfortable with success, and although he continued on Polydor and then went to Atlantic, he was subject to depression and alcoholism, and was found hanged with his own shirt in a Virginia jail in August 1988.

Another ill-fated monster guitarist in the early '70s was Lowell George, who'd been around LA during the height of the Sunset Strip scene, and played in an early version of the Mothers of Invention, from which he was fired. Teaming up with a guy he'd had a previous band with, drummer Richie Hayward, along with keyboardist Bill Payne and former Mother Roy Estrada on bass, he formed Little Feat, who got picked up by Warners for a single, "Strawberry Flats" backed with "Hamburger Midnight," that got a rave from *Rolling Stone*. Their self-titled first album didn't sell too well, the band didn't tour much, and they were in questionable shape by the time their second, *Sailin' Shoes*, came out in 1972, although it introduced LA eccentric illustrator Neon Park's cover artwork, which would become their trademark. Replacing Estrada with Kenny Gradney and adding percussionist Sam Clayton (Merry Clayton's brother) and second guitarist Paul Barrere allowed George to cut loose, especially with slide work, so the band tried again. They began to get more touring work but never actually caught on nationally, although they had packets of fandom in places like Atlanta; Washington, DC; Austin; and New York that enabled multi-day sold-out shows. In 1977, two of these, one in London and one in Washington, were recorded for what became *Waiting for Columbus,* one of the era's best live albums, released the following year. But George, who had multiple drug problems, was already acting erratic, and in the spring of 1979, he left the band (which broke up) and announced his solo career. His first, and only, solo album, *Thanks I'll Eat It Here,* came out almost simultaneously with his death by overdose that June.

Another American guitar-centric movement around this time was, ironically, due to the death of Duane Allman. The Allman Brothers released a posthumous album, *Eat a Peach,* of live and studio tracks, which sold like crazy. In the aftermath, the surviving lead guitarist, Dickey Betts, took over leadership of the band. Then, in November 1972, bassist Berry Oakley, who was suffering from depression, died in a motorcycle accident a few blocks from where Allman had died the year before. This made the band more determined than ever to keep going and, after the gaps in the lineup were filled, *Brothers and Sisters* was released in the summer of 1973, on Capricorn, a boutique label owned by the band's manager, Phil Walden. It became the bestselling album of the Allmans' career. Less overtly bluesy, it had a distinct country feel, exemplified by Betts's tune "Ramblin' Man," which became a smash single.

Suddenly it became apparent to record companies that there was a score of bands following the Allmans' lead: Florida's Lynyrd Skynyrd appeared on MCA boutique label Sounds of the South (run by Al Kooper, of all people), and Capricorn debuted the Marshall Tucker Band, from South Carolina, at about the same time. (Lynyrd Skynyrd was named in homage of a hated high school gym teacher, Leonard Skinner. There was no Marshall Tucker; the name probably came from one stamped on the key to the band's rehearsal hall.) Soon, "Southern rock" was all the rage, with bands like the Charlie Daniels

Band, the Atlanta Rhythm Section, the Outlaws, and 38 Special (fronted by Donnie Van Zant, brother of Lynyrd Skynyrd's Ronnie). It was even better if it came from a hippie commune such as the Allmans lived on: Black Oak Arkansas, a momentarily popular band of the time, was one such, churning out boogie the way Grand Funk Railroad did. Capricorn was the Cadillac of the movement, and released some of the better bands—but there was no shortage of them, some of them sporting Confederate imagery, although some band members were black (even if the music had zero crossover appeal with black fans). Nor was Allman-esque tragedy far from Southern rock: Lynyrd Skynyrd was approaching superstar status with singles like "Sweet Home Alabama," which skewered Neil Young's "Southern Man," and their live guitar epic, "Free Bird," when they lost several members, including their charismatic vocalist Ronnie Van Zant, in a plane crash on October 20, 1977, three days after the release of their career-defining album *Street Survivors*. The members who lived eventually picked up the pieces and re-formed, and Southern rock in general, with its long solos, catchy songs, and defiant regional pride, would become not only a long-lasting genre—several of these bands are still in existence, although in greatly altered form—but a building block in the next country music revolution, as well as a staple of FM radio in the South.

Pop was trying its best, but it needed AM airplay to begin to develop sales and move to FM, and few bands were able to achieve this; Steely Dan was an outlier. One of the great legendary pop bands of the time came out of Memphis. Alex Chilton was the rough-voiced teen fronting the Box Tops, and when their contract expired, he went back to Memphis and, with some friends who were learning audio engineering there, gained access to downtime at Ardent Studios, a new outfit partially funded by Stax, where it recorded its rock acts. Chilton's partner in crime was Chris Bell, a kid in search of pop stardom who genuinely felt he should have been a Beatle. Before long they'd recruited two other like-minded kids, drummer Jody Stephens and bassist Andy Hummel. Because most of the work at Ardent in 1971 was jingles for radio, there was all night to work out songs, and one night, while the quartet was taking a break outside, they decided they were a band and needed a name. There were two buildings across the road, one an ice-cream joint called Sweden Kream, the other a branch of the local grocery giant Big Star. They liked that; it was a joke nobody outside the South would get, and was an ironic commentary on their ambitions, as was the title of the album that came out of their sessions: *#1 Record*. It contained several songs that were as good as any pop-rock numbers since the Beatles, but with a distinctly American feeling. "When My Baby's Beside Me" and "Thirteen" (with its teenage protagonist telling his younger girlfriend to remind her father "what we said about 'Paint It Black,'" a savvy pop-culture reference). The album could have been a monster, with Stax behind it, but at just that moment in 1972, Stax was changing distributors from Atlantic to Columbia, and somehow the album barely sold a thousand copies. This drove Chris Bell crazy, literally. His obsessive attention to detail and his finely wrought songs, which nicely set off Chilton's over the course of the album, were two of the things that had made the album what it was. Before long, he was out of the band and in a psychiatric hospital. When he emerged, he started making an album by himself. (Only a single, "I Am the Cosmos," emerged during his lifetime; he died in an auto accident in 1978.) Meanwhile, the remaining three made a second album a year later, *Radio City*, with its memorable cover of a red wall and a lightbulb, by fabled Memphis art photographer William Eggleston, a fan. Again, Stax ruined the band's hopes, and again, they went into the studio. This time the label rejected their record outright. And that was that, for a while.

One thing Chris Bell had nailed was the idea that if you were going to be an American pop band, it helped to be an Anglophile. One notable band that was on the same wavelength preceding all this was the Aerovons, from St. Louis. Capitol flew them to England to record at Abbey Road—they impressed some of the Beatles' crew (and Beatle George Harrison)—whereupon EMI and Capitol both passed on the resulting album, which wasn't heard until 2003. Bands such as the Wackers, from Montreal; Stories, who were remnants of the Left Banke; Hackamore Brick; and Crabby Appleton all got this, but for the most part, AM radio wanted nothing to do with them; there was too much safer product being released. The only band that actually succeeded, although not in a big way, was the Raspberries, from the Cleveland suburb of Mentor, whose chief songwriter, Eric Carmen, possessed a gift for pop songwriting that somehow touched a chord. Their "Go All the Way" was a top 10 hit in 1972, and they kept going right up to their mordantly titled last hit, "Overnight Sensation (Hit Record)," in 1974, at which point Carmen jumped ship for a solo career and songwriting for others. His first solo record, the unfortunately inescapable "All By Myself," based, as he liked to tell people, on a melody from Rachmaninoff's second piano concerto (yes, he had conservatory training), went to number one.

The Brits didn't make as many distinctions between pop and rock; a band tended mostly to want to appear on *Top of the Pops* and on the charts, to sell records, and, if they were lucky, to tour the States. The British pop band with the best pedigree was Badfinger, former Apple signees whose biggest success was "Without You," a number-one hit . . . for Harry Nilsson. Despite support from various Beatles and a successful transfer from Apple to Warners, they were up against an American AM radio scene that wasn't interested. The songwriting team of Pete Ham and Joey Molland ended in 1975, when Ham hanged himself, leaving a cryptic note about their management. Although the band would re-form in 1979, suicide again tore them apart in 1983, with the death of bassist Tom Evans.

Then there was Fleetwood Mac, who suffered from the opposite problem from Badfinger: they wouldn't die or give up, even though at one point they probably should have. After losing both their original guitarists to mental illness and a cult, they'd added an American, Bob Welch, who'd come from Paris and a career of white soul, and a new guitarist, Danny Kirwan, who suddenly changed his mind about wanting to be in the band and was fired, to be replaced by Bob Weston, and vocalist Dave Walker, who left fairly quickly. They toured America, mostly playing midlevel festivals, during which time Weston started an affair with Mick Fleetwood's wife, causing the band to quit the tour and return to England. Incensed, their manager claimed he owned the name, and he called Bob Welch to see if he was interested in joining the "Fleetwood Mac" he was putting together to fulfill the missed dates. (He wasn't.) The imposters were surprised when they went out on tour (sometimes with "The Yardbirds," another group performing under a fake name) and discovered there were real Fleetwood Mac fans who knew the band's repertoire and weren't hearing any of it from these guys onstage. Welch alerted the real band and talked them into moving to Los Angeles, where he rejoined them, and they got their attorney to file a lawsuit to get the name back to the original musicians. Fleetwood Mac then recorded an album, *Heroes Are Hard to Find,* and went on an extensive tour of the States in 1974, taking bottom dollar so that they could atone for the screwup and get as much exposure as possible. Worn out, Welch quit the band in December, and Mick Fleetwood, knowing they owed the record company a lot of money, went in search of a producer and studio to record their next album.

At Sound City Studios, producer Keith Olsen expressed an interest and showed off his producing chops by playing a track off an obscure album he'd done with an unknown duo two years earlier. Lindsey Buckingham and Stevie Nicks had been in an unsuccessful San Francisco band, Fritz, and had moved to LA to become famous. Their Olsen-produced album, *Buckingham Nicks,* was released on Polydor, with a cover showing them both naked, courtesy of the ubiquitous Norman Seeff, a South African whose heavily treated photos of rock stars were all the rage in LA in the mid-'70s—Seeff shot the elite of the rock world, often in sexualized situations, as on the cover of Carly Simon's *Playing Possum* album and Buffy Sainte-Marie's *Buffy*—but the album stiffed. Buckingham had been doing tours and sessions, while Nicks waitressed, but he happened to be in the studio when Fleetwood was there, and by chance, they started talking; this led to an audition, which led to the duo's being added to the Fleetwood Mac lineup. After all this while, something clicked, and the resultant album, *Fleetwood Mac,* released in August 1975, turned them into stars. Warner Bros., delighted with the tapes it had heard, placed an ad with a picture of the band in *Rolling Stone* and *Billboard,* hailing them as "The Great British-American-male-female-old-new-blues-rock-ballad band" and placing each member's name above his or her head in the photo: "Lindsey" was a girl's name, right? And whoever heard of a chick named Stevie? (The mistake was corrected in *Billboard,* though, the next week.) The configuration worked well: with Christine McVie, Stevie Nicks, and Lindsey Buckingham writing the songs, the group began having pop success with singles like "Over My Head" and "Rhiannon (Will You Ever Win)." It would take a while before they hit number one, but after all they'd been through, they weren't complaining.

To be fair, calling Fleetwood Mac "British" isn't quite accurate. After they'd hired Bob Welch, they became Anglo-American, and remained even more so when they put the new band together. A previous fusion had given a lift to a modestly talented singer named Joe Cocker. A former pipe fitter from the steel city of Sheffield, Cocker fancied himself a soul singer, and assembled a band he called the Grease Band. They were picked up for production and management by Denny Cordell, who got them a slot at Woodstock, where Joe's mush-mouthed singing and jerky body movements went over well, and introduced him to Americans. Soon the Grease Band was history, and Leon Russell, the LA studio musician who'd become a Cordell client, heard that Cocker, with a surprise hit on his hands (the Beatles' "A Little Help from My Friends"), needed a band to tour with. Russell was nothing if not connected, and he whipped together a twenty-one-piece band with backup vocalists called Mad Dogs and Englishmen, who somehow managed to perform sixty-five shows in fifty-seven days in early 1970, which wore out poor Joe, forcing him to take a year off. The self-titled double album they'd recorded live became a smash in the United States, and was followed by a film the next year. This made the public aware of Russell and his entourage as much as it helped Cocker, so Russell and Cordell formed Shelter Records, to release Russell's projects, and a succession of albums followed, including a triple live one by Russell. (Spin-offs from this event involved the duo Delaney and Bonnie, Eric Clapton, and others.) Cocker, however, wasn't doing so well, having added a heroin habit to his already obvious problems with alcohol, and despite recording a new album with a new band under the direction of ex–Grease Band keyboardist Chris Stainton, his performances were becoming legendary for all the wrong reasons. Eventually Stainton could take no more, Cocker moved to LA, and his label, A&M, got ready for his next album, *I Can Stand a Little Rain*. As a teaser, he was booked at the Roxy to showcase it, only to wind up vomiting and falling to the floor in a fetal position after four songs. When the album was scheduled for release in September 1974, A&M bought full-page ads that began "Despite an uneven public appearance schedule in recent years . . ." The album did okay, and as his star faded in the United States and Britain, Cocker found a niche in Germany's Schlager scene (a rock-inflected form of MOR), where he was extremely popular (playing the official concert for the fall of the Berlin Wall in 1989) until his death in 2014.

Russell's career followed a different trajectory. His fans were approximately the same as the emerging Southern rock fans, and merged with some of the boogie crowd, as documented in Les Blank's 1973 film *A Poem Is a Naked Person*, shot on the road and at Russell's compound in his home state, Oklahoma. The film infuriated Russell so much that he refused to have it released until 2015, after Blank's death, when he supervised a reedit. However, he didn't necessarily know what was best for him, given that his big move in 1973 was an album called *Hank Wilson's Back, Vol. I*, a country album recorded with A-list Nashville sidemen. It confused his fans as much as the next one, 1974's *Stop All That Jazz*, on the cover of which Russell was depicted in a cooking pot surrounded by his black backup trio, the Gap Band, dressed like movie Africans. There was no jazz to be heard, and the band quickly abandoned Russell, whose career slowly tapered off as 1980 approached. His legacy, though, was largely through Cordell's wise picks for Shelter: co-owning pioneering reggae label Mango, with Chris Blackwell; Austin songwriter Willis Alan Ramsey, not a big star himself but the writer of a couple of songs that were smashes; and most important, J. J. Cale, a Tulsa songwriter who virtually defined "laid-back" in his infrequent tours, and the writer of many hit songs for others.

By mid-decade, a number of important things were changing in the United States. For one, Richard Nixon, a divisive president who'd lost his vice president, Spiro T. Agnew, to corruption charges, and who'd never been popular with young people—*Rolling Stone* went after him with all it had, including Hunter Thompson—especially after

burglars working for his 1972 reelection campaign were caught breaking into the Democratic Party headquarters in the Watergate building in Washington, managed to make himself so unpopular that in
March 1974, a Harris poll reported that 43 percent of Americans favored his impeachment. Nixon resigned in August. The Vietnam
War, too, was going poorly: Nixon had lied about a "secret strategy"
to end it, and it was widely apparent that American soldiers were dying
for nothing. The new president, Gerald Ford, announced the end of
the war on April 23, 1975, and on the twenty-ninth, the last Americans in Saigon were airlifted out. It was evident the next president
would be a Democrat, and a party atmosphere reigned in the rock
world. Maybe John Lennon would finally get his green card. Big
changes were in the air.

chapter eight

WAITING FOR THE RENAISSANCE

The New York Dolls on stage *(© Bob Gruen/www.bobgruen.com)*

As 1975 began, there was a sense of stagnation in popular music. Numbers aren't everything, and the *Billboard* charts, especially in this era, can be viewed with a touch of skepticism, but the fact remains that in 1974, thirty-five records went to number one, and in 1975, that number would be repeated. (You can compare that to 1971, when there were only eighteen.) There were a number of conclusions one could draw from this without even looking at a list to determine which records they were. For one thing, there was no overwhelming trend: although somebody had to be at the top of the charts, there was no one song for fans to remember the year by, no particular style of music predominating. Only one record in 1974 held the position for more than two weeks (Barbra Streisand's "The Way We Were," at three weeks), unlike 1971, when Carole King's "It's Too Late" was there for five weeks, tying with "Maggie May," by Rod Stewart, but outgunned by Three Dog Night's "Joy to the World," which managed six weeks. The album charts tell the same story: 1974 saw an unprecedented twenty-three albums hit the top slot, with the champ, at ten weeks, being *Elton John's Greatest Hits*. Three other greatest hits albums also made it, the Carpenters' *The Singles 1969–1973*, *John Denver's Greatest Hits*, and *So Far*, by Crosby, Stills, Nash and Young. Apparently, the way to best-sellerdom now was to recycle your past.

Nineteen seventy-four had seen a nostalgia push, too: not the do-wacka-do silliness of the late '60s, but a concerted effort to sell the past via a revival of "oldies"; the continuation of "rock-and-roll revival" shows; the popularity of groups like Sha Na Na and, of *American Graffiti* fame, Flash Cadillac and the Continental Kids; rerecordings of "oldies" by the likes of Tony Orlando and Dawn and Ringo Starr; and, most egregiously, songs *about* rock and roll that weren't rock and roll themselves, ranging from the Carpenters' "Yesterday Once More" to B. J. Thomas's "Rock and Roll Lullaby" to various recordings of "Rock and Roll (I Gave You the Best Years of My Life)," not to mention actual rock and rockish numbers like Led Zeppelin's "Rock and Roll" and a weird, monotonous song of the same name by one Paul Gadd, who styled himself as Gary Glitter to ride the coattails of the glitter-rock fad. His follow-up had the weirdly horrible title "I Didn't Know I Loved You (Till I Saw You Rock and Roll)." There was also the retro approach of Bette Midler, the Pointer Sisters, and Manhattan Transfer, although they were more part of the emerging camp scene. Clearly, this was a movement running out of ideas.

You can see Gary Glitter up close in all his sweaty, pop-eyed, beer-bellied glory in *All You Need Is Love,* the entire history of popular music presented as an ambitious but flawed, nearly seventeen-hour 1977 television series made by British director Tony Palmer, who, as 1975 began, was just wrapping up the filming of the contemporary bits. One of his interviewees was Clive Davis, the forty-three-year-old former Columbia Records president who'd been forced out of the company after it was revealed that he'd used company funds to partially pay for his son's bar mitzvah. (He defended this by saying that enough of the record business was in attendance at the ceremony that it was, indeed, a business expense.) Davis was the sort who landed on his feet, and sure enough, after a decent interval, Columbia Pictures (no relation to Columbia Records, which was at the time owned by CBS) discreetly asked if he'd like to deal with a property it had acquired, Bell Records (on which Gary Glitter's records were released in the United States, along with Tony Orlando and Dawn, the Partridge Family, the 5th Dimension, and many more). Bell's longtime president, Larry Uttal, quit to form Private Stock Records, and Davis announced that the mess he'd inherited would now be released under his new label, Arista. In his brief time on camera, Davis made the point to Palmer that record executives like him don't make trends; they spot them. And from where he sat at that moment, he didn't see any. As it was, his first successes would be with modern MOR, with his new signings Melissa Manchester and Barry Manilow. But just as he'd been at Monterey, he was eager to find contemporary trends to jump on.

Palmer's cameras also traveled to Birmingham, Michigan, a sub-urb of Detroit, where he interviewed the editor of *Creem* magazine, Lester Bangs. This was a wise but offbeat choice, given that the obvi-ous thing would have been to interview *Rolling Stone*'s editor/publisher Jann Wenner. *Creem*, though, had its ear a bit closer to the ground and wasn't currying favor quite so heavily with the movers and shak-ers of the record business, noticing from its midwestern vantage that there was a lot of stuff (Bowie, for one) that kids liked but that *Roll-ing Stone* disdained. Bangs had grown up in Southern California, an autodidact who flooded *Rolling Stone* with record reviews, which, early on, it selectively published. Dismissed as a freelancer in 1973 for dis-respecting musicians (specifically boogie-sludge purveyors Canned Heat, whose love of the blues extended to their making a record with Alvin and the Chipmunks), he turned his verbal fire hose onto *Creem*, which saw in his populism and unhinged intellectualism exactly what the magazine needed as it went national and original editor Dave Marsh was itching to move on. An iconoclast in the swamp of medi-ocrity, Bangs is worth quoting at length:

> *My generation had everything handed to them. I never paid any dues . . . There was no intellectual energy behind the revolt of the '60s. The hippies differ from the beatniks in that they were illiterate. And most of the other generations of American youth we've seen in the past few years, they've become progressively more illiterate—not illiterate, but ignorant.*
>
> *Theatricality is a red herring and is distracting you from the fact that something's gonna have to happen pretty soon. It's like waiting for the Renaissance when everybody thinks it has to happen. It's*

commonly said that every ten years there's gotta be a big star in the middle of the decade . . . Sinatra, Presley, the Beatles. Well, it's been two years and nothing's happened. Here we are half-way through the '70s and the counter-culture hasn't even begun.

Of course, if he'd been contacted a year later, he'd have had a much different perspective.

The theatricality Bangs referred to was, indeed, a big thing at the moment, from Alice Cooper's wild assault, featuring at various times a snake and a hanging, to Bowie's carefully scripted Ziggy Stardust, to two bands that grew up in the same venue in New York.

The Mercer Arts Center was, in fact, a couple of ballrooms in a decrepit downtown hotel, the Broadway Central, whose former kitchen (known as the Kitchen) was also a center of avant-garde video art and music. Original rock bands had very few outlets in Manhattan proper, due to the city's antiquated and destructive cabaret card laws. No performer could appear in a place where alcohol was served without a card, and these were given only to people who had a clean record, one that stayed that way. (Jazz great Thelonious Monk lost his card for being in a car with Bud Powell, who was found by a policeman in possession of heroin, and only regained it after a Herculean effort.) And although the Lower East Side and other downtown bits of Manhattan had bands, they had no real place to play until they were big enough for the concert circuit—or were willing to play New Jersey and/or Long Island, heaven forbid. Thus, a few of them began to do shows at the Mercer. The first was the New York Dolls, who fit right into the scene. Sounding a bit like a looser version of the Rolling Stones, but visually all over the map, they wore dresses, hot pants, platform shoes, and a bit too much makeup. (Guitarist Sylvain Sylvain was an accomplished tailor, which helped.) Their lead guitarist, Johnny Thunders, looked like Keith Richards, but more dangerous, and their lead singer, David Johansen, looked enough like Mick Jagger (and, more important, moved like him) to complete the effect. They somehow got a Mercury Records A&R guy, former *Rolling Stone* writer/editor Paul Nelson, down to hear them. Nelson, a former running buddy of Bob Dylan's in college, was impressed, and turned Rod Stewart onto them.

Stewart invited the Dolls to tour with him in England, and while they were there, they solidified their legend when their drummer, Billy Murcia, went to a party and overdosed on heroin. Attempts to revive him with coffee led to his choking to death. The band recruited a new drummer and acquired manager Marty Thau, Nelson came up with a contract, and they recorded a self-titled album in late 1972, with Todd Rundgren producing. It didn't sell, but they got another chance with the aptly titled *Too Much Too Soon*, produced by former Shangri-Las producer George "Shadow" Morton, which *Creem*'s savvy readers voted the best album of 1973, and the worst. It, too, sold miserably, and Mercury dropped the band, but not before the Dolls had joined the Velvet Underground and Big Star in the growing pantheon of influential failures.

One of the drummers the Dolls auditioned and rejected after Murcia's death was a New York rock veteran named Peter Criscuola, another Mercer habitué, whose current band, Wicked Lester, had recorded an album for Epic, tossed some members, and was now down to Criscuola, Paul Stanley, and Gene Simmons. They'd experimented with a gimmick of wearing makeup onstage to obscure their identities, and despite everyone's industry connections, they were turned down by all who saw them. They added another member, Ace Frehley, on lead guitar, and suddenly things clicked. A week later, they changed their name to Kiss. After acquiring a manager, Bill Aucoin, they signed with a brand-new label, Casablanca, started by former Buddah wunderkind Neil Bogart, in November 1973. (Their labelmates were Parliament, George Clinton's latest iteration of his group, and Clinton was watching Kiss very, very closely.) Aucoin helped Kiss solidify their image, perfecting the makeup and adding costumes, and put the band on the road immediately. Bogart released a single, "Kissin' Time," which rose to a magisterial 83 and then vanished. Kissing these guys was the last thing on any teenage girl's mind; singles wouldn't be Kiss's path to success (nor would girls: their audience was overwhelmingly male), as their live show, increasingly dependent on gimmicks, would show. Perhaps not unexpectedly, they were an instant hit in Japan. Very expectedly, *Rolling Stone* ignored them. *Creem* did not. The Broadway Central Hotel, having given birth to the

Kitchen (now relocated, and a key venue for the emerging downtown avant-garde music scene of Philip Glass, Laurie Anderson, and Steve Reich), and having done its bit to reestablish live rock in New York, bid adieu and collapsed on August 3, 1973.

Clive Davis may have been on the move, but in 1974, his star was eclipsed by David Geffen's. Bob Dylan had left Albert Grossman's management and, soon enough, was refusing to record further for Columbia, which took revenge by releasing two fairly awful records of outtakes and weird cover versions, *Self Portrait* and *Dylan,* to help fulfill his contract obligations. The split was official in November 1973, and at the same time, Dylan announced a tour with the Band backing him, a major event. They gathered at his house in Malibu to rehearse, and there, on the sidelines, was David Geffen, watching and talking to them. In December, he announced that Dylan was forming his own label, Ashes and Sand, and that Geffen was making it a subsidiary of Elektra, with which he'd merged Asylum. A new record, *Planet Waves,* was due imminently, and appeared in February (albeit on Asylum), hitting the top spot on the album charts two weeks after breaking in at number two. In its March 9 issue, *Billboard* printed a puff piece headlined, "Geffen Going Great," which reported that the young mogul, who'd turned thirty-one the week before, was insanely busy—he'd never married, the story noted, oddly—and had achieved something never before seen in the record business: this week, Geffen product held the number-one (*Planet Waves*), -two (Joni Mitchell's *Court and Spark*), and -three (Carly Simon's *Hotcakes*) slots on the *Billboard* Hot 100. (Apparently nobody in his organization was dealing with singles, given that the first single from Dylan's album, "Forever Young," which would go on to plague weddings throughout the '70s and beyond, never charted.) There was a lot of muttering that this commercial miracle was due to a shady industry practice called transshipment, in which product that wasn't ordered was "mistakenly" received by retail outlets, who had the option to return it for full credit, at which point it went somewhere else that had ordered it. Or not: for the moment, the accountants would register this as sales. This allegation has never been proven or disproven, but there was a widespread wisecrack that *Planet Waves,* which wasn't a very good album and had two versions of one of its songs on it, had "shipped gold and returned platinum."

Dylan was on tour, though, and in July the live double album of the tour, *Before the Flood* (which really was a good album, giving a lot of space to the Band), was released on Asylum. That same week, it was announced to the industry that Atlantic and Elektra-Asylum were merging, with Ahmet Ertegun and David Geffen as cochairmen and Jerry Wexler as vice chairman. (The actual merger would take a while longer as administrative matters were ironed out.) In mid-August, Dylan announced his re-signing to Columbia, reportedly "furious" (*Billboard*'s word) at the Elektra-Asylum deal, the actual sales figures for his album, and the heavy returns. As for the Band, they owed Capitol a couple more albums, which they announced they'd deliver.

Another record company drama was drawing to a close, too. Ever since breaking with Atlantic, Stax had been doing well, but the partnership with Paramount wasn't a good idea. Paramount had been the last of the film studios to start a label, but it was rudderless, so Stax made plans to sever that relationship as soon as it could, and by 1972, it had signed a distribution deal with Clive Davis at Columbia. This was a coup: Columbia already had Philadelphia International, and now it had another successful black label. Maybe Davis's dream of conquering the soul charts could become a reality. "We were off to the races," Al Bell said of Stax, and it was: the *Wattstax* film premiered at the Cannes Film Festival to much approbation; Johnnie Taylor, William Bell, the Soul Children, and the Staple Singers ruled the charts; the label paid off its outstanding loans; Isaac Hayes announced a private construction company to build affordable housing; and in May 1973, Clive Davis was escorted from CBS's headquarters. Stax's deal had proved to be more a pact with Davis, and its details hadn't been worked out. Investigators were not only looking into his dealings, but those of Stax. The label was still breaking talent: the young comedian who'd appeared in *Wattstax*, Richard Pryor, signed with Stax and recorded an album called *That Nigger's Crazy*, for which Stax had to set up the Partee label when Columbia's new overseers balked at releasing it. In fact, Columbia was concerned that Stax was releasing more product than it should, and began holding back 40 percent of the money it owed the label to cover returns. Stax contended that if Columbia just distributed the damn records, they'd sell, given that distributors were saying they couldn't get the records they'd ordered. Then, in April 1974, Columbia held back over a million dollars it owed the label. (This dispute was one of the things that had killed both of Big Star's albums.) Then things got seriously silly: there was a bidding war for a ten-year-old Scottish girl named Lena Zavaroni, who'd had a smash in England with "Ma! He's Making Eyes at Me." Her shtick was singing standards—not a typical Stax act, but it won her and released her single, which struggled into the 90s in late summer, and her album, which didn't chart.

Just when Stax should have been narrowing its focus to deal with Columbia, some of its people were doing things like opening an office in Paris and trying to land a South African musical in exchange for an hour-long radio program there that played only Stax material. These things cost money, and thanks to the problem with its distributor, the money wasn't coming in. Stax's debt to Union Planters National Bank in Memphis was over ten million dollars. Jim Stewart, in retirement, put up a chunk of his fortune to keep the label afloat. Isaac Hayes had gotten a check for $270,000 to pay his taxes, and it bounced. He sued and asked to be let out of his contract so he could sign with ABC Records, and won, taking with him the Dramatics, a fairly successful vocal group. Richard Pryor also had problems with the label, and it reluctantly gave him his release. He was quickly snapped up by Warner Bros., which rereleased *That Nigger's Crazy* and began a series of releases that made Pryor a huge star. (Of course, it didn't hurt that Warners was also a film studio.) It was flat-out war: Al Bell faced down Arthur Taylor, the head of all of CBS. The result, the visible result, was a fleet of trucks returning the records Columbia had bought. The packing was intact: the records had never left Columbia's warehouses. By the end of 1974, Stax had defaulted on its payments to Union Planters, and the bank seized the label's publishing wing, its most reliable source of income. The bank needed the money: eight of its officers had just been indicted for embezzlement, including Joe Harwell, who was in charge of Stax's loans. Stax itself staggered on through 1975, releasing a flood of greatest hits albums, and in September, Al Bell and Harwell were served with an indictment in federal court alleging that they'd embezzled $18.9 million. The label kept looking for money, and had almost reached a deal with King Faisal of Saudi Arabia when he was assassinated.

Then something symbolic happened: Al Jackson Jr., who'd drummed with Booker T. and the M.G.'s in Stax's early days, was now part of the studio band that Willie Mitchell was using at Hi Records for Al Green and others, and who'd been talking to the other M.G.'s about a reunion, was shot to death by robbers at his home in Memphis. Packy Axton, whose band the Mar-Keys had created the label's first hit, died of alcoholism in January 1974. The next moves weren't symbolic at all: On December 5, the assets of East/Memphis Music were auctioned on the courthouse steps. The only buyer was Union Planters Bank, which bought the company for Stax's outstanding debt. Next, Union Planters coordinated a petition for involuntary bankruptcy over debts to three suppliers totaling $1,910.13. On December 19, Al Bell was escorted from the building, and it was fitted with a new padlock. Stax was over. Fortunately, Southern soul music wasn't, thanks to Willie Mitchell, Bobby "Blue" Bland, and B.B. King doing well at ABC (where Isaac Hayes soon fizzled out) and to an interesting scene developing in Hialeah, Florida, that would soon be making waves. But the times, they were a-changing.

One factor was television. TV had helped make rock and roll as far back as Dick Clark's original *American Bandstand* in 1957, but rock and roll hadn't really made it on to prime-time network television. Clark had tried a nighttime show presented on a stage, but it flopped, and fans hoping for a sight of their favorite stars had to wait for Ed Sullivan or one of his competitors to book them. After the British Invasion, shows like *Shindig!* and *Hullabaloo* did their best but were hampered by poor production values, even when, as in *Shindig!*'s case, the house band was first rate. In 1966, veteran disc jockey Bill "Hoss" Allen produced twenty-six episodes of *The !!! Beat*, a blues/soul show filmed in Dallas, with Clarence "Gatemouth" Brown as bandleader and an amazing lineup of stars appearing. The program was syndicated but failed to make much of an impression, although the tapes were saved and reissued decades later by Bear Family Records. One thing was certain: post-Woodstock, enough potential viewers existed to make a rock show a success, but they wanted better camerawork, acts that might not be coming to their town, more of a concert feeling, and no condescension.

The best minds in television were working on it: Dick Clark for ABC; Don Kirshner, who'd been following the story from Teen Pan Alley's Aldon Music through the Monkees and the Archies; and NBC's Burt Sugarman, who'd produced two Grammy telecasts. By late 1973, they had come up with three shows, all of which were broadcasting in the stoner-friendly hours after midnight. Clark was incensed that his longtime network, ABC, would pick Joshua White, a former stage manager at the Fillmore East, and Sunny Schnier, who'd worked as a publicist there, to produce the series *In Concert*, its initial offering, and fumed to *Rolling Stone* that only he had the expertise to run such a show. Meanwhile, NBC's *Midnight Special* had gotten off to a rocky start with Canadian MOR sensation Anne Murray as host, thinking that because the show broadcast after Johnny Carson's popular late-night talk show, they'd hold on to that audience. Ratings proved them wrong, and by late 1973 they were scrambling for a new approach; they managed a coup when, after the shortest retirement of all time, David Bowie reemerged at London's Marquee Club to tape an episode for the program. Meanwhile, *Don Kirshner's Rock Concert* was syndicating itself across the country. A year later, not much had changed. A sardonic piece by Ben Fong-Torres in *Rolling Stone*'s October 10, 1974, issue noted that the three programs "are thriving. And keeping out of each other's way. And beginning to look and sound more like each other than ever before." But that's not the only thing that was problematic: television sound was awful. It always had been. Nobody recorded and mixed television sound with high fidelity in mind because the speakers on televisions were tiny and had limited range. Even college-dorm-style record players had better sound than a much more expensive color television, and that was where the fans first encountered the music. As Black Oak Arkansas's manager, Butch Stone, said a year later, "TV people are used to mixing *I Love Lucy*, and don't know shit from beans about mixing rock." Something could be done—for years, CBS had partnered with its radio network for special televised classical events where you'd turn down your TV sound and use your FM stereo hi-fi rig to hear the orchestra in glorious sound. As of Fong-Torres's article, ABC's *In Concert* and NBC's *Midnight Special* were setting up simulcast possibilities with their networks, but another show was reaching far more ears: *King Biscuit Flower Hour* was a syndicated radio show that recorded in high fidelity and distributed each week's show on tapes or private LP records to hundreds of subscribing stations. Unlike the television shows, for which artists had to make space in their touring schedules, these could be recorded on tour without inconveniencing the band much at all. But that didn't deter PBS, the public broadcasting system, which had started to broadcast *Soundstage* from WTTW, its Chicago outlet, a show that would preserve some great moments of blues; and Chip Monck, who'd been a stage announcer and technician at Woodstock, launched a late-night syndicated rock talk show, *Speakeasy,* which came and went. Fong-Torres, following up on the story in October 1975 with another article, noted that *In Concert* had been unceremoniously dumped, *The Midnight Special* had reinstated Helen Reddy as host, and *Don Kirshner's Rock Concert* was now about to air Pure Prairie League, Ruby Starr, and the Commodores. "A lot of the 'A' groups," Don Kirshner told Fong-Torres, "won't do TV any more." ABC was going to test *Saturday Night Live with Howard Cosell* (a beloved sportscaster), and NBC was also developing a program called *Saturday Night Live,* a comedy/variety show with 20 percent music in the course of each show. NBC won the battle of the titles, and the latter show would, indeed, become very important, and not just for the opportunities it gave rock bands. For the moment, though, as Columbia's old slogan had it, phonograph records were still "your best entertainment value."

Well, phonograph records and tapes, which were now firmly established as a portable medium and one with a very profitable subfeature: they cost very little to duplicate, and with a few thousand blank cassettes and a photocopying setup, you could make counterfeit tapes that were almost indistinguishable from the original, set up a display in a nontraditional venue like a truck stop or barbershop, and print money. The industry, sometimes with the help of the FBI if interstate commerce could be proven, was going after the counterfeiters.

Records were a bit harder to counterfeit, but they, too, were a menace: there were never-confirmed rumors that in order to make big numbers fast, some labels were hiring counterfeiters to manufacture records. (Records were also costing more to manufacture: the OPEC retaliation for U.S. support of Israel in the Ten-Day War was to hike the price of oil, and oil was the starting point for polyvinyl chloride, the stuff records were made of.) But even darker clouds were about to burst. In the spring of 1975, the U.S. Attorney's office in Newark, New Jersey, released the first of its indictments of music industry figures, the result of a two-year investigation into the record business that ran out of offices in Newark, New York, Los Angeles, and Philadelphia. A number of charges were announced, including tax evasion and commercial bribery, that last being the ghost of the industry's old friend, payola. Among those indicted were Clive Davis, Kenny Gamble, Leon Huff, and just about everybody involved with Chicago-based Brunswick/Dakar Records, including its president, Nat Tarnopol, who got his start as Jackie Wilson's manager, and a vice president, Carl Davis, who was responsible for two of its biggest stars, Tyrone Davis and Otis Leavill, and had brought a number of acts from his previous gig at OKeh. There was (as there had been the last time around for a major record-biz scandal) an air of belief that these silly kids today wouldn't listen to this trash if someone weren't getting paid to force it on them, an idea that was even less viable at this point than ever. It's notable that no progressive-rock FM stations were involved, and indeed, once again the alleged malefactors seemed to have been selling black music. In truth, the black record business had always had colorful characters involved with it, and questionable promotion tactics, but the prosecutors had learned a bit from the last time, and a lot of the charges were very specific, particularly in Brunswick/Dakar's case.

Clive Davis shrugged off his charges, and Columbia Pictures backed him up, while Gamble and Huff kept going on as if nothing had happened—and in fact, they were about to enter yet another golden period. But the charges against the Chicago folks were tawdry and, it seemed, correct: stories of large amounts of records being traded for cars and other goods outside the normal wholesale framework, and for below wholesale prices, cutting out of the picture not only the wholesalers, but also the artists. Brunswick/Dakar's Tarnopol, it appeared, was also not paying taxes on all this black-market cash, which meant that the IRS started looking at the artists, which resulted in the Chi-Lites' discovering that their managers hadn't taken care of their cash, and the subsequent mess destroyed the group. Eugene Record, their longtime leader and chief songwriter, tried an unsuccessful solo career with Warners, and the other guys went on without him and signed to Mercury, but this was the end for them, and for the Chicago soul scene—except for Curtis Mayfield, who was putting out some odd records indeed at this point. As a sort of coda, on September 29, 1975, Jackie Wilson was playing a Dick Clark oldies show in Cherry Hill, New Jersey, ironically, performing "Lonely Teardrops," and while singing the words "My heart, my heart," he fell to the stage, the victim of a massive coronary. He was in a coma for close to four months, and woke up, but was irreparably damaged. Tarnopol was too busy with his other problems, but some prominent soul artists did benefits, the proceeds of which went mostly to the IRS; Jackie, too, had been neglected. He finally died in 1984, at which point several "widows" appeared to fight over what little was left. Tarnopol died in 1987, aged fifty-six.

As for the rock biz, all seemed well. A kind of formula existed now, a way to deal with the volatility of its performers. Sales were so huge that it was okay to humor your big acts by offering band members the chance for solo work—the Who were basically Pete Townshend's backup, but 1975 saw all the band's members release solo albums, even their madman drummer, Keith Moon; while even the Moody Blues' flutist, Ray Thomas, got two solo albums while the band was trying to figure out if it still existed—and encouraging more or less temporary reshufflings of unemployed members of other groups. The permutations of Crosby, Stills, Nash and Young alone were staggering. The best illustration of this is literally a bunch of illustrations: a fanzine publisher in Buckinghamshire, England, Pete Frame, was a former draftsman for the local electric utility company, and using his keen memory, massive cache of interviews, and draftsman's skills (including calligraphy), he began to publish "rock family trees" in his 'zine *Zig Zag*. These were later collected in three volumes and make for fascinating browsing.

In practice, though, it went sort of like this: Free broke up in 1973, and vocalist Paul Rogers and drummer Simon Kirke were up for something new, so they hired guitarist Mick Ralphs, recently departed from Mott the Hoople, and bassist Boz Burrell, from King Crimson, a band that was always shedding members, and formed Bad Company. Taken on by Led Zeppelin's manager, Peter Grant, they had great success in America, with five chart-topping albums between their debut in 1974 and their stop for a pause in 1979. Or take a band like the Small Faces. Dropped by their label and unsuccessful in America, they were at a low ebb when Rod Stewart, needing a regular band to tour and perform the songs he'd recorded with studio musicians, asked them to join him. Face Steve Marriott, however, went off to Paris to record with French rocker Johnny Hallyday, at which sessions Marriott met Peter Frampton, who'd left his own band, the Herd. Something clicked, they recruited a rhythm section, and Humble Pie was born. A&M Records saw a chance to get in on the ground floor of a good thing and signed them, and they began to tour the United States to great success on FM radio and live from 1971 to 1975, at which point Frampton, who'd had a side career as a solo act with A&M, released *Frampton* and followed it up with 1976's bestseller, *Frampton Comes Alive!*, recorded live at San Francisco's Winterland Ballroom to a crowd so indifferent that cheers had to be overdubbed. (Bill Graham, desperate to attract a crowd, had booked more popular bands like Santana to open the show, so there'd be an audience.) Once released, though, the album sold ten million copies, a record for a live LP at the time, and was inescapable on FM radio. Also in Britain, the Move had broken up, and guitarist Roy Wood formed the poppish Wizzard. Then he got the idea to add electric strings, and Wizzard turned into the Electric Light Orchestra, with another ex-Move member, Jeff Lynne, which cranked out hits until the mid-'80s, when Lynne turned his attention to other matters. On the West Coast, singer-songwriters were all over the place, and with the Eagles and Linda Ronstadt establishing the country-rock sound as a cornerstone of AM and FM radio, ex-Byrds aplenty, and record companies in the backyard, a massive number of albums poured forth, not only from country-rock bands like Pure Prairie League, Poco, Dr. Hook and the Medicine Show, Michael Nesmith's First and Second National Band, the Nitty Gritty Dirt Band, and countless others that fell by the wayside, but also from temporary aggregations like the Souther–Hillman–Furay Band (respectively a songwriter for the Eagles, an ex-Byrd, and an ex-Poco), Firefall (comprising ex-Byrds, ex–Burrito Brothers, and an ex-Spirit), and Neil Young's various countryish combos. Up north in San Francisco, Bill Graham's next big discovery, Journey (ex-Santana, ex–Frank Zappa), was signed to Columbia, which had high hopes for them.

Another source of talent (or product, at least) were boutique labels. Elton John was given Rocket Records by MCA, as an inducement to re-sign with them—the $8 million they gave him might also have helped—and immediately came out of the artistic closet by signing Neil Sedaka and soft-rock singer Kiki Dee. We've already seen the Jefferson Airplane's Grunt, which signed nearly everybody in Marin County before cutting way back to finally achieve success with Jefferson Starship's 1975 chart-topper *Red Octopus,* and Leon Russell's Shelter Records, which continued to put out J. J. Cale's albums until 1979. The Grateful Dead managed a mostly peaceful separation from Warner Bros. in 1973, and started up an audacious project of running Grateful Dead Records (for their own albums) and Round Records (for outside projects by the band, such as Jerry Garcia's bluegrass project, Old and In the Way), which, predictably enough, given the chaos that ruled the Dead organization, foundered in a couple of years but served as a (mostly negative) example to others who'd try the same thing later. Their neighbors, the Youngbloods, had Raccoon Records, administered by Warners, which not only released various Youngbloods' solo efforts but also gave a major-label platform for the wildly eccentric songwriter (and sometime Holy Modal Rounder) Michael Hurley. The Moody Blues got their own label, Threshold, and of course, the Rolling Stones had Rolling Stones Records, which, after a silly vanity project of a jam album at the start, was almost exclusively for their own albums or side projects. Frank Zappa was a master at juggling labels, and channeled a lot of his work through a Warners-affiliated outfit called DiscReet. Warners also wound up hosting Warner-Spector, the legendary producer's latest effort, and having mild success with albums by Cher and Dion.

And slowly, another factor was gaining force. By 1970, rock itself wasn't strictly an Anglo-American thing. Progressive rock, in particular, was eagerly adopted early on in odd places like Germany, home of psychedelic excess from Popul Vuh, Birth Control, and Ash Ra Tempel; Finland, where a number of very odd bands started putting out records; and Denmark, where a classically trained pair of brothers formed Savage Rose to do soundtracks, only to be upstaged by the wife of one of the brothers, who called herself Annisette and had a voice, as one critic memorably put it, "like Minnie Mouse on helium." From behind the Iron Curtain, Locomotiv GT signed to Mercury, and Emerson, Lake and Palmer's Manticore boutique label signed the Italian PFM (Premiata Forneria Marconi), whose three earnest prog albums scraped the bottom of the American charts. Pop, as it always does, fared a bit better: Atlantic scooped up Focus, from Amsterdam, in 1973, and its flute-led instrumental "Hocus Focus" was a top 10 hit; and EMI scored with Blue Swede, from Stockholm, whose "Hooked on a Feeling," with its stupid "ooga-chacka" hook, was a number-one hit in 1974. After the psychedelic scare died down, Germany's charts were pretty much locked into their Schlager genre, a sort of light rock mixed with syrupy sentimentality, with its fan magazines detailing the trials and tragedies of its many stars; and try as they might, their prog bands got nowhere in either Britain or the United States, although the canny British band Nektar, a prog outfit, aimed their sights on the Continent instead of the United States and managed a fine career thanks to a large German fan base. A four-piece from Cologne and Düsseldorf, Kraftwerk ("power station"), was part of an emerging scene there that was heavily influenced by classical electronic music, much of which was composed at WDR radio's studios in Cologne. After a rather lame debut (picked up later in the States by Mercury's prog subsidiary Vertigo), they recorded a bizarre side-long piece called "Autobahn," where electronics were employed to mimic the sound of cars zooming along the superhighway, while

occasionally voices intoned, "Wir fahr'n fahr'n fahr'n auf der Autobahn" ("We're driving, driving, driving on the autobahn"). Edited
down, the song actually became a mild international hit. And up in
Sweden, you had to give music publisher Stig Anderson props: the
man hustled each year at the international music-biz confab MIDEM,
trying to sell a couple of singers he had under contract. The first label
to bite was Playboy, an ill-fated subsidiary of the magazine, bunny on
label and all, which released a couple of singles by Benny and Björn
which were lost in the flood, but Anderson kept going. The two boys
had girlfriends who also sang, and when he put them all together and
cowrote songs with the boys, he loved what he heard, so the group
was dubbed ABBA, for Anni-Frid, Benny, Björn, and Agnetha. In
1974, Anderson entered the quartet in the Eurovision Song Contest
with their song "Waterloo," and they won. England went wild: the
song went in at number one immediately. Atlantic took a chance and
released it in America, and sure enough, the song made it into the
top 10. But this, of course, was a fluke like Blue Swede, and ABBA's
Waterloo album was barely promoted upon release. Still, Stig knew he
was onto something, so he kept going.

Another big factor at mid-decade was a changing attitude toward
drugs. By now, most rock fans had smoked weed and decided if they
liked it, and large amounts of it began to cross the Mexican border
and come in from Hawaii on boats, while entrepreneurs in various
Stateside locations began growing it outdoors in remote areas. Rock
concerts in cavernous halls were, when certain acts played, redolent
of marijuana smoke. Drinking, too, enjoyed a revival. Beer, of course,
with its low alcohol content, was big, but so were sweet "wine" drinks,
most famously Boone's Farm, Annie Green Springs, and Ripple (the
latter immortalized in a Grateful Dead song), with Boone's Farm advertising in *Rolling Stone* for its apple and strawberry flavors. Tequila,
a formerly obscure spirit made from agave cactus, suddenly enjoyed a
spurt of success, one encouraged by the West Coast country-rock scene
and a hit by the Eagles called "Tequila Sunrise" after a suddenly popular cocktail that popped up. A Florida-based, Mobile-raised singer-
songwriter with some Nashville experience, Jimmy Buffett, made
his name being or pretending to be shitfaced during his show, which

consisted of songs about drinking, pirates, parrots, and a beach-based lifestyle, which eventually got him a hit, "Margaritaville." This led to an ongoing career that has made him a multimillionaire, overseeing cruises, theme bars, "Parrothead" conventions, and a short-lived Broadway "jukebox musical." (There are now plans for "Margaritaville" retirement complexes.)

But the two new entries on the dope scene—not actually new, of course, but ominously growing in popularity—were heroin and cocaine. Heroin had enough history with jazz musicians that one would think that so-called hip rock musicians would have given it a wide berth, but from Janis Joplin and Jim Morrison and Keith Richards and John and Yoko on, its dark lure continued to attract acolytes. Every now and again, one of them would hit the news, as when Gram Parsons fatally overdosed in 1973 and his road manager, Phil Kaufman, was busted trying to burn his coffin in the California desert; or when the Average White Band, a remarkable Scottish instrumental soul outfit that Atlantic signed away from MCA, was celebrating their number-one hit "Pick Up the Pieces" in Hollywood, at a party for Gregg Allman, and two of them accidentally took some heroin. Cher called for a doctor and finally got her gynecologist on the line, who, from her description, told her that one guy could be saved by keeping him walking, but that the one who'd turned blue was probably a goner. That was Robbie McIntosh, Average White Band's drummer, who was twenty-four when he died. (Ironically, he was replaced by the only black member the band ever had, Steve Ferrone, who went on years later to play with Tom Petty and the Heartbreakers.) Lou Reed was doing his Velvet Underground song "Heroin" in concert, and while one of his guitarists took a solo, Reed tied himself off with the microphone cord, produced a hypodermic, and pretended to shoot up, handing the needle to someone in the audience afterward. But an awful lot of rock musicians were more discreet about it, and able to ensure a steady supply of relatively untainted heroin for years, until they could go into rehab—or not.

The really dangerous drug was cocaine: heroin could leave you warm and muzzy, but users developed a physiological craving that Beat junkie author William S. Burroughs had loudly warned about. Cocaine, hell, it was *fun*! It didn't turn people into sullen junkies because it was like speed, only without speed's awful crash. The high lasted about an hour, although it could be helped along with a little bump from time to time, and it opened your mind to endless possibilities, ideas, and situations that you couldn't help wanting to talk about—and talk and talk. Plus, it wasn't supposed to be addictive. Eminent medical authorities had said so! Freud himself had used it and praised it! Its chief drawback was that it was considerably more expensive than pot or heroin or alcohol: it was sold by the gram, and that gram could cost between fifty and a hundred dollars, rock star prices in the mid-'70s. And, although you could shoot it, like heroin, it was easier and safer to have on hand a mirror, a single-edged razor blade, and a rolled-up bill (fifties were popular). The drug came in crystals that were very sensitive to humidity, so it had to be chopped to ensure it didn't make your nose bleed, which is where the razor came in. (The mirror was just a smooth surface; a hotel room desktop or the top of a toilet tank would work just as well.) Cocaine was snickered about in *Rolling Stone* and alluded to in songs, and everybody, *everybody* was using it, or so it seemed, and not just the musicians. It was making large inroads into record companies (and, to be fair, the film business and places like Wall Street; the only rule was you had to be able to afford it). That talk about its being a dangerous narcotic? The drug was classified right along with marijuana in the federal law making it illegal, and we all know how accurate *that* was, right? But the sad truth was that it was, in fact, addictive, although not in the same way heroin was. Worse, it distorted judgment something crazy, sometimes on a very basic phys-iological level: original pressings of many of this era's most popular records had a very tinny high end and not much bass because that sounded good to a coked-out engineer. Cocaine played a decisive role in a lot of careers, beginning with Sly Stone (an early adopter), who more or less flamed out in 1975 after a much-publicized wedding cer-emony on June 5, 1974, during a show at Madison Square Garden in New York, only to have his wife divorce him in December. Musicians would walk offstage mid-show, letting the band cover for them while they got a bump. Eric Clapton, wearing a T-shirt reading, NO SNOW, NO SHOW, opened his show in Birmingham on August 8, 1975, by going on a rant about "wogs" (a racial slur for non-Caucasians) and Britain's being a white country. This, surprisingly, didn't sink his career, although it was widely reported. David Bowie went through a radical personality change, adopting the Thin White Duke persona and wearing Nazi-like regalia while being driven around in a vintage Mercedes. Songs like "Fame," from his 1974 album *Young Americans,* are the very model of a cocaine mix. The '60s were over: pot and acid had been supplanted by pot, cocaine, and alcohol. Consciousness expansion was a thing of the past.

Cocaine was almost certainly involved that same year when John Lennon (cowriter on "Fame") and Harry Nilsson had their public contretemps with the staff at the Troubadour (for heckling the Smothers Brothers and allegedly assaulting a waitress), and there's a reason the album they did together, *Pussy Cats,* isn't held up as a high point in the Lennon or Nilsson canon. John and Yoko's marriage was on the rocks—he was having an affair with his longtime personal secretary, May Pang—and all this was very likely the result of the pressure from the years of trying to get legal immigration status so they could stay in New York, a city Lennon had come to love, something strongly opposed by elements of President Nixon's Justice Department. The government's objection wasn't so much about the pot bust, which it held up as evidence of Lennon's moral turpitude, as it was the very public, and very naïve, politics Lennon and Ono espoused: ending the war in Vietnam, legalizing marijuana, freeing political prisoners. Yoko had consulted an astrologer, who believed that the configuration of stars in other places on the globe meant that people could travel there to benefit from more auspicious vibrations, and had sent John to Los Angeles, thereby enabling the situation with Nilsson and Pang. Six months later, Lennon returned to New York to produce and record his next album, *Walls and Bridges,* on which one of the musicians was Elton John, who bet Lennon that the song he played on, "Whatever Gets You Through the Night," would be a number-one record and that if it did make the top slot, Lennon would have to appear with John in concert that Thanksgiving. (It was, and Lennon did; Elton, no fool, recorded the show, and got his own number one out of it with his duet with Lennon on "Lucy in the Sky with Diamonds.") Backstage, John and Yoko were acting lovey-dovey, and it was apparent that they were back together. It would be Lennon's last concert appearance. The next year would see him embroiled with notorious New York music-biz gangster Morris Levy over an album of classic rock-and-roll numbers he'd wanted to record forever. He'd started the project with Phil Spector producing two years earlier, but they quarreled, and Spector disappeared with the tapes. Lennon, with a self-produced hit album behind him, promptly rerecorded the record. Then Levy, who at this point owned Arc Music, Chess's publishing company, leaned on Lennon about his use of some of Chuck Berry's lyrics in the Beatles tune "Come Together," and John agreed to record several Chuck Berry songs for the album, and gave Levy the tapes to approve. The next thing anyone knew, there were ads on television for a mail-order John Lennon album on the previously unheard-of Adam VIII label, called *Roots*. Apple then leapt into action, releasing the actual master tapes as an album called *Rock 'n' Roll,* while Lennon bravely sued Levy and managed to collect forty-five grand in damages from him, an unprecedented victory that must have warmed the hearts of Levy's previous victims—those who were still alive, that is. In October, the New York State Supreme Court overturned Lennon's deportation order, and shortly afterward, Yoko successfully delivered a child, Sean, and John decided to retire to help raise the kid.

Bob Dylan wasted no time in recovering from his experience with David Geffen and Asylum: he had a bunch of new songs he wanted to record and was running around playing them for Michael Bloomfield, David Crosby, and Shel Silverstein. He also played them for John Hammond, who suggested that he had an album, so Dylan grabbed Eric Weissberg and his semi-bluegrass band, Deliverance, and recorded one. Then he had second thoughts and played it for his younger brother, David, who suggested that he could use a better band and a better ambience, so David assembled some musicians in Minnesota, and Bob sat down with them and recut much of what he'd done. The album that resulted, *Blood on the Tracks,* sold better than anything by Dylan had in years and proved to be a classic, provoking discussion among fans about just what was going on. Was the blood on the album's tracks? Was the Dylan marriage in trouble? Were these long story-songs filled with hints to other things? Still, one thing was clear: this was the best stuff he'd delivered in years, and the public sent it to the top of the charts fast. Dylan started showing up in the Village, haunting the folk clubs on hoot nights, gathering together friends old (Ramblin' Jack Elliot) and new (journalist/poet/songwriter Patti Smith, who'd written for *Creem* and performed with electric guitarist Lenny Kaye at poetry readings), and generally having a good time. Well, and trying out an idea for his next album, which he was already writing, mostly in collaboration with Jacques Levy, a psychologist, theater director, and songwriter who'd worked with Roger McGuinn, who'd introduced them. Dylan convened a large band, mostly Eric Clapton's backup band Kokomo (plus Clapton himself) and spent some time trying to record. It didn't work, so he went back in with a bassist (Rob Stoner) and drummer (Howie Wyeth), plus a mysterious violinist, Scarlet Rivera, and Emmylou Harris, a rising star on the LA country-rock scene. The result, *Desire,* was yet another enigmatic Dylan record: its first single was "Hurricane," about imprisoned fighter Rubin "Hurricane" Carter, a middleweight boxer who had been convicted for a murder he hadn't committed, which was Dylan at his protest best. Another song, "Joey," though, hymned "Crazy Joey" Gallo, who'd been shot to death in Umberto's Clam House in New York's Little Italy by a member of a rival Mafia family. A violent psychopath who'd touched off one of New York City's largest interfamily crime wars, Gallo was hardly the kind of person Dylan had memorialized in the past, and the song is a weird artifact. Both songs were cowrites with Levy, as were all but two of the tracks on the album. One of the solo efforts was "Sara," Dylan's emotional plea to his wife, with whom he had, indeed, been having trouble, and one of the few Dylan songs that mentions specific facts of his life, such as admitting what fans had already suspected: that he'd written "Sad Eyed Lady of the Lowlands" on *Blonde on Blonde,* for her.

Dylan wanted to go on tour again, which was another motivation for all the glad-handing in the Village: putting a band together for it. This time he didn't want a big-stadium Bob Dylan Tour, but a kind of variety show, where others would get to sing and play, with, of course, Dylan playing songs from the new album. This meant the musicians from the record (minus Harris); Ramblin' Jack; Joan Baez; Dylan's old friend Bob Neuwirth; McGuinn; Mick Ronson (who, post-Bowie, had been working with Ian Hunter after Mott the Hoople's demise); a lanky guitarist from Fort Worth, J. Henry "T Bone" Burnett; Steve Soles, another guitarist/songwriter; percussionist Luther Rix; a multi-instrumentalist from a band called Quacky Duck and His Barnyard Friends, David Mansfield; and an actress named Ronee Blakley, who'd been in Robert Altman's film *Nashville* (where all the actors playing country musicians were to write their own songs, for verisimilitude; fortunately, Blakley had talent) and who was working out an act at a Village club when Dylan walked in. For companionship and literary cred, Dylan had Allen Ginsberg (and his companion, Peter Orlovsky) along and a guy named Larry "Ratso" Sloman covered it for *Rolling Stone*. Oh, and because it wasn't already chaotic enough, Dylan decided to shoot an improvised film called *Renaldo and Clara*, with members of the troupe, now dubbed the Rolling Thunder Revue, taking acting roles in it.

The tour began before *Desire* was even released, and its first stop was in North Falmouth, Massachusetts, at a motel where a mah-jongg convention was under way, and Dylan and Baez played for the old ladies in attendance, after which Ginsberg declaimed some poetry. The crowd loved it. The tour rattled around New England, with occasional cameos by the likes of Arlo Guthrie, Joni Mitchell, and Gordon Lightfoot, while Sara Dylan came onto the bus after a while, and Dylan's mother, one of his biggest fans, would show up onstage to clap her hands. It was big, expensive, disorderly, visually bizarre—early into the tour, Dylan started wearing eyeliner and white face makeup—and apparently a lot of fun. (This, however, cannot be said of *Renaldo and Clara*, which is rarely screened.) It was the beginning of the next phase of his career, in which he began to tour more or less constantly, a practice that continues to this day.

The Dylan tour was also an explicit repudiation of the Band, another relationship, only this time among five supposed equals, that was in danger. Their 1970 album, *Stage Fright*, was, like their previous ones, a collective effort, but all the songs on the second side were by Robbie Robertson, who, from the evidence on the next year's *Cahoots*, was taking over—and not in a good way. Then, as 1971 turned into 1972, they took a breather by recording a two-disc live album at the Brooklyn Academy of Music, *Rock of Ages*, with a horn section helmed by jazz tuba player Howard Johnson, who played arrangements by New Orleans master Allen Toussaint, complete with a quick cameo from their old boss, Dylan. Late 1973 saw them doing a pallid oldies album, *Moondog Matinee*, its title a tribute to rock-and-roll pioneer deejay Alan Freed, and then there was the Asylum interregnum and tour with Dylan. In 1975, they released *Northern Lights–Southern Cross*, which was supposed to be the Band's examination of their blend of Canadian and (via Ronnie Hawkins and Levon Helm) Southern, and again all the songs were by Robertson. The album didn't sell very well, and the group hauled itself out on the road again, but it didn't help. Finally, Robertson, who'd been doing a lot of side projects, came to the rest of the group with an idea: The Band was in decline, so they should break up, but spectacularly, with a final concert with dozens of guest stars, mostly people he was playing with or producing. They'd get Martin Scorsese to film it and turn it into a theatrical release, and also release the soundtrack on an album. Turning to Bill Graham, master of rock spectacle, they arranged for it to happen at Winter-land on Thanksgiving 1976, with a full Thanksgiving dinner served to holders of higher-priced tickets. (The rest of the audience sat up-stairs on cold concrete seats that had been hosed off hours earlier but were still damp.) The hours-long show featured not only the Band, Bob Dylan, and Ronnie Hawkins, but also another Allen Toussaint horn section; Neil Young and Joni Mitchell representing Canada; and Eric Clapton, Neil Diamond, Paul Butterfield, Dr. John, Ringo Starr, Van Morrison, Bobby Charles, Ron Wood, and Muddy Waters. There were also several poets reading, and of course a jam session. Backstage, a designated "Jean Cocteau room" was painted all white, with plastic noses mounted on the wall, a huge glass-topped table in the center, and piped-in sounds of sniffing. After it was over, the Band retreated to Malibu, where they had their own recording studio, Shangri-La, and they knocked out one more album, *Islands*, which had a few new recordings and a few things they'd had lying around, and fulfilled their Capitol contract so that they could put the film soundtrack out on Warners, which had underwritten Scorsese. Robbie, too, signed with Warners and announced he was going to do a lot of soundtracks and solo albums. *Islands* was a critical and sales bomb, although it did have Richard Manuel singing "Georgia on My Mind," and after additional film was shot of Emmylou Harris and the Staple Singers, the film, now titled *The Last Waltz*, premiered in April 1978. It's definitely an attempt to take a snapshot of the end of an era, with many participants coked out of their heads—Neil Young was shot from below, and had a large coke booger in his nose that had to be painstakingly edited out—and a few notable performances, including Muddy Waters, who was mesmerizing, and whose filming almost started a panic when it was discovered that all the cameras except one had mysteriously ceased to work; what was that again, about having your mojo working?

The Last Waltz was hardly the end of an era. Its participants had been enshrined by *Rolling Stone* (which had its own end-of-an-era moment when it moved its offices to New York in 1977) as rock royalty, a rather odd concept if one stops to think about it. By the mid-'70s, the record business was raking in tons of money, and the concept of some kids somewhere getting a deal with a big label seemed to have vanished. Kids still formed bands, but an overwhelming majority seemed content simply to consume the spectacle, attending rock festivals and mass outdoor concerts put together by successful promoters in the summer, cramming into big venues in the winter, and reading in the rock press about what they were missing. This last had expanded to include alternative weeklies (including the *Village Voice*, now a national cultural as well as local political force, whose music editor, Robert Christgau, "the dean of American rock critics," wrote a monthly "Consumer Guide" in which he assigned letter grades to albums), *Rolling Stone*, *Creem*, *Zoo World*, *Circus*, and a revived *Crawdaddy* (minus its exclamation point and Paul Williams). Other eras were ending, too: Led Zeppelin lasted the decade out, but turning in fewer and fewer memorable moments: they disbanded officially at the end of 1980, after the death by alcohol of their drummer, John Bonham. A new generation of bands following the decade's aesthetic was popping up—

Queen, Aerosmith, Rainbow, and Bob Seger, who finally started selling records—and there was never a shortage of product from the likes of Elton John, not to mention the cocaine cowboys of the West Coast. The "good old" Grateful Dead had taken a break in 1974, only to come roaring back shortly thereafter to find themselves more popular than ever. Classic rock would endure, even if some dissenting voices were beginning to be heard.

epilogue

AUGUST 16, 1977

Elvis souvenirs at Graceland Too, Jackson, Mississippi
(Photo courtesy of Tom Graves)

As might be expected, the new eras of rock and roll swept the past behind them, and many a great performer was left behind. Some did not go quietly: Rick Nelson had performed at a "rock-and-roll revival" show at New York's Madison Square Garden after performing around LA with a fine country-rock band, the Stone Canyon Band. The experience disgusted him so much that in 1972 he wrote a song called "Garden Party" repudiating the whole experience, and had a decent hit with it. In it, he declared that "But if memories were all I sang / I'd rather drive a truck." He kept on skirting the line between country and country-rock until his death in a plane crash in 1985. Another "revival" perennial was Chuck Berry, by now 100 percent in it for the money: he'd show up to a gig, get paid in cash, and then go on to meet his backup band, whom he often didn't pay. God help them if they didn't know the tunes; his tongue was as sharp as ever. But he did have something of a right to his bitterness: in all the years he'd been performing and making classic records, many of which were hits for himself and others, he'd never hit the number-one slot on the charts. With the demise of Chess Records, his home from the beginning, he'd signed with Mercury, who made a mess of his career, putting him in front of the Steve Miller Band at the Fillmore for an album. When Marshall Chess revived the label, Berry went back in 1972 and recorded another live album, in

Coventry, England, on which (backed by the Average White Band) he played a song that an obscure group called the Bees had recorded in the early '50s. They called it "Toy Bell," but Chuck, to whom subtlety was a foreign country these days, called it after its chorus: "My Ding-A-Ling." The London audience sang along to this crude nursery rhyme, Chess released it as a single, and for the first and only time in his life, Chuck Berry had a chart-topping single. (He took writer's credit, of course, but he knew better.) The various "revival" shows gave gigs to many (sometimes deservedly) but forgotten artists: Little Richard and Fats Domino, both of whom had short careers at Warner Bros., played some of them, and Jerry Lee Lewis occasionally got onto the bill, although he was doing just fine with country music.

Then there were the more obscure musicians. A lot of rockabillies wound up with gigs in country backup bands, or else, like the Rock and Roll Trio's Paul Burlison, retired entirely: he operated a radio/TV repair shop for decades until fans demanded that he perform again, which he did, if only rarely. Sun Records veteran Billy Lee Riley did session work around Memphis, mostly playing harmonica; made a couple of *Folk Rock Harmonica* albums for a Mexican label (one of which included "Como Piedra Que Rueda," aka "Like a Rolling Stone"), and even cut an obscure but excellent song, "Sun Goin' Down on Frisco," for a Stax subsidiary. International rockabilly fanatics kept him going until he died in 2009. Johnny Otis put together a revue that featured loads of talent from the old days, including Ruth Brown, Pee Wee Crayton, Roy Brown, Esther Phillips, Roy Milton, Eddie "Cleanhead" Vinson, and his own son Shuggie Otis, and got Epic to record them at the 1970 Monterey Jazz Festival, which resulted in increased visibility for all the performers, although few of them wanted to work with Otis afterward. (He didn't mind: Shuggie was looking to develop into a star, and Johnny had other hustles, including the ministry and an organic apple juice farm, in his future.) Others weren't so lucky: most of the "5" Royales had left music after their last recordings for Smash in 1964, but their guitarist and songwriter, Lowman Pauling, continued to record with various groups until it was evident nothing was happening. He then signed on as guitarist for Sam and Dave's road band, but his drinking was getting worse, and finally they had to let him go. He died on the day after Christmas 1973, employed at the time as the janitor in a synagogue in Queens.

Not that the post-Invasion acts got off without some tragedies besides the headlining ones like Jimi, Janis, Brian, and Jim. Ron "Pigpen" McKernan of the Grateful Dead died of alcohol poisoning on March 8, 1973. He was still performing onstage with the band but was being supplemented by another keyboardist, Keith Godchaux. Nick Drake, a Joe Boyd discovery considered by many to be one of Britain's preeminent rising young songwriters, accidentally took an overdose of antidepressant and died in 1974, aged twenty-six. And it wasn't too surprising when Keith Moon, the wild-man drummer for the Who, overdosed on several legal drugs, including one designed to block the effects of alcohol, in late 1978: he'd already collapsed onstage, in the middle of a show at San Francisco's Cow Palace, and a young fan, Scott Halpin, had responded to Pete Townshend's call for a drummer, and finished the show with the band quite well, by all accounts. Michael Bloomfield remained in seclusion in California, emerging occasionally with an album by a band that probably broke up before the records were out of the pressing plant, but remarkably, he started getting clean in the early '80s, and his slips from sobriety were primarily with alcohol. Nobody has ever explained how he came to be found dead in his locked car on February 15, 1981. The toxicology report showed cocaine-related chemicals in his blood, unusual for a guy whose biggest problem was insomnia.

Nor were drugs the only danger: onstage wiring was still an evolving art, and in 1972, Stone the Crows, an up-and-coming band managed by Led Zeppelin's manager, Peter Grant, was performing in Swansea, Wales, when guitarist Les Harvey caught a spark from a microphone, which killed him. Keith Relf, one of the original Yardbirds, was playing guitar in the basement of his home in 1976 when it electrocuted him. Graham Bond, whose band had birthed Cream and had been in on the very beginning of the British blues scene, threw himself in front of a London Underground train in 1974. Marc Bolan, formerly of T. Rex (but relegated to hosting a musical variety show on British TV after his last album, *Light of Love,* on Casablanca, tanked), was driving with his American girlfriend, Gloria Jones, when she drove into a tree, killing him instantly, in 1977. And on April 28, 1975, Tom "Big Daddy" Donahue, San Francisco's pioneering disc jockey and sometime label entrepreneur, had a couple of reggae fans on his show to discuss Bob Marley's new *Natty Dread* album and reggae in general; at the program's end, he turned the air over to the next guy, went home, and died. He was a big man, weighing more than four hundred pounds, with a gray beard, but only forty-six years old. In his last interview, he said, "Music freaks . . . That is what I'm looking for in disc jockeys. I want people who are really involved in the music. I do not want anybody who is told what to play." He died right in time to miss huge changes that would take over his industry, and it was radio's, and San Francisco's, end-of-an-era moment, although this wasn't yet apparent.

And then there was Elvis. His 1968 Christmas show had liberated him from the old grind and put him back on the road, but as much as audiences loved seeing him, some of the same problems he'd had before persisted. The Colonel was still choosing the material, still taking his 50 percent. Elvis was touring, but still doing monthlong residencies in Las Vegas, surrounded by girlfriends and the Memphis Mafia. His marriage was in trouble: it came out that Priscilla was involved with her karate instructor, Mike Stone, and the couple filed for a legal separation in February 1972. The divorce became final in October 1973, with Priscilla getting two million dollars, alimony, and child support for their daughter, Lisa Marie. But Elvis's weight was ballooning, and although he was practicing karate (and doing moves in his stage show), he was also beginning to depend heavily on drugs, provided to him by Dr. George Nichopoulos, known as "Dr. Nick" to Elvis's entourage; he'd been Elvis's personal physician for some time. Nichopoulos has been painted as a villain, but other Memphians praise him: journalist Stanley Booth, who had toured with the Rolling Stones and picked up a drug habit, wrote a fine essay about his recovery at the hands of Dr. Nick. But there was only so much a doctor could do. Elvis was losing it, lonely and isolated, not much interested in anything. RCA kept trying to get him back into the studio, and he'd go record singles and the occasional album, but with the exception of his recording of Dennis Linde's "Burning Love" in 1972, nothing much after his 1973 *Aloha from Hawaii via Satellite* soundtrack was catching on with any but his hard-core fans. He was behaving erratically, too, reading all manner of odd books on spiritualism, and spending large amounts of money, on cars and an airplane, which he dubbed the *Lisa Marie*. He collapsed with pneumonia in 1973 and stayed in the hospital for two weeks, and then went back in twice in 1975, for exhaustion brought on by touring. RCA finally became so desperate for product that they allowed the Colonel to grab bits from Elvis's rambling between tunes in his live shows and released a thirty-seven-minute-long album, *Having Fun with Elvis on Stage*, in 1974. It was greeted with incomprehension, at best. As "Fat Elvis" jokes began to circulate, the King ripped his trousers doing karate in his act one night at the end of 1975.

In June 1976, Elvis, still touring, started his next tour in Landover, Maryland, where Elton John was in the audience. "He had dozens of people around him, supposedly looking after him, but he already looked like a corpse," John told *Rolling Stone*, and at tour's end, on July 5, he played Memphis and then slunk off with a girlfriend, ignoring the fireworks he usually hosted at Graceland. A week later, Sonny and Red West, key members of the Memphis Mafia, brothers who'd been his bodyguards almost from the beginning, found out in separate phone calls from Elvis's father, Vernon, that they'd been let go, with a week's salary apiece, because of vague financial issues that Vernon didn't expand on. Elvis also fired his karate trainer, Dave Hebler—or, rather, Vernon did. There were also rumors that Dr. Nick had been replaced by another doctor, based in Las Vegas. Rumors went both ways, though: the West brothers and Hebler were rumored to be writing a book, using tabloid reporter Steve Dunleavy as a ghostwriter. (They had to: Red West had had to sell his house to keep his family afloat; a week's salary didn't go all that far.) The book, *Elvis: What Happened?*, appeared on August 1, 1977. It was an instant shock, with its tales of shooting televisions out, wild behavior with women, and absolutely amazing amounts of drugs (prescription, of course) being consumed. It also showed why Elvis's shows and records had gotten so bad: he just didn't care. And he didn't: earlier that summer, remaining Memphis Mafia member George Klein decided that Elvis needed a tonic in the form of a new girlfriend and brought three sisters to visit him, all girls Klein had dated, including the current Miss Tennessee. Elvis picked her sister, twenty-year-old Ginger Alden, the current Miss Traffic Safety, to accompany him to Las Vegas for a few days, then came back to Memphis and holed up in his room, watching what was going on at Graceland via his video surveillance cameras. On the afternoon of August 16, Ginger, looking for Elvis, walked into a bathroom and found him lying on the floor, holding a book called *The Scientific Search for the Face of Jesus.* She called a couple of bodyguards, who called an ambulance; one of the EMTs trying artificial respiration kept muttering, "Breathe for me, Presley," under his breath. The ambulance reached Baptist Memorial Hospital at 3:30, and Elvis Aron Presley was declared dead. He was forty-two years old.

The news went out instantly. President Jimmy Carter issued a statement that said, in part, "Elvis Presley's death deprives our country of a piece of itself. He was unique and irreplaceable." The newsrooms of both Memphis papers were in turmoil. (In fact, an entire book about the news of Elvis's death—a pretty good one, at that—titled *When Elvis Died* was later written by a husband-and-wife team of journalists.) Although the official cause of death was listed as cardiac arrhythmia, an autopsy showed the presence of Butabarbital, codeine, morphine, Pentobarbital, Placydil, Quaalude, Valium, and Valmid in his stomach, a mighty combination of downers. Elvis's body was laid in state in Graceland, and on the seventeenth, more than 25,000 people filed past the open coffin. The next day, 150 people attended the funeral, while a crowd of 75,000 stood outside. Elvis was buried next to his mother at the Forest Hill Cemetery in Memphis. (The graves of Elvis; his stillborn twin, Jesse; and his mother, Gladys, were eventually relocated to Graceland.) In New York, Lester Bangs, freelance again after his stint editing *Creem,* wrote an elegy in the *Village Voice* that concluded, "If love is truly going out of fashion forever, which I do not believe, then along with our nurtured indifference to each other will be a nurtured indifference to each others' objects of reverence . . . We will continue to fragment in this manner, because solipsism holds all the cards at present; it is a king whose domain eclipses even Elvis'. But I can guarantee you one thing: we will never again agree on anything as we agreed on Elvis. So I won't bother saying good bye to his corpse. I will say good bye to you." Angry words, somewhat opaque, but containing an important fact: Elvis was the first consensus pop star, and the last. Then came the Beatles/Stones. The fragmentation would continue. Another new landscape was just over the hill.

In a not very fashionable part of London, Andy Jakeman, former roadie for Jimi Hendrix and others, now trading as Jake Riviera in his capacity as part of a very small record label, was preparing a box of new releases to mail to an American journalist. He wrote a nice cover letter, hoping they'd be well received, and took it out of the typewriter as the bulletin came over the radio. He grabbed a pen to sign the letter, then scrawled over it, "ONLY ONE ELVIS LEFT NOW!"

BIBLIOGRAPHY

Books

Boyd, Joe. *White Bicycles: Making Music in the 1960s*. London: Serpent's Tail, 2006.

Bradley, Lloyd. *Bass Culture: When Reggae Was King*. London: Penguin Books, 2000.

Brown, Peter, and Steven Gaines. *The Love You Make: An Insider's Story of the Beatles*. New York: McGraw-Hill, 1983.

Chusid, Irwin. *Songs in the Key of Z: The Curious Universe of Outsider Music*. London: Cherry Red Books, 2000.

Dickinson, Jim. *I'm Just Dead, I'm Not Gone*. Jackson, MS: University Press of Mississippi, 2017.

George, Nelson. *Where Did Our Love Go?: The Rise and Fall of the Motown Sound*. New York: St. Martin's Press, 1985.

Goodman, Fred. *Allen Klein: The Man Who Bailed Out the Beatles, Made the Stones, and Transformed Rock & Roll*. New York: Houghton Mifflin Harcourt, 2015.

———. *The Mansion on the Hill: Dylan, Young, Geffen, Springsteen, and the Head-on Collision of Rock and Commerce*. London: Jonathan Cape, 1997.

Gordon, Robert. *Respect Yourself: Stax Records and the Soul Explosion*. New York: Bloomsbury, 2013.

Green, Jonathon. *Days in the Life: Voices From the English Underground, 1961–1971*. London, Minerva, 1988.

Gregory, Neal and Janice. *When Elvis Died*. Washington, DC: Communications Press, 1980.

Guralnick, Peter. *Careless Love: The Unmaking of Elvis Presley*. New York: Little, Brown, 1999.

————. *Dream Boogie: The Triumph of Sam Cooke*. New York: Back Bay Books, 2005.

Hagan, Joe. *Sticky Fingers: The Life and Times of Jann Wenner and Rolling Stone Magazine*. New York: Alfred A. Knopf, 2017.

Hoskyns, Barney. *Small Town Talk: Bob Dylan, the Band, Van Morrison, Janis Joplin, Jimi Hendrix & Friends in the Wild Years of Woodstock*. Boston: Da Capo Press, 2016.

————. *Waiting For the Sun: A Rock 'n' Roll History of Los Angeles*. New York, Backbeat Books, 2009.

Jackson, Blair, and David Gans. *This Is All a Dream We Dreamed: An Oral History of the Grateful Dead*. New York: Flatiron Books, 2015.

Kramer, Wayne. *The Hard Stuff: Dope, Crime, the MC5 and My Life of Impossibilities*. New York: Da Capo Press, 2018.

Miles, Barry. *In the Sixties*. London: Jonathan Cape, 2002.

Norman, Philip. *Shout!: The Beatles in Their Generation*. New York: Fireside Press, 1981.

Oldham, Andrew Loog. *Stoned*. London: Vintage, 2001, 2003.

Perry, Charles. *The Haight-Ashbury: A History*. San Francisco: Rolling Stone Press, 1984.

Rees, Dafydd, and Luke Crampton. *The Guinness Book of Rock Stars*. London: Guinness, 1991.

Richards, Keith. *Life*. New York: Little, Brown, 2010.

Riley, Tim. *Lennon: The Man, the Myth, the Music—The Definitive Life*. New York: Hyperion Books, 2011.

Selvin, Joel. *Altamont: The Rolling Stones, the Hells Angels, and the Inside Story of Rock's Darkest Day*. New York: Dey Street Books, 2016.

Smith, RJ. *The One: The Life and Music of James Brown*. New York: Gotham Books, 2012.

Steffens, Roger. *So Much Things to Say: The Oral History of Bob Marley*. New York: W. W. Norton, 2017.

Wald, Elijah. *Dylan Goes Electric!: Newport, Seeger, Dylan, and the Night that Split the Sixties*. New York: Dey Street Books, 2015.

Ward, Ed. *Michael Bloomfield: The Rise and Fall of an American Guitar Hero*. Chicago: Chicago Review Press, 2016.

Whitburn, Joel. *Hot Country Songs, 1944–2012*, 8th ed. Menomonee Falls, WI: Record Research, 2013.

————. *Hot R&B Songs, 1942–2010*, 6th ed. Menomonee Falls, WI: Record Research, 2011.

⸺. *Top Pop Albums,* 7th ed. Menomonee Falls, WI: Record Research, 2010.

⸺. *Top Pop Singles, 1955–2010,* 14th ed. Menomonee Falls, WI: Record Research, 2011.

Wyman, Bill. *Rolling with the Stones.* London: DK Publishing, 2002.

Liner Notes

Bowman, Rob. *The Band.* Hollywood, Capitol Records, 2000.

Dahl, Bill, Keith Hughes, Janie Bradford, and Todd Boyd. *The Complete Motown Singles, Vol. 4: 1964.* Universal City, CA: Hip-O Select, 2006.

Dahl, Bill, Keith Hughes, Al Abrams, and Todd Boyd. *The Complete Motown Singles, Vol. 5: 1965.* Universal City, CA: Hip-O Select, 2006.

Dahl, Bill, Keith Hughes, Edward Holland Jr., and Stu Hackel. *The Complete Motown Singles, Vol. 6: 1966.* Universal City, CA: Hip-O Select, 2006.

Dahl, Bill, Keith Hughes, Barney Ales, and Herb Jordan. *The Complete Motown Singles, Vol. 7: 1967.* Universal City, CA: Hip-O Select, 2007.

Dahl, Bill, Keith Hughes, Otis Williams, and Herb Boyd. *The Complete Motown Singles, Vol.8: 1968.* Universal City, CA: Hip-O Select, 2007.

Dahl, Bill, Keith Hughes, Shelly Berger, and Stu Hackel. *The Complete Motown Singles, Vol.9: 1969.* Universal City, CA: Hip-O Select, 2007.

Dahl, Bill, Keith Hughes, John Reid, and John Anthony Neal. *The Complete Motown Singles, Vol.10: 1970.* Universal City, CA: Hip-O Select, 2008.

Dahl, Bill, Keith Hughes, Harry Webber, and Andrew Flory. *The Complete Motown Singles, Vol.11A: 1971.* Universal City, CA: Hip-O Select, 2008.

Dahl, Bill, Keith Hughes, Scott Regan, and Andrew Flory. *The Complete Motown Singles, Vol. 11B: 1971.* Universal City, CA: Hip-O Select, 2008.

Edmonds, Ben. *What's Going On (Deluxe Edition).* New York: Motown Records, 2001.

Flanagan, Bill, and Clinton Heylin. *Bob Dylan: The Complete Album Collection, Vol. 1.* New York: Columbia Records, 2013.

Gordon, Robert, Bill Mehr, and Alec Palao. *Keep an Eye on the Sky: Big Star.* Burbank, CA: Rhino Records, 2009.

Heylin, Clinton and Sid Griffin. *The Complete Basement Tapes.* New York: Columbia Records, 2014.

Nathan, David. *Lorraine Ellison: Sister Love, the Warner Bros. Recordings.* Burbank, CA: Rhino Handmade, 2006.

Zax, Andy, and Bud Scoppa: *Woodstock 40 Years On: Back to Yasgur's Farm.* Burbank, CA: Rhino, 2009.

Periodicals

Billboard, Cincinnati, Ohio, 1964–1975 inclusive, accessed via books.google
.com.

Crawdaddy! Issues 1–8, New York, 1966–1968.

Rolling Stone, The First Forty Years. New York: Bondi Digital Publishing, 2007.

Films

All You Need Is Love. Directed by Tony Palmer. London: Isolde Films, 2008.

Bang! The Bert Berns Story. Directed by Bob Sarles. Ravin' Films, 2016.

The Complete Monterey Pop Festival. Directed by D. A. Pennebaker. New York:
The Criterion Collection, 2002.

Dont Look Back. Directed by D.A. Pennebaker. New York: DocuDrama Films,
2006.

Festival. Directed by Murray Lerner. Patchke Productions, 1967.

A Hard Day's Night. Directed by Richard Lester. United Artists, 1964.

Help! Directed by Richard Lester. United Artists, 1965.

Long Strange Trip. Directed by Amir Bar-Lev. Amazon Studios, 2017.

Sir Doug and the Genuine Texas Cosmic Groove. Directed by Joe Nick Patoski.
Artist Labor, 2015.

The Trip. Directed by Roger Corman. Hollywood, 1967.

LINER NOTES

The publication of a book should be a wonderful event in the life of its author, and I was really looking forward to the first volume of this work coming out in late 2016 because, a few months earlier, I'd watched as my Michael Bloomfield biography, long out of print, but newly revised, was published. I'd had to do publicity for it, being interviewed by Michael's fans and people who'd only discovered him through records. Most of it was fun, but what was coming would be a much bigger deal. Since I had some time before I had to get to work again, I took a vacation. I decided I wanted to see more of Spain, and planned a route around part of the country that turned out to be exactly what I needed.

Until, that is, I reached Valencia. There, in the most luxurious hotel I've ever stayed in, I set up my iPad and checked my email. There were a couple of disturbing photos from the guy who was checking my house, who, it turned out, had had a family emergency and had turned the job over to his assistant, who'd noticed water pouring out my front door one day and shot photos of it with his camera. The key was in possession of my friend, who was halfway across the country. From Austin to Buffalo to Valencia and back to my landlord in Austin those photos went, and the next day I learned that a valve in one of the toilets had broken, sending the tank lid flying, taking out a couple of walls and part of the ceiling with super-high-pressure water. The water was standing a couple of inches deep, and there was extensive damage to my books and CD collection. The vacation was almost over, the damage had been done. In a few days I could see it for myself.

And I did: by the time I got back, my landlord's insurance agency had paid for an emergency cleanup crew to pay a visit. Wet books had been put in cardboard boxes labelled WET and were now furry with mold; CD box sets and workers' water bottles littered the backyard; piles of wet clothing were moldering. The work of restoration, I was told, would take at least four weeks. I checked into a long-stay residential hotel in downtown Austin, which was a bad solution, and then got rescued by a Facebook friend with an Airbnb space that wasn't in use in the dead of winter. There I learned about winter winds, pecan trees, and a tin roof, but at least I picked up a year's worth of pecans.

Four weeks turned into four months, during which I found out that the radio show for which I'd been doing rock and roll history for almost thirty years wouldn't have me on to discuss the book. We parted ways, but I did a bunch of other interviews thanks to Flatiron's publicist, Steven Boriack, and picked up some great reviews in the press and on various websites. Eventually, Nate Wilcox and I developed the *Let It Roll* podcast to explore the themes in these books, and I can't wait to start in on a new session based on this one!

But the house was a mess, so the writing of this volume was interspersed by much unpacking, shelving, rebuilding, and replacing reference materials. Thanks to all who helped, including Kelly Saragusa McEntee, Jennifer Milbauer, Andrew Halbreich, Richard Luckett, Tony Romano, Roland Swenson, Bob Simmons, Chris Walters, and Gary Rice. My ever-understanding landlord, Jeff Kramer, deserves special thanks.

Much of the research comes from not only the pages of *Billboard* and *Rolling Stone*, but from my own experience, since the era depicted here coincides with the beginning of my writing career, so thanks to Sis Cunningham and Gordon Friesen at *Broadside* magazine for kicking it off; Paul Williams and Tim Jurgens at *Crawdaddy!*; John Burks,

John Morthland, John Lombardi, Baron Wolman, and Robert Altman at *Rolling Stone;* Lester Bangs, Jaan Uhelszki, and Dave Marsh at *Creem*; and the countless publicists and record biz folks who helped me understand what was going on in front of me as it happened. Big thanks to the folks on Pine Street: Luria Castell, Ellen Harmon, Lynne Hughes, and Alton Kelley for an unforgettable week in 1967, and Quentin Fiore and his family, who encouraged my interest in social and cultural history. Musicians like Michael Bloomfield, Nick Gravenites, Ian Hunter, and Ray Benson provided insight along with entertainment, and John Goddard of Village Music continued to educate me and open new vistas. And thanks to Tim Page and Mark Satlof for last-minute fact-checking.

Outside the U.S., thanks to Pete Frame and the folks in North Marston, Charles Shaar Murray, and Andrew Lauder in the U.K., the Berlin crew from my years there, Gérard Bar-David and Michelle Campbell in Paris, Dr. J.-C. Marrache and Etienne Podevin in Montpellier, Tapio Korjus and Pekka Lainen in Finland, and Rikke Rask in Copenhagen.

As usual, my super agent, David Dunton of the Harvey Klinger Agency kept things smooth, and at Flatiron, Jasmine Faustino has made turning this into another real book absolutely painless.

I'm sure I'm missing some folks here, but the deadline is calling. One last observation: it's only fair, in a book that covers this period of cultural history, to give thanks to my dealer, so here's to Anderson's Coffee in Austin, who did their part to get this book written.

INDEX

ABOUT THE AUTHOR

Ed Ward was the rock-and-roll historian on *Fresh Air* for more than thirty years, reaching fourteen million listeners. Currently he is the cohost of the *Let It Roll* podcast. His writing has appeared in *The New York Times*, *The Wall Street Journal*, and countless music magazines. He is also the author of *The History of Rock & Roll, Volume 1* and *Michael Bloomfield: The Rise and Fall of an American Guitar Hero*. He lives in Austin, Texas.